CHOOSING ETHNICITY, NEGOTIATING RACE

CHOOSING ETHNICITY, NEGOTIATING RACE

Korean Adoptees in America

Mia Tuan and Jiannbin Lee Shiao

Russell Sage Foundation • New York

The Russell Sage Foundation

The Russell Sage Foundation, one of the oldest of America's general purpose foundations, was established in 1907 by Mrs. Margaret Olivia Sage for "the improvement of social and living conditions in the United States." The Foundation seeks to fulfill this mandate by fostering the development and dissemination of knowledge about the country's political, social, and economic problems. While the Foundation endeavors to assure the accuracy and objectivity of each book it publishes, the conclusions and interpretations in Russell Sage Foundation publications are those of the authors and not of the Foundation, its Trustees, or its staff. Publication by Russell Sage, therefore, does not imply Foundation endorsement.

Library of Congress Cataloging-in-Publication Data

Tuan, Mia, 1968-
   Choosing ethnicity, negotiating race : Korean adoptees in America / Mia Tuan and Jiannbin Lee Shiao.
      p. cm.
   Includes bibliographical references and index.
   ISBN 978-0-87154-875-7 (alk. paper)
      1. Interracial adoption—United States. 2. Interracial adoption—Korea (South)
   3. Intercountry adoption—United States. 4. Intercountry adoption—Korea (South)
   5. Adoptees—United States. 6. Adoptees—Korea (South) 7. Korean Americans.
   I. Shiao, Jiannbin Lee, 1970– II. Title.
      HV875.64.T83 2011
      306.874—dc22

2010028843

Text design by Genna Patacsil.

RUSSELL SAGE FOUNDATION
112 East 64th Street, New York, New York 10065
10 9 8 7 6 5 4 3 2 1

CONTENTS

ABOUT THE AUTHORS

Mia Tuan is professor of education studies, director of the Center on Diversity and Community, and associate dean of the graduate school at the University of Oregon.

Jiannbin Lee Shiao is associate professor of sociology at the University of Oregon.

ACKNOWLEDGMENTS

It seemed like a reasonable idea at the time. Jiannbin ("J") had just joined the University of Oregon's Sociology Department, where Mia, an assistant professor, was finishing up her first book on later-generation Asian Americans. J was writing on the role of large philanthropies in establishing diversity goals in post–civil rights America, but had a long-standing interest in the Asian American experience. Why not pull our mutual interests together to do a project about Korean adoptees? As Asian Americans, we were both drawn to this unique population and what they had to teach us about race, inclusion, and identity. Furthermore, Holt International Children's Services, the agency responsible for pioneering Korean adoption, was located a mere two and a half miles away from campus. The hubris of youth and inexperience had us believing that the entire project would take no more than three years tops, from grant writing and data collection all the way to completing the book. Alas, life kept getting in the way of our grand plans. And so, after ten years that included a courtship and marriage (for J), children (for both), other book projects (for both), tenure and promotion reviews (for both), a one-year move to Dartmouth (for J), and a new career direction (for Mia), we finally completed the book. To quote the Beatles, it's been a long and winding road.

We would like to thank the people who kept us on track and helped make this book a reality. First, our sincere thanks to the adoptees who are the subjects of this book. It took courage to participate in this project, as well as an act of faith to entrust us with their life stories. The same is true for the non-adopted Asian Americans we interviewed—thank you for taking the time to be part of this project. Holt International Children's Services believed in the project from the start, and we wish to thank them for helping us in recruiting adoptee participants. Special thanks to Carole Stiles and Laura Adler for their assistance.

Next up are our spouses, Nancy Toth and Michael Welch, and kids, Macy, Cleo, and the newest edition, baby Maia. You have our love and gratitude for tolerating the trips away, the endless meetings, and the accompanying stress of trying to finish an overdue project. We would also like to thank our parents, Wen-Tsai and Fang-Zu Lee Shiao and Winnie and Chang Chih Tuan.

The Russell Sage Foundation saw the promise of this project over ten years ago and patiently waited for us to get on with the business of completing it. We owe many thanks to Eric Wanner, Stephanie Platz, and Suzanne Nichols for believing in our vision and potential. Thanks also to the anonymous reviewers who provided critical feedback that helped us distill the original 560-page manuscript into the leaner book before you.

Various colleagues provided feedback on numerous draft analyses and chapters as well as invaluable advice during key stages of the project, and we would like to acknowledge them: Kathleen Bergquist, Larry Bobo, Ellen Herman, Ken Hudson, Nadia Kim, John Lie, Linda Liu, Dina Okamoto, Yung-Yi Diana Pan, Liz Rienzi, Ellen Scott, Rick Tessler, and the anonymous reviewers at the *American Journal of Sociology, Du Bois Review,* and *Race and Society.* A special thank you to H. David Kirk, who generously sent copies of unpublished manuscripts and other texts that he thought would be useful to our work.

Important assistance with research, production, and grant management was provided by Jessica Alvarado, Andrea Coukos, Diane Hayashino, Rachel Kovensky, Barbara Luton, Diane Marcell, Ariel Masters, Liz Rienzi, and Joel Schoening. Thank you for helping with all the behind-the-scenes details!

Last but not least, special friends deserve mention: Anne Allanketner, Annie Bentz, Tony Chen, Meleah Drews, Janet Golden, Susie Hanner, Jan Harris, Jocelyn Hollander, Robin Holmes, Steve Hsu, Ken Hudson, Ray Lin, Eve Montanaro, Jennifer Pratt, Kesho Scott, and Erwin Tan. Thank you for your friendship and support, which have kept us afloat over the years.

CHAPTER 1

Korean Adoptees in America

To hear Caleb Littell recount the story, life was good growing up during the 1980s.[1] Adopted as an infant from South Korea, Caleb joined a loving family consisting of his parents and, a few years later, a sister, Holly, also adopted from Korea. John and Deborah Littell raised their children in the predominantly white suburb of Renton, Washington, just outside of Seattle. Deborah, an attorney, and John, the director of a nonprofit as well as a minister, chose Korea because of its reputation as a reputable source of healthy children. Caleb was the answer to their dreams, and his arrival was cause for a grand celebration: "It was a *huge* deal [Caleb's emphasis]. I think that they were pretty open about my mother not being able to have children. . . . The whole family came out there, and when I arrived home, everybody came over to see me with gifts and this and that, and so it was a pretty big production." As his words convey, Caleb grew up surrounded by love and knowing that he was fiercely wanted by his parents.

Still, despite a "borderline picture-perfect" childhood, Caleb increasingly struggled to make sense of who he was and what it meant to him and others to be Korean, Asian, and adopted by white parents. To be sure, his difficulties did not start at home, but when he stepped outside the front door. By the time Caleb was nine or ten, "Oriental" jokes and "Asian" jokes were a regular occurrence in the schoolyard as well as on the streets. The teasing not only hurt Caleb but confused him because, among family, being Asian was an interesting but largely irrelevant part of his identity. In fact, Caleb mainly identified with his white family and friends, who were at a loss as to how to support him when he was made fun of for being racially different. His parents made efforts to connect their children to Korea and its culture, but they largely followed the children's lead, choosing to expose rather than impose. As for the taunting, they urged their son to accept his differences and not get so riled up, a response that did little to assuage Caleb's growing hurt and anger. "What I think is, they had no clue of what was in store for them as far as the identity crisis as I became older, through the preteen era and through my teens," Caleb said. By fifteen, his challenges came to a head as, to use his own words, he hardened and numbed himself to the teasing. "In fact, in my opinion, adolescents have adolescent problems that they go through. And I think mine were to the extreme where I pushed my family and my parents and my sister away." From about age fifteen to twenty-one, Caleb said, he "wouldn't go to family functions . . . lots of substance abuse, was in a gang, a wannabe gang, when I was younger. Lot of trouble, was in jail a couple of times."

Now fast approaching his thirties and at a good stage in his life, Caleb reflected on why, as an adolescent, he was drawn to a lifestyle that emulated a bad Hollywood movie involving armed robbery, drugs, frequent danger, and, eventually, a stint in rehab:

> I didn't know why I was doing it. Again, this is all reflecting. I didn't know why I was self-destructing, why I was living the life that I did. But looking back now, I realize it was because I was scared. I didn't want any—I didn't want to get teased like that again. . . . So I hung out with people [with whom] that just wasn't going to be an issue.

Caleb's story, while extreme in its trajectory, captures many of the unique elements of the Korean adoptee experience: loving white families who are ill prepared to aid their Asian children as they encounter racial prejudice; discomfort over being a visible minority in predominantly white communities; and confusion over the meaning of being Korean, Asian, and adopted by white parents. While clearly an outlier in terms of his response, the conditions that Caleb faced as a transnational and transracial adoptee are familiar to many Korean adoptees.

In this book, we examine the experiences of Korean adoptees in the United States. Our study includes members of the "pioneer" generation—those who were among the first to be raised by white families in the aftermath of the Korean War—as well as adoptees like Caleb Littell who arrived a generation or two later. Four central questions guide our study of this exceptional population. First, how do Korean adoptees learn about their racial and ethnic identities when their parents and kin are white? Second, what variables lead some adoptees to embrace their ethnic and racial identities while others remain indifferent or reject them altogether? Furthermore, how does ethnic exploration, or the absence of it, vary by life stage and circumstance? Third, how do Korean adoptees choose to identify, and what meanings do they attach to those identities? And finally, how does the study of Korean adoption contribute to our understanding of the significance of race, ethnicity, and group identity in the United States? More specifically, how does it contribute to our understanding of the Asian American experience?

Before proceeding further, some definitions are in order. By race we mean the visible physical markers (skin color, facial features, hair texture, and so on) that are used to sort individuals into broad ancestral groupings (such as black, white, Asian, Native American, or Latino) and have long been the object of social use and abuse in the United States. Like most sociologists, we view race as a social construction rooted in social, economic, and political processes (Omi and Winant 1994). Nevertheless, race has very real and tangible consequences in people's lives because it informs where they are located in a larger hierarchy of power, privilege, and preference. By ethnicity we mean the specific ancestral groupings (such as African American, Haitian, German, Irish, Korean, or Chinese) that are used to sort individuals into cultures, often nation-based, with distinct practices (linguistic, aesthetic, culinary, and so on) and beliefs. As scholars interested in identity development, we focus our work on how individuals relate to the racial and ethnic groupings to which they are assigned, the ways in which they pursue ethnic exploration, and the factors that influence or diminish identity salience for them.

Korean adoptees are an important population for scholars interested in racial and ethnic identity development to consider. On the one hand, they are raised deep within white mainstream culture because of their family circumstances. On the other hand, they are racial minorities in a racially stratified society. Korean adoptees provide scholars with a valuable opportunity to observe identity construction with a unique population for whom the "natural" transference of racial and ethnic knowledge between parent and child cannot be assumed. How are race and ethnicity learned when Korean adoptees grow up

Figure 1.1   Cumulative International Adoptions
into the United States, 1948 to 2009

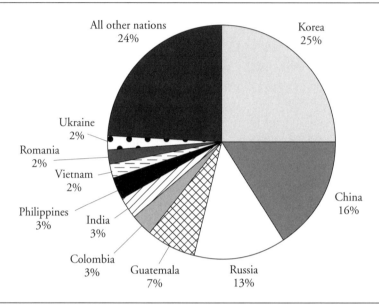

Source: Authors' compilation based on Altstein and Simon (1991) (for 1963 to 1987, total adoptions: 137,437) and U.S. Department of State (2010) (for FY1989 to FY2009, total adoptions: 290,958); 1988 data are unavailable.
Note: Data for "all other nations" from the U.S. Department of State include only the top twenty or more source countries and therefore are an underestimate.

in white families and communities where there are few Asians? In the absence of the "natural" opportunities of a coethnic family, what avenues do Korean adoptees pursue to explore their heritage, and what exactly do they learn about race and ethnicity?

Since 1948, roughly half of all individuals who were adopted as children from outside the United States have come from Asia; they represent the largest fraction of the 11,000 to 22,000 children who have migrated annually over the last decade to join their American families (Krieder 2003; U.S. Department of State 2008). While China has dominated since 2000 as the leading source of adoptable Asian children, South Korea alone accounts for 25 percent of all children ever adopted from abroad (see figure 1.1). Because Korean placements stretch back to the end of the Korean War, there are more adoptees from Korea than any other country. By some estimates, somewhere between

120,000 and 160,000 Korean adoptees currently reside in the United States, ranging in age from infancy to their fifties. This age range is important to emphasize because compared to contemporary Chinese adoptees, the oldest of whom have just entered adolescence, most Korean adoptees grew up under very different social and historical circumstances. Even adoptees like Caleb came of age when the Internet was primarily a military and higher education network, adoptee associations and resources (books, heritage camps, motherland tours) were less common, and the promotion of multiculturalism within the family was barely gaining momentum. Keeping in mind the historically specific periods during which the practice of Korean-white adoption arose and then matured, the pioneering experiences of this population serve as an important theoretical and empirical benchmark for studying Asian-white adoption more broadly.

Korean adoptees are also an understudied *Asian American* population. While scholars in psychology and social work have extensively assessed adoptee social adjustment and other developmental issues (physical, language, cognitive, self-concept, psychosocial), research linking adoptee experiences to the broader Asian American experience has been lacking. What challenges faced by adoptees are generally shared with other Asian Americans? Evidence of rising anti-Asian sentiment, combined with the perception that Asians, irrespective of generational status, are "forever foreigners," poses hurdles that all Asian Americans face in developing healthy racial identities in the United States (Lowe 1996; Tuan 1998). Yet there has been no exploration of how these challenges might be exacerbated or mitigated because an Asian American has white parents. Are Asian adoptees more or less race-conscious because they have grown up in white families? Are the ways in which they develop identity and coping strategies for dealing with racism different from those of Asian Americans raised by biological parents? These are additional questions informing the direction of this study.

As our book title suggests, we believe that Korean adoptees have significant choice concerning the degree to which ethnicity matters in their private lives, the question of whether to engage in ethnic exploration, and the types of exploration they can pursue. Race, on the other hand, is significant precisely because it is not a private matter. Whether they consciously embrace their racial identity or not, adoptees still must negotiate the expectations, judgments, and stereotypes that others have of them based on their racial status. In this regard, they have much in common with their non-adopted Asian American counterparts. We have argued elsewhere (Tuan 1998) that even Asian ethnics with roots stretching back several generations struggle to be embraced as legitimate Americans because of long-held racial stereotypes portraying Asians as perpetually foreign. How Korean adoptees negotiate others' racialized expectations of them and the effect these expectations have on their identity development and relationships with other Asian Americans provide important insights into how race continues to operate and influence life in American society.

Korean adoptees are also a compelling case for exploring the relative significance of race precisely because their adoption into white American families suggests that barriers between racial groups have eroded in recent decades (Simon and Altstein 2000). However, the belief that race has declined in significance (Wilson 1978) is only one of three camps within the research on the post–civil rights significance of race. A second camp counters that racial prejudices have declined more in public culture than in private expression or social consequence (Bobo, Kluegel, and Smith 1997; Bonilla-Silva 2003; Sears, Sidanius, and Bobo 2000), and a third camp argues that the significance of race is shifting from the white-nonwhite boundary to the nonblack-black boundary (Bobo and Zubrinsky 1996; Yancey 2003). Less optimistically, the second camp would be suspicious of the color-blindness imputed to white adoptive parents and the actual experiences of Korean adoptees themselves, whereas the third camp would accept the declining significance of race for the white-Asian boundary but be suspicious of its implications for other intergroup boundaries. Still others would argue that the three major camps are too narrowly focused on domestic race relations and therefore miss the importance of the transnational context for how Americans, particularly white Americans, perceive and treat Asian Americans. Rather than simply regarding Asian Americans with more tolerance than they do African Americans, whites also perceive Asian Americans as perpetual foreigners—forever tied to their ancestral homelands and colored by the homeland's relation to the United States as threat, ally, or dependent (C. Kim 1999; N. Kim 2007b). These researchers would suspect that Korean adoption represents neither the color-blind acceptance of Asian Americans nor an emerging solidarity against blacks, but instead the invisibility of their specific racial experiences to whites. In sum, the experiences of Korean adoptees have important implications for ongoing debates about the character and scope of recent changes in racial attitudes and racial inequality. Therefore, we ask: What is "the Korean adoptee experience"? And what does it suggest about the state of race relations in contemporary America?

We argue that the experience of Korean adoptees indicates that far from simply declining or rising in significance, race has become increasingly contradictory in how it shapes the lives of Americans. Despite being raised in racially integrated families, Korean adoptees have racial experiences that contradict their apparently color-blind upbringing. Although the result is a nearly universal interest in exploring their ethnicity, we find no single path for ethnic exploration but instead a wide range of individual strategies for exploring and asserting their social citizenship—that is, their sense of belonging in a hegemonically white nation. What most of their strategies share, however, is the achievement of an exemption from the persistent association of authentic Americanness with whiteness. The fact that Asian adoptees are able to achieve—but also must regularly achieve—honorary whiteness in their everyday lives illustrates a critical aspect of the state of race relations in the contemporary United States. In brief, racial hierarchy persists into the present in the very ways in which whites accept nonwhites into their social networks, neighborhoods, and even families: primarily as individuals shorn of their groups, that is, as exceptions to unchallenged attitudes, assumptions, and beliefs about their race or ethnic ancestry.

RESEARCH ON KOREAN ADOPTION

Until recently, there has been a general lack of research on Korean-white placements and their impact on the lives of adoptees and their families and on the implications of the phenomenon for broader race relations. Early studies assessed adoptee social adjustment (DiVirgilio 1956; Child Welfare League of America 1960; Valk 1957), but more extensive research was not conducted until the mid-1970s, nearly twenty-five years into the practice (D. S. Kim 1977). Other studies followed, with the majority coming from scholars in psychology, social work, and, to a lesser degree, sociology. To be sure, Korean adoption research benefited from the added attention paid to transracial adoption when controversy erupted in the 1970s over placements of African American children with white parents (Lee 2003a). With critics charging that transracial placements ultimately did more harm than good for adoptees and supporters denying such claims, Korean adoption, with its long-standing placement history, came under increasing interest and inspection (Simon and Altstein 1977; Feigelman and Silverman 1983; Benson et al. 1994).

Borrowing from Richard Lee's (2003a) fine review of the transracial adoption field, we have grouped the available social science research on Korean adoption into three, non-exclusive categories:

1. *Outcome* studies, including physical, linguistic, cognitive, psychological, and social adjustment: Andresen (1992), Brooks and Barth (1999), Cederblad

(1982), Cederblad et al. (1999), Clark and Hanisee (1982), Feigelman and Silverman (1983), Hoksbergen (1991), S. P. Kim, Hong, and Kim (1979) Simon and Altstein (1977, 1992, 2000), Tizard (1991), and Winick, Meyer, and Harris (1975).

2. *Identity development (racial, ethnic, cultural)* studies: Baden (2002), Baden and Steward (2000), Brooks and Barth (1999), Friedlander (1999), Friedlander et al. (2000), Grotevant et al. (2000), Hollingsworth (1997), Huh (2007), Huh and Reid (2000), Koh (1993), Meier (1999), and Westhues and Cohen (1998).

3. *Cultural socialization* studies: Carstens and Julia (2000), Friedlander et al. (2000), Johnston et al. (2007), Kallgren and Caudill (1993), E. Kim (2007), Kim Park (2007), Lee and Quintana (2005), Vonk et al. (2007), and Yoon (2004).

Korean adoption research is dominated by outcome studies, which assess the psychological, behavioral, and developmental consequences of placing children with parents who are of a different race and culture. For the most part, this research has shown that Korean adoptees raised in white families thrive and do not differ significantly from same-race adopted children or non-adopted children once other factors are taken into consideration (see especially Benson et al. 1994; Simon and Altstein 1977, 2000; Feigelman and Silverman 1983). Significant mitigating factors include age at adoption, gender, adoptive family structure, and pre-adoption history (Benson et al. 1994; Bimmel et al. 2003; Brooks and Barth 1999; Cederblad 1982; Cederblad et al. 1999; Friedlander 1999; D. S. Kim 1977; Verhulst, Althaus, and Versluis-den Bieman 1990a, 1990b). In general, adoptees appear to be well adjusted, to perform well in school, and to be free of growth or developmental problems.

Differences emerged, however, in the areas of racial identification and exposure to, and comfort interacting with, same-race peers. Some studies found that Korean adoptees were less comfortable identifying as Korean as opposed to American or white, had few opportunities to interact with other Koreans or Asian Americans, and experienced discomfort over both their physical appearance and their interactions with other Asians (Brooks and Barth 1999; Feigelman and Silverman 1983; D. S. Kim 1978; Meier 1999). In the comparative study conducted by Peter Benson and his colleagues (1994) of 715 adoptive families, both same-race and transracial, the authors found that Asian adoptees, the majority of whom were Korean, were the least likely of various transracial adoptees to say that they felt "really proud" of their racial background. Furthermore, in response to the question "Which has made growing up difficult for you: your race, being adopted, both, or neither?" one out of three Asian adoptees (35 percent) said that their race had made growing up difficult. Although it is important not to overstate these findings, they do suggest that a substantial minority of Korean adoptees have some difficulty relating to their racial and ethnic identities.

Identity development studies are a more recent addition to Korean adoption research. Although outcome research also explores identity issues, the approach is typically limited to asking questions that assess adoptee accuracy in self-identification, willingness to identify racially and ethnically, and association of attributes to racial background. In contrast, research on identity development is more deeply concerned with how adoptees relate to their racial and ethnic identities and whether having a sense of racial-ethnic pride aids them in coping with racial prejudice and discrimination. These studies recognize that identity formation is a complex process for all adoptees (Hoopes 1990; Grotevant et al. 2000), but that, for transracial adoptees, both domestic and international, the challenges are further compounded by differences of race and culture (Friedlander 1999).

The research of Amanda Baden and Robbie Steward (Baden 2002; Baden and Steward 2000), in particular, captures the nuanced ways in which transracial adoptees can identify racially and ethnically. Their cultural-racial identity model emphasizes the need to acknowledge the diversity among transracial adoptees in how they relate to both their own racial and ethnic origins and their parents' racial and cultural backgrounds. One adoptee may identify strongly with her mother's Norwegian culture, but also acknowledge the significance of being Asian in the predominantly white community where she lives. Another adoptee may dismiss her own racial and cultural background altogether and simply identify as white, both racially and culturally, in solidarity with her adoptive family. Baden and Steward's model allows for sixteen possible combinations, each representing a distinct " 'face' of transracial adoption with a unique set of experiences and related issues" (Baden and Steward 2000, 18).

Overall, research has found that Korean adoptees do not strongly identify in ethnic terms. Dong Soo Kim's (1977, 1978) study of 406 Korean adolescents captures the prevailing theme in this body of research. Most of these adoptees had "little Korean identity" and preferred to think of themselves as American or, in some cases, as Korean American. Since few adoptees have opportunities to interact with individuals from their native country on a consistent or meaningful basis, it is not surprising that they have little sense of what it means to be Korean (Friedlander 1999). Lacking a positive reference group to identify with, most adoptees are left to form their own conception of Korean people based largely on media images and stereotypes, images that often gloss over ethnic-specific differences in favor of a generic Asian stereotype. In the absence of something meaningful and positive to associate with, adoptees are more likely to opt out of identifying as Korean.

It is important to note, however, that adoptees' relationship to their identities does vary based on the historical period when they came of age and that it can change over the life course and in response to new opportunities and institutional contexts (Shiao and Tuan 2008b). Going to college, moving to a community with larger numbers of Koreans or Asian Americans, traveling abroad, and having children are just a few of the milestones that can have an impact on adoptee access to, and familiarity with, Korean culture and peers, as well as on adoptees' willingness to explore or claim an ethnic identity.

Finally, cultural socialization studies address how Korean adoptees learn about race and culture, both within and outside their white families. Particular emphasis has been placed on the role of white parents in creating a racially aware family setting and providing their children with opportunities to explore their racial and ethnic backgrounds. According to Richard Lee (2003a, 719), "An underlying assumption of [this] research is that healthy psychological development is contingent on positive racial and ethnic experiences." Similarly, Carl Kallgren and Pamela Caudill (1993) argue that a family's "racial stance" can strongly influence whether adoptees develop healthy relationships to their racial identity. Families who are "racially dissonant" and express ambivalent or openly negative attitudes toward acknowledging racial differences may inadvertently contribute to adoptees' development of a poor self-image.

Beyond the family, Eleana Kim (2007) has conducted fascinating research on "motherland" tours and attempts on the part of the South Korean government to "grant Koreanness" to overseas Korean adoptees visiting the country of their birth. Responding to the negative press that the country received during the 1988 Olympic Games—which highlighted the international exportation of "its greatest natural resource"—the government sought through its Overseas Korean Foundation to reconnect with its former citizens by offering cultural enrichment opportunities, including "trips to ancient palaces and courses on Korean 'traditional' food and customs" (E. Kim 2007, 57). While simultaneously a good-faith effort and a public relations spectacle, Kim argues that these trips amounted "to little more than a quick and dirty introduction to Korea's 'rich culture' that feels contrived and forced (53)." Rather than encourage cultural pride and a greater sense of connection to the country, these official efforts often left adoptees feeling alienated, ethnically inauthentic, and even resistant. In contrast, Kim argues, some U.S.-based community-building efforts—such as "The Gathering," a Korean adoptee–centered conference that took place in 1999 in Washington, D.C.—provide a more meaningful socialization experience for adoptees. At the "Gathering" conference, for instance, emphasis was less on Korea and Korean culture and more on the emergence of a Korean adoptee identity and subculture (Freundlich and Lieberthal 2000).

Identity development and socialization studies stand apart from earlier outcome studies in several important ways. First, early outcome studies generally assumed the goal of assimilation into the adoptive family as well as American society. That adoptees might benefit from maintaining a bicultural perspective or that the family's overall identity or cultural orientation might change was generally not considered. Instead, the onus for change rested squarely on the child's shoulders. As Toby Alice Volkman (2005, 85) has noted:

> When Oregonians Harry and Bertha Holt launched adoption from South Korea as a Christian "rescue" mission for mixed-race orphans fathered by American soldiers, it seems that little thought was given to how such children would fit into a society where sameness was the unquestioned norm. The prevailing "clean break" model of domestic adoption was transposed, in intercountry adoption, into a "clean break" from biological progenitors and from the national or cultural origins of the child.

Early research did not question whether a "clean break" was truly in the best interests of adoptees. It is only with more recent work that such assumptions have been challenged by parents, adoption professionals, and scholars. Recent research on Chinese adoption, in particular, reflects this paradigmatic shift (Dorow 2002, 2003, 2006a, 2006b; Johnston et al. 2007; Tessler, Gamache, and Liu 1999; Volkman 2003).

OUR APPROACH AND RESEARCH DESIGN

Our own work spans the categories of identity development and cultural socialization research and reflects our sociological training, particularly in the areas of ethnicity, identity, and the Asian American experience. Sociology problematizes the concept of an essentialist identity—a consciousness natural, primordial, or necessary for members of a group (Espiritu 1992; King and DaCosta 1996; Nagel 1994). Instead of static inheritances from family and kin, racial and ethnic identities are understood as active and ongoing processes whose meanings can change over the life course and in response to emerging opportunities and contexts (Gans 1979; Song 2003; Tuan 1998). Emphasis is placed on (1) how the very categories available for identification are historically dynamic (Omi and Winant 1994); (2) how groups reconstruct collective identities in nontraditional forms (Jeung 2002, 2004; Kibria 2000; Nagel 1994, 1996; Song 2003; Tuan 1998; Vo 1996); (3) how individuals negotiate their identity in relation to broader stereotypes, discourses, and collective identities (Frankenberg 1993; Lee 1996; Spickard and Burroughs 2000; Waters 1999); and (4) how individual identities develop in interactions with coethnics and racial others (Nagel 1996).

Thus, whether Korean adoptees develop identities as Americans, whites, Koreans, Asians, or Asian Americans becomes an issue of broader social and political conditions, personal relations, and stage of life rather than psychological health. Rather than focusing on the relative identification with a taken-for-granted category or participation in a distant foreign culture, the sociological perspective emphasizes how these and other categories and social practices are chosen, discarded, or revised over time and looks at the factors triggering these shifts. These areas of research point to new ways of thinking about Asian adoption and the broader contexts in which adoptees and their families encounter consequential racial-ethnic constructs.

To further highlight how our approach differs from earlier research, we return to Caleb Littell, the adoptee with whom we opened this chapter. First, existing research relies heavily on the perspective of adoptive parents rather than that of adoptees and focuses largely on family social adjustment (Hollingsworth 1997; D. S. Kim 1978). In Caleb's case, his parents could have reported, in good faith, that their child had adjusted well to their family (especially at earlier stages in his life), and still miss the depth of his racial and ethnic identity struggles. Second, the literature has not been consistent in exploring the distinct yet related contributions of family and extrafamilial influences (such as peers, strangers, the neighborhood, the community, institutions) in shaping adoptee identity. As Caleb's story indicates, what happens outside the home is just as important as what happens within it. Third, existing studies typically use survey data that are not designed to speak to an adoptee's qualitative relationship with his or her ethnic identity and changes over the life course. Caleb, for instance, actively rejected being Korean and Asian early on, but today is gradually experiencing a change of heart as he matures and gains more perspective on his experiences. Lastly, the available research sheds little light on what is unique, if anything, about the identity formations or coping strategies of Asian adoptees like Caleb compared to Asian Americans more broadly.

We designed our study of Asian adoption with these considerations in mind. First, we directly focus on adult adoptees rather than on adoptive parent evaluations of their children. Moreover, we interviewed adults who were in a position to reflect on the development of their ethnic identities and racial experiences not only within their families but also in broader social contexts. Second, we examine adoptees' experiences not only in their adoptive families but also with extrafamilial institutions and influences. Other environmental factors include those chosen in adulthood, such as organizational affiliations, leisure activities, career and employment contexts, political participation, and experiences with racism and discrimination (Frankenberg 1993; Meier 1999; Nagel 1996; Waters 1990, 1999).

Third, we concentrate on the understudied population of Korean adoptees who make up the largest proportion of international adoptions in the last half-century, as well as the largest proportion of transracial adoptions. Fourth, we empirically compare identity formation in Korean adoptees with identity formation in Asian Americans raised by their biological parents, but under similar geographic and historical circumstances. And finally, we capitalize on the fact that multiple generations of adopted Korean children have come of age since they first began migrating to the United States in the 1950s. Included in our study are members of the "pioneer" cohort, the first generation of adoptees to join their American families, as well as those who came decades later and during different historical moments in U.S. race relations.

The Asian Immigrants in White Families Project

Data for this book come from our Asian Immigrants in White Families Project, funded by the Russell Sage Foundation. The study consists of life-history interviews with sixty-one adult Korean adoptees recruited from a gender-stratified random sample of international adoption placement records. We restricted the range of placement years in order to interview adoptees who were twenty-five years of age or older at the time of the interview in 2000 and who could thus reflect with sufficient distance on their childhood and its salience for their adult lives. Our sampling frame is one agency's 3,255 placements of Korean children with families living in the West Coast states of California, Oregon, and Washington between the years 1950 and 1975. In sum, our study is the first to collect in-depth interviews from a random sample of adult Korean adoptees.

We examine the experiences of Korean adoptees at four moments in identity development: (1) early childhood, (2) young adulthood, (3) current practices and lifestyles, and (4) reflections on societal perceptions. Our interview questionnaire is divided into four sections corresponding with these four moments of identity formation. Furthermore, some sections include different but parallel questions to explore internal differences based on gender, urban or rural experience, and generational cohorts. We designed the questionnaire around a narrative comparison of past and present experiences and beliefs. Each section asks questions related to significant factors identified in the sociological and popular literature on Americans' experience of diversity.

In section 1 of the questionnaire, on *childhood experiences,* we probe for retrospective data and reflections on adoptees' lives up through high school. This section establishes important facts about the social milieus and family members shaping adoptees' pre-adult experiences. We explore extrafamilial experiences and inquire about the places they lived, the schools they attended, their contacts with others "like" themselves, and their consciousness of being Asian and adopted. We also explore familial experiences and ask the interviewees about how their parents (and other kin) influenced their attitudes about and involvement in ethnic culture and prepared them to deal with discrimination. Lastly, we ask adoptees about the circumstances of their adoption; the social characteristics defining their adoptive families; their earliest memories, both abroad (if any) and in the United States; and how their parents included their adoption in the "family story." This section addresses the sociological literature on (1) the influence of childhood neighborhoods, ethnic places, region, gender, and local demographics on early experiences with racial others; (2) the role of family in shaping cultural transmission and responses to racism; and (3) the role of family in reconstructing family narratives to include adoption and international migration.

Section 2 covers the *early adulthood years.* Here we probe for information and reflections on adoptees' lives after high school, asking distinct but comparable questions of college-goers and non-college-goers. As in the previous section, section 2 retrospectively identifies important facts about adoptees' initial years of independence from their families. We ask college-goers about the racial-ethnic demographics of their institution and their friends in college and the role that college played in their postsecondary identity development. We ask non-college-goers about the racial-ethnic demographics of their postsecondary friends and the relative opportunities they had to explore their racial-ethnic identities. This section addresses the sociological literature on the relative importance of new social contexts in significantly channeling adult perspectives on race and ethnicity.

Section 3 gives us a look at *later adulthood.* This section explores the scope and meaning of ethnic-racial practices in adoptees' mature lifestyles and the role of race and ethnicity in their romantic involvements. First we ask about the racial-ethnic demographics of their workplace and their closest current friends and how regularly they explore their ethnicity-race by means of personal associations, ethnic foods, ethnic holidays, linguistic practice, domestic or foreign travel, and organizational participation. Next we ask distinct but comparable questions of respondents who are in either interethnic or intraethnic romantic relationships. With intraethnically partnered interviewees, we explore the formation of the relationship, the influence of ethnicity on their lives together, its role in their child-rearing practices and beliefs, and whether and how they have prepared their children to respond to discrimination. We ask interethnically partnered respondents the same questions, but preface them by asking how "difference" has played a role in the relationship, how their respective families have reacted, and how familiar their respective families are with interethnic relationships. This section addresses the sociological literature on the relative decline and renewal of ethnic practices across a variety of dimensions: food and holidays, romantic relationships, and ethnic organizations.

In the final section, on *personal identity and societal perceptions,* we probe the public-private interface of adoptees' racial-ethnic identities. We ask what meaning their self-identification has for them, which social interactions make race and ethnicity more salient for them, and how, and their opinions about discrimination against Asians in the United States. Section 4 addresses the sociological literature on the public-private juncture that has distinguished the "ethnic options" of white Americans (Waters 1990) and Asian Americans (Tuan 1998).

Holt International Children Services provided access to its placement records through procedures that protected the confidentiality of adoptees and their families. We invited equally sized samples of men and women to participate until we reached a total sample size of sixty-one adoptees. The complex recruitment process began with the agency sending letters to the adoptive parents for randomly selected placements at their last known mailing address, which was typically from when the adoptee had reached eighteen years of age. The letters asked parents to forward the invitation materials to their adult children, who in turn were asked to mail or fax their consent forms to us, the principal investigators.

Out of the original sixty-one adoptees we interviewed, we eventually disqualified two respondents for geographic reasons. Two additional respondents required special consideration. Matt Riley was born with developmental disabilities and still lives with his parents; we include his data in chapters addressing adolescence but decided to exclude his experiences from analyses involving adulthood. Another respondent, Ella Scott, has racially mixed parents: her adoptive mother is Korean, and her adoptive father is white. After much debate, we decided to keep Ella's data in the sample but to note her unique circumstances where appropriate.

The final sample consists of thirty-nine women and twenty men (nineteen when Matt's data are not included), approximately the same proportions as in the target population despite their equal stratification during recruitment. The age distribution ranges from twenty-five to fifty-one, with a mean of 35.9 years; age at adoption ranges from two months to thirteen years, including 46 percent who were one year or younger at arrival and 29 percent who were three years or older.[2] Also included in the sample are twelve biracial adoptees, all of Korean and white American ancestry. Biracial adoptees lend a methodological twist to our study design, since their identity development may differ from that of monoracial adoptees. As Leslie Doty Hollingsworth (1997) has noted, there is a dearth of research on mixed-race adoptees and how their experiences converge or diverge from those of monoracial adoptees. Where relevant, we spotlight this subpopulation with an eye toward highlighting their unique experiences.

We also interviewed a smaller sample of Asian Americans who are not adoptees. Existing transracial adoption research frequently compares transracial adoptees with white adoptees or the biological children of white adoptive families. Although these studies are useful for capturing the special dynamics within adoptive families, they are less useful for determining how the experiences of transracial adoptees compare with those of their non-adopted counterparts, particularly on issues of racial and ethnic identity development. To pursue these issues, we decided to compare Korean adoptees with same-ethnicity as well as same-race non-adopted Asian Americans who grew up in the same geographic communities as the adoptees in the study, or in similar ones. Where appropriate, we replace questions having to do specifically with adoption history with questions that probe their families' immigration histories.

Our initial plan was to interview up to sixty non-adoptees matched with each adoptee on the basis of region *and* gender *and* either ethnicity *or* race. Comparing Korean adoptees with same-ethnicity as well as same-race non-adoptees, we reasoned, would allow us to vary the possible axes of social difference—race, ethnicity, and adoptive status. Locating matched non-adoptees, however, proved to be much more difficult than we imagined. We had hoped that adoptees would refer us to non-adoptees among their friends and acquaintances who grew up in the same communities and attended the same schools as them. As it turned out, many adoptees grew up in communities where they were the only Asian, excluding their adopted siblings. Moreover, we were often unsuccessful in locating the non-adoptees whose names some of the adoptees were able to offer us, despite numerous efforts and strategies to do so.

In the end, we interviewed twenty-nine non-adoptees obtained through adoptee references, snowball sampling, and general word of mouth.[3] The sample is exceedingly diverse with respect to ethnic background, migration status, generation, and class background. Suffice to say, the sample is far from ideal and does not allow for a strong test of how adoptees and non-adoptees compare on racial and ethnic identity development. Our original plans to prominently feature this comparison group have fallen by the wayside. Instead, we cautiously include data from these interviews in the interest of identifying fruitful areas for further study rather than drawing any definitive comparisons between adoptees and non-adoptees.

Few studies live up to their authors' initial ambition (fantasy, really), and ours is no exception. The challenge we encountered recruiting a viable non-adoptee sample is just one of several limitations we need to acknowledge up front. Another concerns our response rate: we cannot make a valid estimate of the response rate because an unknown number of envelopes were returned to the agency for incorrect addresses and the agency destroyed them in the interests of confidentiality; however, we can calculate its lower bound to be 16.3 percent. This potentially low rate of response raises the question of sample bias—that is, whether and how our respondents differ from the nonrespondents in ways that limit our analysis of ethnic exploration.[4] To put this limitation in perspective, however, our sampling procedures remain an improvement on the convenience sampling typically necessary for studying such populations. It is practically a tradition within the sociology of transracial adoption to recruit subjects through adoptive parent organizations (Feigelman 2000; Feigelman and Silverman 1983; Silverman 1980; Simon 1984, 1994; Simon and Altstein 1977, 1987, 1992, 2000; Tessler et al. 1999). This form of sampling increases the representation of parents who actively identify as transracial adoptive parents, a bias that might bear more directly on the identities of their children. By comparison, our sample is less constrained with respect to our central theoretical and measurement constructs.

Another limitation is that the use of retrospective data typically introduces bias related to memory failure and social desirability. In particular, older subjects may not accurately remember their early and middle twenties. We cannot be sure of the validity of every interview; however, we were able to clarify claims that appeared questionable or vague and correct them if necessary by probing for connections to other self-reported events.

THE ORGANIZATION OF THE BOOK

In the next two chapters, we explore how adoptees and non-adoptees experienced their childhood and adolescent years. In the first half of chapter 2, we historicize Korean adoption's rise and institutionalization in the United States, paying particular attention to how the practice has been juxtaposed against another form of transracial adoption, black-white adoption. In the second half, we explore why the adoptees' parents chose to adopt Korean children and whether they had ever considered adopting an African American child. In sum, we reveal how the racial history of Korean adoption misled white parents into assuming that race would not matter in the lives of their adopted children.

In chapter 3, we focus on family life and how parents approached the topics of adoption, race, and culture. In particular, we explore the role of the family in setting up the earliest expectations regarding how adoptees *should* respond to being Korean, Asian, and transracially adopted. Although white parents were largely unprepared for the challenges faced by their children, their responses ranged widely, creating significant variation in the lessons that adoptees absorbed about the meaning of family, race, and ethnicity.

In chapters 4 and 5, we shift the focus to adoptees' lives after high school and during their initial years of independence from their families. These chapters address the sociological literature on the relative importance of new social contexts in channeling adult perspectives and opportunities to explore race and ethnicity. Chapter 4 focuses on adoptees' forays into ethnic exploration in early adulthood. We examine whether and how adoptees and non-adoptees explored their ethnic identities during their initial years of independence from their families. We demonstrate that their social environment was a critical influence on the conditions for exploration and the content of exploration experiences. For most adoptees, attending college full-time mattered more for how they explored their ethnicity than whether their parents were open to discussing racial and ethnic issues during childhood.

Chapter 5 follows the life-stage progression by moving to our respondents' ethnic explorations and practices in mature adulthood. We demonstrate that exploration in later adulthood also depended on whether opportunities were available and whether the available activities fit the interests of individual respondents. In addition, we find that of the two major paths for exploration introduced in chapter 4, *exploring their cultural heritage* is what commanded the most interest among adoptees in later adulthood; however, it also resulted in the most frustrating outcomes, whereas *pursuing social exposure,* such as socializing with other Asian Americans, most fulfilled and sustained adoptees' interest in their ethnicity.

Chapter 6 focuses on the state of adoptees' current racial and ethnic identification and the meanings they attach to their chosen identities. In brief, we reveal that the labels with which they choose to identify themselves are less important than the reasoning behind their choices and the shared experiences for which their ethnic identities provide an answer.

In chapter 7, we offer our concluding thoughts about the state of Korean adoption and the implications for broader race relations and social policy.

CHAPTER 2

Historicizing Korean Adoption

Before turning to the interviews, we believe it is important to situate Korean adoption within the context of U.S. race relations. The history of the practice coincides with momentous social, political, and cultural changes in the United States that have had significant bearing on the lives of Korean adoptees. The first wave, those who came in the 1950s and 1960s, joined their families as the civil rights movement was gaining momentum. The evening news was dominated by accounts of protest marches, unrest, and legal action contesting the prevailing racial order. At the same time, adoptees were influenced by popular television shows that idealized white, middle-class, and suburban family life, such as *Leave It to Beaver, The Adventures of Ozzie and Harriet,* and *The Donna Reed Show.* In short, the pioneer generation of Korean adoptees came of age at a turning point in this country's racial history. They, more than any other adoptee cohort, were subject to mixed messages concerning race, assimilation, and identity. In contrast, contemporary Korean adoption occurs within a period of race relations characterized by a contested but institutionalized belief in the value of multiculturalism (Shiao 2005). Adoptees coming of age today are encouraged to pursue cultural exploration and to embrace their multiple identities. Unlike earlier generations, young adoptees today may avail themselves of social and material resources such as support groups (online as well as in person), heritage camps, motherland tours, and consumer items (food, books, dolls, clothing). Similarly, adoptive parents have abundant resources for emotional and practical support. Advice and fellowship are available twenty-four hours a day and at the tap of a keyboard.

One of the main points we make in this chapter is simply that racial history matters in the study of Korean adoption. Not only does the experience of growing up a Korean adoptee vary depending on the historic period when the adoptee arrived, but the ways in which white parents relate to the differences (adoptive, cultural, racial) embodied by their children and their reasons for adopting from Korea have shifted over time. While the earliest families were motivated by humanitarianism as well as by a desire to raise children, contemporary couples, and now even individuals, are more likely to be motivated by the latter reason. Today many couples delay having children to pursue careers, there is less secrecy surrounding infertility and adoption, and single-parent families have become much less stigmatized; all these changes have made adoption, whether domestic or international, an attractive and socially acceptable choice (Carp 2000, 2002).

In this chapter, we historicize the rise and institutionalization of Korean adoption in the United States. The first section introduces Harry and Bertha Holt, the Oregon couple responsible for popularizing the practice. We frame the national embrace of the Holts in the context of the broader international and domestic struggles of the time. The second section contrasts the rise of Korean adoption with the controversies that emerged over black-white adoption. Importantly, this section looks specifically at how and why the two practices have been juxtaposed, both explicitly and implicitly. The third section explores the impact of these historical forces on our respondents' families and their adoption decisions. We focus on why their parents chose to adopt Korean children and whether they ever considered adopting an African American child.

THE HOLTS MAKE HISTORY

In 1955 Harry and Bertha Holt transformed U.S. adoption practices by adopting eight Korean children orphaned by the Korean War. Three years of military conflict between the Communist North and the democratic South had left "hundreds of thousands of lost, abandoned, neglected, and orphaned children both in the North and South whose needs for care and support were unmet" (D. S. Kim 2007, 5).[1] Added to the numbers of children in need of loving homes were the mixed-race children of Korean women and U.S. and European military personnel, who were ostracized in their birth country. Upon learning of these children's plight, the Holts, a white, evangelical Christian couple from Oregon with six biological children, felt "called by the Lord" to open their hearts and home (Holt 1995). In the process, the couple made history.

Although they were not the first to adopt foreign-born children, the Holts received unprecedented media attention. From small-town evening gazettes to the *New York Times,* their actions were greeted with fanfare and intense interest:

"Farmer Adopts 8 Korean Foundlings," *The Independent* (Pasadena, California), October 11, 1955

"Korean Orphans Arrive," *Ohio Lima News,* November 29, 1957

"'Pied Piper' Corrals 12 Korean Babies, Flies Them to America for Adoption," *Washington Post,* October 14, 1955

"Oregon Family of Eight Adds Eight More," *Christian Science Monitor,* October 21, 1955

"Mr. Holt Moves the World," *Oregonian,* April 9, 1956

"Children: New Faces," *Time,* December 23, 1957

"Oregonian Takes 8 Seoul Orphans," *New York Times,* October 2, 1955

"Adopter of 8 Koreans Off to Get 200 More," *New York Times,* March 26, 1956

Local and national media seized on the story with its elements of humanitarianism, war orphans in need, and Christian missionary zeal. The Oregon couple publicly legitimized international and cross-racial adoptions on moral and religious grounds, inspiring thousands of white American families to follow suit. Korean adoption rapidly became a cause that Americans rallied behind for both humanitarian and self-interested reasons. In response to an overwhelming number of inquiries from prospective parents, the Holts founded one of the first, and eventually one of the largest, international adoption agencies, thereby institutionalizing the practice of adopting from abroad.

What should be of particular interest to observers is the historical timing of this movement. Adoptions from Korea and their creation of interracial families preceded both the liberalization of U.S. immigration policy in 1965 and the elimination of antimiscegenation laws in 1967. Asian migration to the United States was not an option for much of the first half of the twentieth century because of racist exclusionary laws designed to maintain America's white, Eurocentric dominance (Ancheta 1998; Glenn 2002; Steinberg 2001). In fact,

Congress had to pass special legislation to allow the Holts' children entry into the United States. Furthermore, prior to the 1967 Supreme Court decision in *Loving v. Virginia,* sixteen states still barred interracial marriage between whites and nonwhites, evidence that interracial families were still very much a taboo in many parts of the nation. Against the backdrop of these de jure racial restrictions emerged the practice of white American families adopting Korean children and its celebration in the public eye.

Another intriguing aspect of Korean adoption is that it came into practice despite the controversies that were emerging over other forms of transracial adoption. Criticism regarding the appropriateness of placing African American children with white parents came to a head in the 1970s when the National Association of Black Social Workers (NABSW) issued a statement denouncing the practice (Bremner 1974). While the actual number of placements was quite low during the 1940s and 1950s, by the 1960s social service agencies and private advocacy groups were encouraging the practice as a positive step toward racial integration (Day 1979; Quiroz 2007). Even then, the numbers were modest compared to total adoptions: when such placements peaked in 1971, approximately 2,500 African American children joined their white families that year (Silverman 1993). Still, criticism mounted based on the assumption that harm was being done to children's racial identity development and also to the communities from which they were taken.

It was in this spirit that NABSW took a stand. Referring to the practice as "cultural genocide," NABSW called into question whether white parents could prepare children of color for "survival in a racist society." Transracial placements, they argued, left black children in a racial and cultural "no-man's-land," fully accepted by neither white-majority society nor the cultural and racial community from which they originated (Chestang 1972; Chimezie 1975; Courtney 1997; Simon and Altstein 1992). Critics further charged that the child welfare system put little effort into rehabilitating black parents estranged from their children, working with extended families, or encouraging prospective black parents to adopt (Willis 1996). Attention was also called to the fact that the majority of adoption workers and supervisors in public as well as private adoption agencies were whites with little cultural competency working with or evaluating black families (Gelles and Kroll 1993). In sum, NABSW stated in the strongest of terms its opposition to the practice, setting off an equally strong reaction among social service agencies, children's rights organizations, and white adoptive parents, both prospective and actual. Some responded by complying with

NABSW's wishes to cease pursuing such placements, while others defended the practice and sought to show its appropriateness.

The controversy that followed received substantial attention despite the fact that the actual number of black children placed with white families constituted a small fraction of all adoptions (Abdullah 1996; Bartholet 1995; Herman 2007; Howe 1995; Nutt and Snyder 1973; Perry 1993; Townsend 1995). Nevertheless, the practice became a highly symbolic and politicized issue given the broader racial struggles being waged at the time (Kennedy 2003). Ensuing research was clearly influenced by the debates, and numerous outcome studies were conducted to assess adoptee social adjustment, racial identity development, self-esteem, and school performance (Altstein and Simon 1991; Brooks and Barth 1999; Feigelman and Silverman 1983; Grow, Shapiro, and Child Welfare League of America Research Center 1974; Ladner 1977; Lee 2003a; McRoy and Zurcher 1983; Shireman 1988; Simon and Altstein 1977, 1987, 1992, 2000).[2]

The 1972 NABSW statement also triggered a serious reexamination of other transracial adoption placements (Fanshel 1972; Unger 1977). The Indian Child Welfare Act of 1978, for example, was passed by Congress to protect Indian children and their birth parents after decades of forced removals of Indian children from their families. According to B. J. Jones (n.d., 1):

> Before 1978, as many as 25 to 35 percent of the Indian children in certain states were removed from their homes and placed in non-Indian homes by state courts, welfare agencies, and private adoption agencies. Non-Indian judges and social workers—failing to appreciate traditional Indian child-rearing practices—perceived day-to-day life in the children's Indian homes as contrary to the children's best interests.

At the high point in 1987, thirty states had established policies against transracial placements, largely in response to the concerns raised by NABSW and other critics. By the 1990s, however, sentiment shifted in favor of color-blind policies that did not emphasize a child's group identities. This shift accompanied broader changes in public opinion concerning minority rights that were fueled by a post–civil rights weariness and backlash toward race-based policies (Schuman et. al 1998; Bonilla Silva and Embrick 2006). In 1994 the Multi-Ethnic Placement Act (MEPA), sponsored by Senator Howard Metzenbaum (D-Ohio), was passed, forbidding any state or entity that receives federal assistance for adoptive or foster care placements from delaying or denying the placement of a child on the basis of race, color, or national origin (Jennings 2006). Bolstered by research showing that children of color are not harmed by being placed with white parents, MEPA moved to eliminate "unreasonable" delays in placement on the basis of efforts to race-match parents and children. The movement away from supporting same-race adoptions reflected an important ideological shift in how the phrase "the best interests of the child" was understood. Earlier, the phrase was interpreted with the importance of preserving a child's racial and cultural heritage firmly in mind; after 1994 the phrase emphasized the need to shorten the time that children must wait to be adopted, with race-matching policies seen as hindering this effort. This interpretation still prevails today for domestic placements.

Although it did not present nearly so heated a controversy as black-white adoption, international adoption also came under scrutiny. Critics argued that the practice amounts to the commodification of children from developing nations, and they took aim at the largely middle-class and white families who adopt these children and the broader systems of global inequality that promote the practice (Anagnost 2000; Freidmutter 2002; Lovelock 2000; Ngabonziza 1988; Smolin 2004; Volkman 2003). Curiously, however, Korean adoption drew little attention during this time, despite representing the largest proportion of cross-racial and international placements in the United States (Yoon 2007). In fact, placements of Korean children with white families not only continued but expanded under a positive and mostly uncontested discourse.

KOREAN ADOPTION: THE UNEXPECTED EMBRACE

How might we account for the unexpected embrace of Korean adoption by the white public as well as the lack of scrutiny by minority rights advocates? According to C. C. Choy (2007) and Christina Klein (2003), white Americans could support Korean adoption because the minorities in question, orphaned babies and young children, were not perceived as threats to the prevailing racial order. In fact, the practice maintained the notion of American dominance right down to the image of white couples "saving" Korean children. Harry Holt, in particular, emerged as a symbol of America's indomitable "can-do" attitude.[3] Choy and Klein also emphasize the significance of the Cold War and the emerging view of adoption as a means for average Americans back home to contribute to the war effort by "liberating" and "saving" children caught up in the throes of Asian communism. An important ingredient of this liberation was a commitment to raising Korean children to be unapologetically American (read: culturally white) and Christian. Rather than being seen as radical or transgressive, adopting from Korea was viewed as patriotic and in alignment with deeply held American values. Far from threatening the prevailing racial order, the practice was actually seen as reinforcing it.

Also contributing to the lack of concern about Korean adoption was the absence of Korean opposition at the time when criticism of other transracial placements was peaking. In the case of African American and Native American transracial adoption, opposition arose directly from those communities because their most precious resources, their children, were being "stolen" from them (Abdullah 1996; Jones, n.d.). There was no Korean American community of comparable size or politicization, owing in part to the racial restrictions on Asian immigration (discussed earlier). Moreover, unlike other children, Korean adoptees were not taken directly from Korean American communities but from a country half a world away, in the aftermath of a devastating war, and against a historical backdrop of U.S. imperialism in Korea (N. Kim 2008; Yoon 2007). Furthermore, many children who first arrived were the mixed-race sons and daughters of Korean women and American and European military soldiers and were viewed by many Koreans as the products of shameful liaisons (Cho 2008). In light of these circumstances, adoption, even to white couples on the other side of the world, was seen as consistent with the best interests of the children and of the country overall (Bai 2007; D. S. Kim 2007; Lee 2007).

Yet another factor was the historical understanding of Asians in the white American imagination. Since the "Asian" has long been a symbol for foreignness in the United States (N. Kim 2008; Lowe 1996; Said 1979; Tuan 1998), it is not surprising that Korean adoptions are more commonly viewed as transnational than as transracial adoptions. This deflection of race into a discourse of national and cultural difference has kept the issues raised by transracial adoption scholars largely focused on black-white adoptions, while international adoptions have mostly evaded the concerns of transracial discourse and other race discourses in general.

So far we have explored why Korean adoption evaded controversy during its early years. Yet even today the practice remains largely uncontested while black-white placements still generate debate.[4] In fact, with the emergence of China as a major figure in international adoption, the popularity of Asian adoption as a whole has skyrocketed. Googling the search term "Korean adoptee" fetches 8.8 million hits; Googling "China adoptee" returns an astounding 24.3 million hits.[5] Corporate advertisers have capitalized on the practice to demonstrate their multicultural leanings (Eng 2003; Shiu 2001). From Kodak and IKEA print ads to Wal-Mart and JCPenney television commercials, images of white parents and their Asian children are now quite popular. We suggest that Madison Avenue's embrace of Asian adoption is both evidence of and contributor to the practice's move toward mundanity. Thanks in part to these advertisements, most whites do not consider adoption from Asia controversial. On the other hand, it is arguable that these commercials would never have seen the light of day if they had been considered too provocative in the first place.

Hierarchies of preference, race-based as well as nation-based, clearly influence which children parents are willing to adopt (Dorow 2006a, 2006b; Fogg-Davis 2002; Jacobson 2008; Kennedy 2003; Maldonado 2006; Rothman 2005; Shiao, Tuan, and Rienzi 2004). As Pamela Quiroz (2007) writes in her book *Adoption in a Color-Blind Society,* race matters in the decisionmaking of white parents. Far from being color-blind, white parents find that racial considerations weigh heavily as they consider the various options available to them. Within these hierarchies, Korea continues to rank near the top because of its long-standing involvement in international adoption combined with (1) racial stereotyping that favors Asians over other racial minority groups and (2) the preferences generally held toward international adoption by prospective parents who are willing to adopt transracially.

Much has been written about Asian Americans and their portrayal as model minorities and honorary whites (Bonilla Silva and Embrick 2006; Lee 1996; Lee 1989; O'Brien 2008; Osajima 1988; Park 2008; Suzuki 1989; Tuan 1998; Yancey 2003). These depictions suggest that Asians are superior to other racial minorities in terms of intelligence, temperament, and capacity for fitting into white society. Scholars and activists have taken a more critical stance toward these stereotypes, but prospective families are more likely to embrace them. Especially for white parents with little firsthand knowledge or experience of other races, such racial imagery can profoundly influence who they are willing to adopt. These stereotypes reinforce beliefs that Korean adoption and Asian adoption more generally are socially acceptable and likely to be successful.[6] White adoptive parents, for the most part, do not anticipate extra challenges beyond those associated with parenting any child.

In contrast, prospective white parents are confronted with abundant antiblack messages that may discourage them from adopting a black child (Quiroz 2007; Dorow 2006b; Rothman 2005; Kennedy 2003). For example, white adoptive mothers in Heather Jacobson's (2008, 33) study avoided adopting black children "because of the negative reactions they anticipated receiving from friends and family" who believed these stereotypes. Her respondents considered it "unfair" to adopt black children because of the racial prejudice they might face from family members and beyond.[7] Prospective white parents also fear disapproval from the black community and shy away from drawing unwanted attention to themselves. Although these parents may have little familiarity with either Asians or African Americans, the societal messages they receive about both populations clearly favor the former over the latter (Dorow 2006a). For couples or individuals just looking to create families rather than controversy, the choice is clear.

To be sure, the model minority stereotype does not exist within a vacuum but functions in tandem with stereotypes about other racial groups (O'Brien 2008; Prashad 2001). Here, it is important to single out Claire Kim's (1999) racial triangulation theory. Kim argues that in a "field of racial positions" racial groups are evaluated not only in comparison with one another but also along multiple dimensions, in particular, insider-foreigner and superior-inferior. Asian Americans are "racially triangulated" between whites and blacks. Relative to blacks, they have been valorized as superior (both racially and culturally). Relative to whites, they have been ostracized on the grounds of being immutably foreign and unassimilable.

In addition to favorable racial stereotyping, Asian adoptees benefit from the preferences that prospective parents willing to adopt transracially have toward international adoption. According to Jacobson (2008, 32), "it was as if domestic adoption was completely off the radar in the decision-making process." Most white mothers in her study sought a particular type of adoption experience— a healthy infant or toddler and no birth parents seeking involvement— and viewed international adoption as the best way to achieve it. Similarly, Dong Pil Yoon (2007, 279) argues that adoptions involving foreign-born children of color are less controversial compared to adoptions of domestically born children of color "because many believe that issues such as ethnic identity and mental health of internationally adopted children are less important when one considers the consequences of remaining in an orphanage or an economically depressed country." In contrast, it is nearly impossible for white parents of domestic children of color to avoid the politics of transracial adoption or the broader implications of their decision to adopt. Seen in this light, it is understandable that the adoption of foreign children of color has come to be framed favorably in contrast to the domestic adoption of children of color, which carries not only a historical legacy of racism and oppression but a modern-day controversy (in the case of black-white adoption) that puts adoptive parents under much greater scrutiny and accountability.

Monica Dalen and Barbro Saetersdal (1987, 44) further argue that geographic distance has an impact on how racial and cultural differences are evaluated by adoptive parents, with foreign-born adoptees of color generally being seen more favorably than domestic adoptees of color: "The cultural background represents few threats to the family unit when it is distant enough. . . . However, the cultural background is more threatening with a geographically present minority group of your own, especially if such a group has a marginal and low-status affiliation to society." According to Evelyn Lamb, director of a children's aid organization, international adoption can seem "tidier" than domestic adoption because "adoptive parents can fantasize . . . about the circumstances that led a birth mother to place her baby for adoption elsewhere. Here [in the United States] . . . blame is often levied on birth mothers for lifestyle choices. You don't hear women in China being blamed for giving up their daughter. . . . You hear about how hard it is to live under communism" (Gabrielle Glaser, "Sending Black Babies North." *Oregonian,* July 4, 2004, L1).

In sum, the rise and institutionalization of Korean adoption is remarkable given the historic period within which it emerged. The practice flourished despite a backdrop of movements challenging the dominance and authority of white people. Whether it flourished in spite of, or in response to, this backdrop remains an open question. What is clear is that the agencies that facilitated placements, the white families who adopted from Korea, and the American public more generally were not concerned by the racial and cultural differences between Koreans and whites as they were with the differences between whites and other racial groups. Instead, the parties involved largely assumed that the children would adapt well to their white families as well as to the broader white society and would not need to seriously wrestle with questions about their racial and ethnic identity.

We turn now to our respondents and situate their families' decision to adopt from Korea within these historical contexts. What did their parents think about adopting children of color given the racial climate in which they were making their decisions? Why Korea? Why international instead of domestic adoption? What would compel white couples, many from small, rural, and all-white communities, to adopt children who not only were from halfway around the world but were culturally, racially, and linguistically different from themselves?

ADOPTING FROM KOREA

Back then, it was the thing to do, to adopt from Korea.

—Ross Green, forty-two years old

At the time, Holt was real big.

—Mona Brown, twenty-eight years old

Harry and Bertha Holt figured prominently in our interviews with adoptees who joined their families in the early years of the practice of Korean adoption. Jennifer Welch, a forty-one-year-old executive at a major financial management firm, shared some family history: After eight years of marriage, her parents, Norval and Marianne Welch, had not produced a child. A laborer who picked up jobs wherever possible, Norval supported Marianne's long-standing desire to become a mother, even though it was a strain on the couple's finances. "They were on a list to adopt here, the typical seven-year . . . you know, the blond-haired bouncing baby boy list. So they'd been on that list for a while. And there was an article in the *Fresno Bee* interviewing a family that had adopted two daughters from Holt, and my mother read that and contacted this woman." Shortly thereafter, Jennifer, then a beautiful six-month-old baby girl, was adopted by the Welches. Jennifer's parents, like others who adopted in the late 1950s and 1960s, pursued Korean adoption after hearing about Harry and Bertha Holt and their mission to find homes for Korean orphans. Inspired by their story and the glowing media coverage that ensued, couples across the country were spurred into action. Some, like Jennifer's parents, were driven by a desire to have a family of their own and saw Korean adoption as the means to achieve their dreams. Others felt spiritually "called" to become involved. After watching a television program highlighting the Holts' activities, the parents of Carmen Krum, a forty-eight-year-old mixed-race woman fathered by a white American GI, felt "led by the Lord" to follow suit. Out of fourteen respondents for whom religious faith was a motivator in their parents' decision to adopt, two-thirds were members of the pioneer generation adopted during the first ten to fifteen years of the practice.

In no time, the practice became self-sustaining. As couples followed in the Holts' footsteps, more chose Korean adoption because they personally knew somebody who had already done so. Couples like Emily Stewart's parents needed the personal connection to initiate the process for themselves. They decided to adopt after members of their church had done so, while Margaret Houston's parents followed in the path of close friends. "At the time [my parents] had some friends that . . . adopted through Holt. And they saw those cute little kids . . . and they decided to see if they could adopt through them. And that's how they ended up with me." Despite adopting in the late 1950s, when the practice was still quite new, Margaret's parents did not consider their actions to be particularly remarkable or socially daring. "Really, it was their only—it was their only way of getting a child. And so it just seemed like a natural thing to do—for them to do. And they never thought about the fact that I wasn't—that I wasn't white. It was just their way of getting a child, and if that's the way they were going to have to do it, that was the way they were going to do it. It was no big deal." Margaret's comments reveal the normative tone that Korean adoption acquired even in its early days. Far from considering their decision to adopt from Korea deviant, our respondents' families considered that decision to be well within social norms, whether they resided in urban areas or small farming towns.

Other parents pursued Korean adoption because of a personal connection to Korea or Asia. Ella Scott's father was stationed in Korea during the Korean War and witnessed firsthand the devastation and turmoil wreaked upon the country. Seeing so many homeless children touched him deeply and inspired him to make a personal commitment to help. After marrying, he came through on that promise when he and his wife adopted six-month-old Ella. Similarly, Matt Riley's mother wanted to adopt an Asian child after numerous miscarriages because she had lived in Indonesia as a child and felt a deep connection to Asian people.

To be sure, the reasons why parents chose to pursue Korean adoption were not mutually exclusive. As we saw in the case of Jennifer's parents, hearing about Harry Holt's work combined with her mother's growing impatience as they waited for the iconic "blond-haired bouncing baby boy" to become available for adoption. Korean adoption emerged as an easier way for couples to adopt. Parents who did not qualify for domestic adoption for any number of reasons (they already had children, they were considered too old, and so on) found in Korea a faster, more lenient way to fulfill their dreams.

There were also parents who adopted from Korea because they considered such an adoption a novel way to be distinctive. These were parents who liked getting attention for being different. According to Dalen and Saetersdal (1987, 44), some white adoptive parents considered their children's cultural and racial differences to be assets, something like a "desirable exotic spice." John Davis's parents fit squarely into this category:

> I really didn't have any trouble acclimating, that I could see. Except that I was—I don't know how to put this delicately—a token, if you will. And this is more perception later in life. I actually was more aware, I was dressed and shown off, "Oh, this is our Korean, you know, adopted son." Almost like a . . . trendy cat or a trendy dog, you know. This "Look what we have." Today I guess it would be like an Elmo doll or [*laughs*] something else.

A mixed-race man adopted in the 1950s, John spoke plainly about the role he played in his family and the expectations they had of him:

> JOHN: To this day [my father] pretty much gives my mother whatever she wants. If she wants this, that's what she gets, and he will work for that. That's his motivation in life, is to give her what she wants. So, trying to extract from that is, she wanted an Amerasian son or an Asian son, and that was going to be what he would get. But I looked very, very Oriental when I was adopted. I almost think at times they were disappointed I wasn't pure-blood. At times I've always had that kind of feeling. It's like, "Oh well, now you're less Asian. And because you're less Asian, you're now not as acceptable because we were really wanting, you know, a little Asian boy."
>
> INTERVIEWER: Were your parents particularly attention seekers? Or did your mother like to have that kind of attention?
>
> JOHN: My mother loves the attention. She loves to be showy and flashy. When everybody else drove Fords and Chevys, they had a big red Thunderbird, you know. And it was always show with them, you know?
>
> INTERVIEWER: And adopting a Korean child was part of that?
>
> JOHN: Yeah. I might as well have had the leash and the leopard outfit on! [*laughs*] I was an object, you know. I was taken places and shown off. Oh, this is her little Korean adopted son.

Without denying other motives, or the love, care, and sacrifice they made, attention-seeking parents such as John's chose Korean adoption because it was a socially acceptable way to stand out in a crowd. While other adoptees spoke of the irritation their parents felt from being stared at and questioned by strangers, attention-seeking parents basked in the interest that others showed in their family, as well as the compliments they typically received for being such "generous," "kind," and "adventurous" people.

In sum, the adoptees we spoke with did not believe that race mattered in their parents' decision to adopt from Korea. Instead, they viewed their parents' choice as a positive action that enabled some to fulfill their wish to become parents, others to help children in need of loving families, and still others to have a way to do good while standing out from the crowd in a socially acceptable manner.

Why weren't racial and cultural differences a concern to these families given how charged the racial climate was during the time when they were deciding on adoption? We believe that families who adopted from Korea were told, implicitly and explicitly, that race and culture *did not have to matter* in their child-rearing, a soothing message at a time when other racialized norms and practices were being called into question. Unlike adoptions involving other children of color, Korean children were framed as racially and culturally neutral subjects who could readily adapt to white American society. A Korean child, they were told and led to believe, could more neatly "fit" into their picture of family and community life.

Seen through this lens, the historic trajectory of Korean adoption takes on a provocative hue. The practice's unexpected embrace in its early years can be understood in relation to mounting criticism of white dominance from African Americans and other racial minorities. Juxtaposed against this domestic power struggle, adopting from Korea enabled whites to avoid criticism for their actions and in fact to feel that they were doing something good in rescuing Korean children half a world away. Furthermore, without the harsh gaze, parents felt freer to raise their children however they saw fit. As a result, few of these parents, their children believe, anticipated the developmental challenges that Korean adoptees might face based on ethnicity or race. This was particularly true for adoptees from the earliest cohorts. Their parents, for the most part, did not concern themselves with issues of social adjustment, cultural mismatch, or psychological well-being. Instead, they fully expected their Korean-born children to assimilate into family life and American society.

ADOPTING A BLACK CHILD

That would have been a little stretch for them.

—Tracey Tulane, forty-seven years old

It was just a prettier picture.

—Carrie Bennett, thirty-one years old

Given what adoptees said about the limited role that race played in their parents' decision to adopt, we wondered whether these beliefs extended to other racial groups, most notably African Americans. In other words, did the parents of the Korean adoptees ever consider adopting African American children in need of families?

We found that, even though these parents were willing to cross racial lines to adopt Korean children, their color-blind and humanitarian impulses had limits. Some racial lines were indeed a big deal—namely, the divide between black and white, a finding confirmed by the research literature (Feigelman and Silverman 1983; Fogg-Davis 2002; Jacobson 2008; Jennings 2006; Kennedy 2003; Kirk 1988; Ladner 1977; Maldonado 2006; Quiroz 2007). Forty-seven-year-old Tracey Tulane shook her head and laughed when asked whether her parents would have considered adopting a black child. "Noooo! That would have been a little stretch for them." With the exception of a handful of adoptees whose parents had adopted, fostered, or considered adopting black children, most adoptees were clear that their parents were closed to the idea.

In a few cases, outright prejudice toward black people eliminated the possibility. For most parents, however, adopting a black child was simply beyond the pale of consideration. As earlier research has shown, fear of disapproval from either other family members or society at large kept them from even considering the option (Dorow 2006b; Jacobson 2008; Kennedy 2003; Quiroz 2007; Rothman 2005). Twenty-nine-year-old Melissa Garvey was certain that her parents would not have been open to the idea:

> MELISSA: I don't see my parents doing that. I don't see them having that much controversy in their life.
>
> INTERVIEWER: Oh, so if they had adopted a black child, it would have been way more controversial?
>
> MELISSA: I think it would have been a bigger deal to them, in the community.
>
> INTERVIEWER: But not adopting Asian children?
>
> MELISSA: No, because I think adopting a child is like saving that child. When it came to my time, it was, you know, Korean adoptees were, you

know, left and right at that time, I think. . . . So many Asian babies were just being abandoned. You know, that's what I was told. At that time there were so many Asian babies that needed adoptive families. In the United States or anywhere. And it's a little less now.

Melissa refers to "controversy" as a factor that would have discouraged her parents from adopting a black child. Put into historical context, her family was making the decision to adopt right at the height of the civil rights movement and just as the NABSW was issuing its statement denouncing black-white adoptive placements. Had they decided to adopt a black child, they most certainly would have courted controversy. In contrast, Korean adoption was entering its second generation and had benefited from glowing media coverage touting the practice as "doing the best thing in the world." For Melissa's conflict-avoidant parents, the choice was easy.

Clearly, white parents saw a meaningful difference between adopting an Asian child compared to a black child. Without downplaying the disapproval that some families faced from kin, friends, and strangers, adopting an Asian child simply did not generate the level of concern that adopting a black child would have done. Adopting from Korea was seen as a good and positive action, while adopting a black child was generally viewed as going out of one's way to look for trouble. Even attention-seeking parents were not willing to adopt the ultimate attention getters—namely, black children—because it might have generated the wrong kind of attention, reflected in harsh looks and judgments.

Carrie Bennett's parents provide another example. They never considered adopting a black child because they were intimidated by the stereotypes they held of the African American community:

From what I've heard, particularly my mom, talk about [pause]. . . . I know that she has this kind of stereotype of, um, of Asian countries and Asian cultures, as being submissive and meek and polite and humble. And, like always [pause] . . . very nice kinds of things. Um [pause] . . . and she did throw in some negative things for me when I was growing up about, saving face and that kind of stuff. But, um [pause] . . . whereas I think, um, more with blacks, there's more, I think there's more of the association with like the Black Panthers, and being more vocal and, and aggressive and [pause] . . . um, I don't quite, I think for my parents, it was, again. . . . It was just a prettier picture, I think, to have Asian children, who were going to be, um, meek and reserved [laughs] and [pause] . . . not hostile to them.

Carrie's comments effectively capture the duality between black and Asian stereotyping (Dorow 2006a; C. Kim 1999). For most parents, deciding to adopt a child was enough of a challenge to assume, and they were not interested in courting more discomfort. Given the choice between "polite and humble" versus "vocal and aggressive," there was little contest for parents like Carrie's.

To be sure, adoptive parents were not consciously manipulating racial inclusion in some Machiavellian fashion. Instead, this selective acceptance was genuinely communicated to and understood by their Asian children as color-blindness. Christopher Hurley, a fifty-one-year-old train engineer raised in Glendale, California, provides a good example:

> INTERVIEWER: Did they ever, did they have any concerns that they were adopting a child who was of a different race than themselves? Did they have any awareness of that?
>
> CHRISTOPHER: You know, I think, from their, the way they are, their character, I think that that was not a, I don't think that really concerned them. . . . I think maybe to some other people, if they had a different type of personality, it probably would have, but to my parents, since they were the way they were, I think that had nothing to do with it.

Christopher speaks with some pride about his parents' strong character as a key reason why they would not let race get in the way of adopting a child. Yet when we specifically asked whether his parents would have considered adopting a black child, the tone of his story changed significantly.

> INTERVIEWER: Would they, would your parents have been willing to adopt a black child, do you think?
>
> CHRISTOPHER: I don't think so.
>
> INTERVIEWER: So they would have drawn a line there?
>
> CHRISTOPHER: Yes, I think so.
>
> INTERVIEWER: What's the difference do you think?
>
> CHRISTOPHER: Well, I don't know. I guess maybe to them the Asians, because of the color and everything, maybe they're more, you know, more close than, just adopting a black was so opposite to the . . . you know,

maybe there'd be so much contrast. . . . I think, maybe because at the time also that the, you know, after the Korean War and everything . . . people were very sympathetic, I think, towards the, towards the orphans.

Christopher's description of his parents epitomizes the curious and contradictory nature of contemporary race relations and how it is captured within transracial adoption. Although the phenomenon of Asian adoption symbolizes the successful growth of interracial acceptance, it also accommodates prevailing patterns of racial segregation.

In keeping with the work of other transracial adoption scholars (Dalen and Saetersdal 1987; Dorow 2006a; Jacobson 2008; Quiroz 2007; Yoon 2007), our research confirms that race matters when white parents decide who they are willing to adopt. This is neither a surprising nor necessarily controversial finding given how pervasive race is in American society. What intrigues us is how some adoptive parents communicated their rationale for adopting from Korea to their children as an example of the irrelevance of race, while simultaneously drawing a firm boundary against blackness.

The juxtaposition of black and Asian adoptees raises an important theme in scholarship on contemporary race relations: interminority hierarchy. A provocative new thesis is that the United States is moving beyond its historic hierarchy of whites over nonwhites to an emergent hierarchy of nonblacks over blacks (Bobo and Zubrinsky 1996; Shiao 2005; Yancey 2003). Focused on statistical patterns in residential segregation, intermarriage, and racial attitudes, this work suggests that white reactions to blacks are qualitatively more negative than to white reactions to other nonwhites. While it is beyond the scope of this study, we believe that further research is needed to flesh out this thesis in the area of transracial adoption. Adoptions from Latin America have recently risen in popularity with nary an eyebrow raised, suggesting that there is something unique about black adoption that sets it apart from other forms of transracial adoption.

Ultimately, our comparison of Asian and black adoptees raises more questions than it can answer. Both groups share in the experience of being racially different from their white family members and, as is often the case, their surrounding community. In this sense, adoptees from both groups must grapple with the identity and social adjustment issues that arise from being marked as different. But as we have seen, there are clear and discernible differences in perception and experiences between being Asian and being black, differences that in turn have an impact on each group of adoptees. One might argue that racial "survival skills" of the kind mentioned by the National Association of Black Social Workers matter less for Asian adoptees because they experience greater social acceptance compared to black adoptees. On the other hand, one could also argue that racially charged incidents are more devastating to Asian adoptees when they occur because they are less likely to expect them or to be prepared to deal with them. We are not aware of any contemporary studies that have been done comparing the experiences of these two groups. More research of the kind conducted by William Feigelman and Arnold Silverman (1983) over two decades ago involving direct comparisons of Asian and black adoptees is needed today.

CONCLUSIONS

In this chapter, we have endeavored to show that Korean adoption occupies a unique position in U.S. race relations history. At the macro level, racial history informs whether the practice of Korean adoption is deemed "patriotic," "inspiring," and "normal" or "risky," "controversial," and "inappropriate." At the micro level, historical context affects how adoptees experience life, from whether they are encouraged or discouraged to explore their racial and ethnic roots to whether there are people and resources available to facilitate their exploration.

Two key findings stand out in this chapter. First, parents who adopted Korean children, particularly those who adopted in the earliest decades of the practice, assumed that their children would adapt well to white society and would not need to wrestle with questions about race or ethnicity. The parents were actively encouraged to hold this view by an American media and public charmed by the practice and invested in seeing its successes highlighted. Despite adopting at a time when other racialized practices were being called into serious question, the soothing messages that adoptive families received from the media and the general public led them to believe that race did not have to matter in their child-rearing and family practices. In the long run, these assumptions would have significant implications for promoting model minority and honorary white stereotypes (Bonilla-Silva and Embrick 2006; O'Brien 2008; Park 2008; Yancey 2003).

Second, our examination of the history of Korean adoption indicates that although the phenomenon symbolized a genuine form of interracial acceptance, it also accommodated prevailing racial attitudes. The unexpected embrace of Korean adoption signaled an important shift in how white Americans conceived of family and in who they were willing to embrace as family. Yet, according to most adoptees in our study, their families were closed to adopting a black child. Our findings lend support to the growing body of scholarship on interminority hierarchy and racial triangulation and the role of the model minority stereotype in elevating the status of Asians over blacks (Dorow 2006a; Fogg-Davis 2002; Jacobson 2008; Kennedy 2003; C. Kim 1999; Maldonado 2006; Prashad 2001; Quiroz 2007; Rothman 2005; Shiao, Tuan, and Rienzi 2004).

In the next chapter, we delve further into adoptee family life and continue our exploration into their adolescent experiences. We explore how their families shaped their attitudes about being Korean, Asian, and adopted, their coping strategies for dealing with prejudice and discrimination, and their relative pursuit of ethnic exploration.

CHAPTER 3

Family Life and Childhood Experiences

Emily Stewart was raised in a small, predominantly Dutch community in the state of Washington. In the mid-1970s, "it was a 'closed on Sundays' type of community, mostly white, blond-haired, blue-eyed Dutch kids." With her dark hair and Asian features, Emily was anything but the norm in her community. Her parents, Faye and Gary, decided that the best way to help their daughter adjust would be to teach her that racial and cultural differences did not matter in family or community life. People were people—individuals rather than members of racial groups.

Then Emily started dating, and their tune changed. "One weird thing about my mom is, she didn't want me dating any guys from other ethnic groups. She kind of treated me as if I was white." Important contradictions and clues to how race is handled in adoptive families are revealed in this excerpt. On the one hand, white parents such as Emily's aspire to a vision of racial and cultural differences playing insignificant roles in the intimacy of family life. Yet race absolutely matters in relations beyond the family—serving, in this case, as a gatekeeper for sorting appropriate boyfriends for their Asian daughters. Of particular note in Emily's case was that "other ethnic groups" meant nonwhites, not non-Koreans.

As this narrative conveys, how white adoptive parents relate to race and other forms of difference embodied by their Korean children defies easy categorization. Far from being color-blind or not color-blind, racist or not racist, these parents reveal, upon examination, a more complex picture. Some of the families who bucked social conventions to love children of a different race could also hold rather familiar racial attitudes. In short, Korean adoptive families both challenged and reproduced the existing racial hierarchy through their daily actions and choices.

In this chapter, we delve further into an exploration of adoptee experiences in childhood through adolescence, a period we refer to simply as "childhood." We explore how parents like Emily's handled issues of difference (race, ethnicity, adoption) within the family and beyond, with a particular eye to the time period when adoptees came of age. We also delve more deeply into two of the central questions guiding this study. First, how do adolescent Korean adoptees learn about their own racial and ethnic identity when their parents and kin are white? And second, what factors lead some adolescent adoptees to pursue racial and ethnic exploration, some to reject exploration altogether, and some to feel indifferent toward exploration?[1]

NEGOTIATING "DIFFERENCE" WITHIN THE FAMILY

The first step in examining how difference is negotiated within Korean adoptive families is to analytically distinguish between adoptive difference and racial difference. Adoption researchers have taken their lead from social work's concerns about successful or nonpathological placements, and consequently they treat race as an internal tension for adoptees who experience otherwise positive psychosocial and behavioral outcomes (Hollingsworth 1997; Kim, Hong, and Kim 1979; W. J. Kim 1995; Silverman 1980; Simon 1984; Simon and Altstein 1987, 2000). "Difference" in these research designs plays the role of a potential barrier to successful clinical outcomes, especially a permanent adoptive placement. By using the absence of difference—that is, color-blindness—as an indicator of how well adoptive families approximate biological families, the transnational adoption literature has shown a preoccupation with difference as a threat to family cohesion and identity rather than as a social fact to which families might respond in varied ways with consequences more complex than simply success or failure by clinical standards. Instead of viewing transracial adoption solely through either clinical assessments of pathology or political litmus tests for parental competence, we suggest exploring how families make sense of and respond to being not only adoptive but also transracial.

We find clues to such an approach in H. David Kirk's (1964/1984) pioneering book *Shared Fate,* where he offers a comprehensive theory of how families created through adoption relate to being different from biological families. Developed during a time when adoption was stigmatized and shrouded in secrecy (Benet 1976), Kirk provides a framework for understanding how adoptive parents relate to their unique family circumstances as a role handicap and deal with the inability of others to see them as normal parents with children of "their own" (biological offspring). Some of the key tenets of the theory include:

1. Childless couples entering upon adoption are confronted with a series of difficulties, which we identified as role handicap.
2. This role handicap is reinforced by the attitudes of other people.
3. To cope with their role handicap and feelings of alienation, the adopters take recourse to various supports for their roles. These coping mechanisms appear to be of two types: those which serve the adopters in denying that their situation is different from that of biological parents ('rejection-of-difference'), and those which serve the adopters in acknowledging that difference ('acknowledgment-of-difference').
4. The greater the original deprivation and the consequent role handicap suffered, the greater the likelihood that the adopters will lean toward mechanisms of coping by 'rejection of difference.'
5. Adoptive parental coping activities of the type of 'acknowledgment of difference' are conducive to good communication and thus to order and dynamic stability in adoptive families. Coping activities of the type of 'rejection of difference' on the other hand can be expected to make for poor communication, with subsequent disruptive results for the adoptive relationship." (Kirk 1964/1984, 98–99)

Out of this work came the categories *rejection of difference,* describing parents who deny that there are any differences between adoptive and biological families; *acknowledgment of difference,* describing parents who accept that differences exist; and the concept of *shared fate,* describing parents who, as a result of acknowledging difference, openly share with their children the uncertainties that arise from adoption and cope with those difficulties alongside them.

Kirk's framework has been modified over the years in recognition that parenting strategies fall along a continuum, change depending on context, and can vary with the developmental stage of the adoptee or family (Brodzinsky 1987,

1990; Kaye 1990). Still, some might argue that the theory, developed over forty years ago, is out of step with major changes within the adoption world. Open adoption, support for access to birth records, and the emergence of a vital adoption culture all signal a clear shift in how adoption is viewed and practiced (Carp 2000; Melosh 2002; Volkman 2003). Most significantly, placement agencies now routinely counsel adoptive parents to not shy away from acknowledging the differences accompanying adoption. In short, the tide has turned away from secrecy and stigma and toward openness and affirmation.

The same cannot be said, however, for acknowledging differences based on race. Deep ambivalence remains in the adoption world and beyond regarding how wise it is to acknowledge racial differences and whether adoptive parents should encourage their children to develop a salient racial identity (Andujo 1988; Feigelman and Silverman 1983; Friedlander 1999). Families who adopt across racial lines still find themselves in the crosshairs of public debate regarding appropriate racial awareness, boundaries, and intimacy (Kennedy 2003; Lee 2003a). Although some agencies evaluate the readiness of prospective parents to adopt transracially and provide parenting classes and counseling on children's racial identity development, others make little or no effort in these areas. As a result, adoptive parents are offered inconsistent and even contradictory advice regarding the stance they should take toward racial differences within the family and beyond (Kallgren and Caudill 1993).

Rather than focusing solely on adoptive difference, we expand Kirk's framework to incorporate how families relate to differences stemming from their children's race and ethnicity. Do parents employ *rejection of difference* and deny any racial or cultural differences between themselves and their children? Do they employ *acknowledgment of difference* and recognize that meaningful differences exist? Or do parents vary their strategies depending on circumstances?

We categorized adoptees based on responses to questions regarding their parents' approach to difference and how they dealt with concrete situations involving adoption, race, and ethnicity. An initial sorting of our respondents based on strategy toward adoptive difference revealed that a little more than half ($n = 31$) grew up in families who employed rejection of difference and the remainder ($n = 28$) were raised in families who employed acknowledgment of difference (see table 3.1).

However, our analysis revealed important variations once we further sorted based on how racial and cultural difference were handled. Although most families utilized the same strategy for adoptive, racial, and cultural difference, there

Table 3.1   Distribution of Korean Adoptees by Family Strategies and Their Consequences

	Family Strategies	
Consequences	Rejection of Difference	Acknowledgment of Difference
Cope alone	74%	46%
	(23)	(13)
Shared fate	26%	54%
	(8)	(15)
Total	(31)	(28)

Source: Authors' compilation based on Shiao and Tuan (2008a).

were subsets of families who resorted to mixed strategies depending on the dimension of difference. For example, some families openly acknowledged adoptive difference but rejected racial difference and were neutral on the subject of culture. We also found variation in the creation of a shared family fate (see table 3.2). For Kirk, only families willing to acknowledge differences are able to create a sense of shared fate. Yet we met some adoptees whose parents employed rejection of difference as an overall strategy but still fostered a shared fate. Moreover, many adoptees came from families who acknowledged differences but did not foster a shared fate as Kirk envisioned. Instead, adoptees were left to cope alone with trying situations. Some of these families proved to be ones in which the parents acknowledged differences based on adoption but drew the line at acknowledging racial differences. That is, they acknowledged their adoptive family status but not their transracial adoptive family status. In other families, especially those with attention-seeking parents, both kinds of differences were emphasized, typically to excessive levels, while the children were still left to cope with prejudice by themselves.

REJECTION OF DIFFERENCE

Families who utilized rejection of difference did so for many reasons, but foremost among them were (1) insecurity over being an adoptive family, (2) a desire to facilitate their children's assimilation into the family and community, and (3) a wish to avoid uncomfortable conversations and feelings.

Stephanie Muller, a twenty-seven-year-old financial consultant, believes that her parents downplayed conversations about her adoption because they wanted

Table 3.2   Pathways from Family Strategies to Consequences for Family Cohesion

Family Orientation	Approach to Race	Family Response to Racial Prejudice	Consequences
Acknowledgers	Acknowledge racial differences	Advocacy and support	Shared fate
	Reject racial differences	No advocacy or support	Cope alone
Rejecters	Reject racial differences	Advocacy and support	Shared fate
	Reject racial differences	No advocacy or support	Cope alone

Source: Authors' compilation.

her to feel completely secure as a family member. It was not that they refused to speak with her about the topic, but rather that they preferred to emphasize her similarities to her father in temperament or the ways she shared her mother's good taste in clothing. In other words, families like Stephanie's chose not to highlight differences because they were concerned that doing so might jeopardize their children's sense of family attachment. Parents set the example by discounting the differences embodied by adoptees and encouraging their children to follow suit.

Adoptees also mentioned insecurity as an important reason for their parents' reluctance to discuss their adoption (Dalen 2005; Friedlander 1999). Some sensed that their parents, particularly their mothers, were threatened by their interest in learning about their birth parents, birth country, or Korean culture. When Jennifer Welch expressed an interest in her Korean roots, her mother became uncharacteristically upset:

> **JENNIFER:** I read books about Korea. I do remember, it probably would have been in elementary school, and I think I revisited the topic once in junior high. My mom got very upset about it, [my] having a deeper curiosity about my roots and her being, feeling very insecure about it. So I didn't bring it up very often. I think only twice actually.
>
> **INTERVIEWER:** Did you ever talk about that insecurity, or was that insecurity . . .

JENNIFER: She was really [*pause*] . . . I think she was very afraid that I really [*pause*] . . . I think she actually said something like, you know, "I'm just really afraid you'll like your other mom more." Um, you know, "And I don't want to lose you. You're my whole world." And so she would get embarrassed and cry really hard about the whole thing. So we didn't talk about it, you know, without [*pause*] . . . we talked about it twice.

Jennifer found herself in a difficult position: she had to subsume her own natural curiosity to assuage her mother's unresolved feelings about being an adoptive mother. Employing Kirk's typology, this is a classic case of a family choosing rejection of difference as a way to deal with role handicap.

Adoptees also felt responsible for shielding their parents from the uncomfortable aspects of their adoption. Without directly saying so, Carrie Bennett's mother communicated that she did not wish to hear about her daughter's difficulties because they upset her. After recalling an unpleasant childhood experience involving racial taunting, Carrie lamented that she could not rely on her mother for emotional support:

And I think it's, on some level, it must be kind of threatening to her that, that I had the experience, because *in her mind they were doing this wonderful thing* [*emphasis ours*]. And, and yes, I know that my life would be very different, and I wouldn't be living in this kind of environment if I'd not been adopted. And at the same time, I feel like, I've had to work through a lot of difficult things, [first] because I was adopted and dealing with abandonment issues and all of that. And then also dealing with being around, [being] in a Caucasian family.

Her mother's inability to deal with her own discomfort left Carrie in a bind. Not only did she have to mind her mother's feelings, but she had to deal with the situation and her *own* hurt feelings in solitude.

For Kirk, it is understandable why some families embrace rejection of difference as a coping strategy. The urge to smooth over differences between parent and child can be great, especially for parents with unresolved feelings about adoption (Friedlander 1999). However, adoptees are likely to have questions about the circumstances that brought them into their parents' lives. "Why was I given up? Why did you decide to adopt me? What is Korea like, and in what ways am I like other Koreans?" Moreover, as they venture farther out into the world they are likely to encounter situations that trigger further feelings and more questions. "Why do people think I am more Korean than American? Why do some people dislike me because I am Asian? What do Koreans and other Asians think about adoptees like me?" By making taboo any discussion of the circumstances that led to the formation of their family, the consequences of being a racial minority, or what it means to be adopted, parents run the risk of eroding their children's ability to confide in them. Topics that might create greater intimacy within the family, if handled thoughtfully and with empathy, can instead undermine it. As Kirk (1988, 49) writes: "Rejection of difference in the short run soothes parental feelings of deprivation but in the long run has destructive consequences for the parent-child relationship." In the case of transracial adoptive families, this admonition seems even more compelling given that adoptees face intense questioning from the outside world about their background and family composition. Put simply, they wear an aspect of obvious difference on their faces.

Rejection of Difference: Race Within the Family

Not surprisingly, families who rejected adoptive difference also rejected racial difference. Rejecter families did not voluntarily bring up the subjects of race and racism in America with their children. Instead, they abided by a color-blind philosophy and raised their children to see themselves as individuals rather than as members of a racial group (Andujo 1988; Dorow 2006a; Gill and Jackson 1983; Howe 1992; D. S. Kim 1978; McRoy et al. 1982).[2] "Color-blind" here refers to the conscious decision to disregard racial differences within the private and public realms in favor of emphasizing a shared identity as human beings. These were families who argued that race was irrelevant to the mundane rhythms of family life (buying groceries, folding laundry, going to the dentist, and so on). Furthermore, most parents focus on fostering healthy family attachment, and these parents were concerned that acknowledging racial differences might interfere with this process. As a result, their child's Asian ancestry was treated as an interesting but downplayed fact.

Still, race had a way of asserting itself in family life, such as when: (1) racially charged comments were made by family members toward other racial groups, (2) comments were made by family members toward adoptees, and (3) adoptees came home after experiencing racial prejudice outside the family.

As we learned at the beginning of this chapter, Emily Stewart's otherwise color-blind mother was quite willing to express racial prejudice when it came to the subject of Emily's potential boyfriends. Dating served as a litmus test for some parents' deeper feelings about race, particularly the parents of daughters. Five adoptees, all women, were raised to be color-blind, yet they received strong messages against dating men who were not white, especially black men. In a twist to the historic policing of the sexual color line between black men and white women, these adoptees found themselves enfolded in what Evelyn Nakano Glenn (2002, 123) refers to as the "mythology of pure white womanhood" and admonished to stay away from men who were not white. In Emily's case, this admonition also extended to Asian men and even fellow Asian adoptees, but for most adoptees the boundary was drawn at black and Latino men.

In short, adopting and loving an Asian child did not necessarily mean that white adoptive families became more tolerant of blacks, Latinos, Native Americans, or even Asians. White parents and kin with questionable racial views were able to fully love the nonwhite children in their lives without having to examine their own prejudice or alter their attitudes toward other groups. In fact, they could point to their children as proof of their tolerance without ever owning up to the fact that they had all but recast them as white. Framing adoptees as white freed them from concerns they might otherwise have felt when making racially charged comments in front of their Asian kin. As Patricia Jennings (2006, 578) argues in her work on white adoptive mothers: "My findings question the assumption that the choice to adopt across racial boundaries is an antiracist choice. Only a small number of women in this study had a critical grasp of race relations." Like Jennings, we found that the decision of rejecter families to adopt transracially was not primarily informed by a desire to further racial and social justice but rather was driven by other motives.

Adoptees could also be the subject of family race talk. A little more than half of adoptees from rejecter families recalled times when they were singled out by kin on the basis of race. Incidents ranged from teasing to outright rejection. Grandparents were most frequently involved: about one out of three adoptees from rejecter families experienced issues with grandparents. As Margaret Houston, a forty-three-year-old ceramic tile store owner, put it, "My grandma is the kind that would introduce my family as her son Brad, his wife, and her two adopted children." Siblings were involved in a handful of cases, with race functioning as one more piece of "ammunition" used to get under each other's skins. Forty-one-year-old Natalie Johnson's sister, to this day, pronounces the word "Oriental" in exaggerated pigeon English to irritate her. Such behavior, while questionable, was not experienced by most adoptees as cruel and did not fundamentally disrupt sibling relationships. However, race was used by several siblings to deliberately hurt and humiliate. Gwen Owens, a forty-one-year-old office manager who grew up in a large and dysfunctional family, recalled how her brothers who were biologically related to her parents used slurs to keep her and the other adopted children in their place and aware of their lower status within the family.

And finally, race asserted itself in family life when adoptees came home after experiencing racial prejudice. School peers were typically the culprits, but sometimes strangers (adults as well as children) were responsible. In most cases, rejecter families were either unable or unwilling to provide aid when their children encountered these situations. They were caught off-guard by these incidents because, as we found in the last chapter, they had assumed that their children would not need to wrestle with racial or cultural differences. As a result, most such parents were ill prepared to aid their children when they experienced prejudice and instead either urged them to "turn the other cheek" or discounted the significance of the incident. Such advice did little to soothe adoptees, however, especially those suffering from recurring problems.

As we sat in his sweltering apartment on a hot summer afternoon, Kerry Nowitsky, a soft-spoken twenty-five-year-old computer support technician, shared the difficulties he faced as an Asian child growing up in a predominantly white and rural Washington community. The way he saw it, others went out of their way to harass him. "I think out there, where, like, a lot of people are, like . . . more rednecky, drive Chevys type stuff. I experienced a lot of racism growing up."

A big man standing well over six feet tall, Kerry once played professional baseball in Japan. Still, he faced his share of racial slurs both inside and outside his home—Kerry's brother, for instance, regularly used racial profanity to hurt him. His parents, despite good intentions, failed to provide either empowering strategies to help Kerry handle racially charged incidents or a safe environment in which to debrief his experiences.

> There were a few, um, instances when I would try to discuss it with them, and I just felt like they couldn't really grasp the concept of where I'm coming from, 'cause they'd never been in my position. . . . Pretty much, like a lot of times I think they didn't really believe me. I'd try to tell them something and they'd be like, "No, you must have done something to them." You know, that kid's picking on me, and then a fight later or something, and they'd be like, "Oh, why'd you pick a fight?"

Over time, Kerry stopped going to his parents for advice. Not only were they ineffective in helping him handle situations, but they made matters worse by doubting his reality. Their skepticism and Kerry's feeling of being unsupported had an impact, in turn, on the family's ability to foster a shared fate. Instead of bringing the family closer together, racially charged incidents pulled families like Kerry's further apart.

According to Anne Westhues and Joyce Cohen (1998), white families adopting transracially often overestimate how comfortable their children feel in mainstream culture. As members of the racial majority, the parents experience racial acceptance in most social situations and see little reason why their adopted children should not feel similarly. When their children come home after painful experiences involving race, many families are at a loss regarding how to support them. They lack the knowledge, awareness, and skills to respond effectively. Some may learn to stretch beyond their familiar comfort zones to support their children, but more often families, either by choice or by default, end up avoiding, denying, or minimizing the harm that their children experience as racial minorities (Friedlander 1999). Adoptees facing these circumstances eventually learn, as Kerry did, not to confide in their parents rather than risk further disappointment.

While most rejecter families did not succeed in creating a sense of shared fate, we were surprised to discover a subgroup ($n = 8$) that did. These adoptees came from families who maintained a high level of intimacy and connection but did not encourage open dialogue concerning the differences (racial, cultural, adoptive) that existed. Still, they were ready to aid their children if *any* situation called for it, racial or otherwise. Put another way, they did not seem to confuse their goal of color-blindness with the means necessary to achieve it. However, the striking observation that the adoptees within this subgroup were all women led us to speculate on the gendered aspects of a shared family fate. Like other rejecter families, the families of these female adoptees did not want to draw attention to the ways in which their children differed from them. Nevertheless, unlike most rejecter families, they succeeded in creating a high level of intimacy and closeness. Perhaps they felt more protective of their daughters and therefore were more involved in their lives compared to families with sons. Despite closing the door on certain subjects, they still succeeded in maintaining a strong bond with their children.

ACKNOWLEDGMENT OF DIFFERENCE

Ultimately, for Kirk, the strategy best suited to the long-term well-being of adoptive families is acknowledgment of difference. Families who are open about how their lives became entwined, who are empathetic toward one another, and who deal with issues that come up as a cohesive unit are able to foster a sense of shared fate. For Kirk (1988, 15), "such parental willingness to listen to and answer troublesome questions increases the child's trust in the parents and therefore the bonds between adopted child and the adoptive parents." A little less than half of the adoptees in our study ($n = 28$) came from families who embraced acknowledgment of difference, but important variations emerged. These variations, in turn, had an impact on whether families succeeded in creating a sense of shared fate.

The first subgroup ($n = 15$) fits neatly within Kirk's vision. Parents in this group encouraged their children to share feelings about being adopted, good and bad, and were supportive if they expressed interest in visiting Korea, learning about their birth culture, or searching for birth parents. Especially for adoptees under the age of thirty, their arrival date was referred to as their "anniversary" or "second birthday"; noted on the family calendar, this day was treated as a time to celebrate by going out to dinner, reminiscing, or, in some cases, receiving presents. Twenty-eight-year-old Brandon Luebke, a river-rafting guide, recalled with pleasure the extra attention he received on his arrival anniversary: "We . . . had two birthdays. Like, we celebrated my birthday and our arrival date as well. So mine was April 15, and we always went out."

The second subgroup ($n = 13$) departs significantly from Kirk's conception of acknowledgers and did not foster a shared fate. According to adoptees, their parents either took things to an extreme by overfocusing on their differences or acknowledged differences but did not provide practical or emotional support for those differences. Most disturbing to us were two adoptees who came from families with rigid hierarchies between the biological, adopted, and foster children. Both came from families who had adopted and fostered an extraordinary number of children. Samantha "Sam" Cawthorne, forty-one-year-old air traffic controller, told us that, after raising four biological children and remarrying, her mother decided to adopt four more children in addition to fostering many others:

> **SAM:** Well, what they did was they would call it, you know, the number-one family, you know, like some family member's number one, and you're from family number two. . . . We were always different families. We were never, we were always classified, when they were talking to other people or, you know, it was, it was very distinctive of . . .
>
> **INTERVIEWER:** Of which group you were in?

SAM: Which family I [*pause*] . . . we were in group two! [*laughs*]

INTERVIEWER: Was group two also as authentic as group one?

SAM: No, oh, no-no-no-no. Oh, no-no, ye—, no. It was very different.

INTERVIEWER: Different in what sense?

SAM: Um, just the way they, you know, just the way they spoke about, you know, my. . . . They would always say, "my real kids." You know, my *real* children [*Sam's emphasis*]. My, you know. . . . And it was always, the real, the real kids that are first family. My mother's first family.

Although extreme, this case aptly captures how the acknowledgment of difference strategy could be taken too far, a point also made by David Brodzinsky (1987; Brodzinsky and Schechter 1990) and Monica Dalen (2005). Milder cases included parents who referred to adoptees as their "adopted Korean children" instead of simply as their "children." Forty-three-year-old Gabrielle Anderson's mother, for example, always referred to Gabrielle as her "Korean adopted daughter" instead of simply as her "daughter," a practice that unintentionally left Gabrielle feeling disconnected from her family. Several adoptees also recounted volatile arguments when an angry and frustrated parent made the statement, "You should be more grateful that we adopted you." Although uttered in the heat of the moment, such comments left their mark, and in some cases they irreparably eroded family trust and goodwill.

Acknowledgment of Difference: Race Within the Family

Parents in the first subgroup were also more willing to acknowledge the significance of race and racism in America. Although only a handful brought up the topic voluntarily—most waited for their children to raise the issue—all were willing to comfort their children and advocate on their behalf when necessary. Twenty-eight-year-old Mona Brown, a corrections officer, was teased regularly during elementary school, but she recalled with satisfaction her mother's response one day when she came home upset.

My mom would just tell me the story of my adoption, that I was, you know, a little different . . . and different good. . . . Oh, she said I could beat them up if I wanted to. That always works, you know . . . ? "If they tease you too much, you can hit 'em." Okay. Or I would tell them that, "you know, at least I was wanted," you know? 'Cause I was adopted. So I was chosen, you know? I'd always tell this one kid, "You weren't chosen. You just happened. You were a mistake." That would get him crying, so it worked! [*laughs*]

Parents like Mona's became personally involved when their children experienced racial bias. Their sense of shared fate meant that what happened to one member of the family became a matter of concern for the entire family.

Parents in the second subgroup, those who acknowledged adoption differences but rejected racial differences, truly confused their children. The experience of forty-two-year-old Ross Green, a construction manager, is illustrative. On the one hand, his mother openly acknowledged that he was different and not really "hers" because he was adopted.

> INTERVIEWER: And how did they acknowledge your adoption while you were growing up?
>
> ROSS: You know, I have a different perception of that. . . . To me, I always thought I was white. . . . And I was really upset when she told me, she used to tell me, "Well, you know, you're not really mine." And I would think, *God, what a, you know, mean thing to say!* [*laughs*]

On the other hand, when Ross tried to seek comfort and counsel during moments when he paid the price for being *racially* different, his mother doubted his account because his sister, also Korean and adopted, did not have the same experiences.

> INTERVIEWER: Did your family ever speak to you about racism or discrimination that you might face?
>
> ROSS: No. I was the one that brought it up.
>
> INTERVIEWER: And what was their reaction to that?
>
> ROSS: Their reaction was, um, "That's not happening to you because it's not happening to Janet," my sister. So they just denied it. . . . Yeah. If I told them, you know, "A guy called me a chink," or, you know, [an]other racial name, [they would say,] "No, they're not." That was my mother.

Ross found himself in the curious position of coming from a family that acknowledged its adoptive status but refused to identify as or take responsibility for being a transracial adoptive family. Families like Ross's selectively sorted through the differences they were willing to recognize and for a variety of reasons drew the line at acknowledging race. Even attention-seeking parents who enjoyed highlighting the ways in which their families were "different" and "unique" could not be counted on when those differences were experienced as liabilities by their children. Although they basked in the praise they received for adopting exotic, foreign-born children, they were not helpful when their children experienced racial taunting and harassment. They were neither willing to comfort their children nor able to provide practical aid. When faced with situations that drew attention to their children's racial difference but did not increase their social status, they left it to their children to cope alone.

Cohort Differences in Adoptive Family Strategies

When we began our investigation of family strategies, we anticipated that earlier cohorts of adoptees were more likely to come from rejecter than acknowledger families. We reasoned that earlier generations of adoptive families, influenced by the assimilation ethos of the period, would downplay racial and cultural differences in the family. In contrast, we believed that adoptees born later were more likely to come from acknowledger families because of the later rise in popularity of multiculturalism.

What we found did not neatly conform to our expectations (see table 3.3). Although our sample sizes are small (especially for the 1960s cohort), we found that, indeed, more adoptees born during the 1950s were raised in rejecter families and more adoptees born during the 1960s were raised in acknowledger families. But the pattern did not hold for the 1970s cohort: slightly more adoptees in this group were raised in rejecter families. Comparing the cohorts by shared fate yielded intriguing findings. The vast majority of adoptees from the 1950s cohort, regardless of family strategy, were left to cope alone, while adoptees from the 1960s and 1970s cohorts were more likely to come from families with a sense of shared fate. It is difficult to know for sure what to make of the differences between the 1950s and later cohorts. On the one hand, American society as a whole has moved toward a more child-centered approach to parenting and pays greater attention to the parent-child bond (in other words, shared fate) (Ginsburg 2007; Lee and Bowen 2006; Miller-Loncar et al. 1997; Zelizer 1994). Adoptive families, as much as biological families, may

Table 3.3   Family Strategies and Consequences, by Birth Cohort

	1950s		1960s		1970s	
	Reject Differences	Acknowledge Differences	Reject Differences	Acknowledge Differences	Reject Differences	Acknowledge Differences
Cope alone	84.6%	87.5%	33.3%	37.5%	73.3%	25.0%
	(11)	(7)	(1)	(3)	(11)	(3)
Shared fate	15.4	12.5	66.7	62.5	26.6	75.0
	(2)	(1)	(2)	(5)	(4)	(9)
Total	(13)	(8)	(3)	(8)	(15)	(12)

Source: Authors' calculations.

be responding to these cultural shifts in parenting by focusing more on the quality of their connection to their children. On the other hand, it is likely that our subsample of 1960s rejecter families is too small to be representative ($n = 3$), whereas their acknowledger counterparts ($n = 8$), along with the 1970s cohort, more accurately indicate a historical shift in the meaning of acknowledging differences from exoticizing adoptees to identifying as mixed families.

ETHNIC CULTURE WITHIN ADOPTIVE FAMILIES

If race was a topic that most families avoided, they were more willing to warm to the subject of ethnic culture. Granted, it is important not to overstate the level of enthusiasm: over half of the adoptees came from families, rejecters as well as acknowledgers, who were neutral on the issue, neither encouraging their children to discuss or engage in ethnic exploration nor discouraging them from doing so. Still, the point remains that far fewer families were resistant to addressing cultural differences compared to how they approached racial differences. In fact, ethnic exploration was seen as a fun endeavor for adoptees, and in some cases families, to pursue.

What most families considered to be exploration, however, was not particularly nuanced. They frequently blended Asian cultural groups indiscriminately and considered each a reasonable stand-in for any of them. Only a handful of families, all acknowledgers, emphasized Korean ethnic exploration by arranging family trips to Korea or otherwise engaging in activities that required sustained effort. More common were parents who made occasional attempts through token gestures: by bringing home a book about or from Korea, by encouraging their children to do school reports on Korea, by purchasing dolls or other artifacts from any Asian country, by preparing or purchasing Korean foods like kimchi, by attending a Korean- or Asian-centered event (including various Asian restaurants), or by attending an adoptee-centered event. The families of about one-third of adoptees, almost all of them acknowledger families, took this approach.

Since we did not speak with parents directly, we can only speculate as to why they were more open to culture than race. Rightly or wrongly, race is seen by most whites as a divisive "hot button" issue (Bonilla-Silva 2003; Dalton 1995; Schuman et al. 1998). It is especially hard for whites who do not define themselves in racial terms to relate to others for whom race is a salient aspect of identity (Kimmel 2002; Rabow 2002).

In contrast, ethnicity and culture are concepts that resonate for many white people, especially since these concepts are often personalized, intertwined with notions of family, and perceived as shared between individuals (Alba 1990; Bakalian 1992; Gans 1979; Waters 1990). And as Andrea Louie (2009), Ann Anagnost (2000), and Anthony Shiu (2001) argue, white adoptive parents typically view culture in purely celebratory and nonthreatening terms, largely purged of any dark historical undertones.

Accordingly, adoptive parents used culture to strengthen bonds within the family and with wider communities. For example, some white parents shared German or Dutch traditions with their adopted Asian children as a way to include them in the family's personal history; Amanda Baden and Robbie Steward (2000) have explored this practice in their research. For families consciously working to build strong bonds, race was a topic simply not worth bringing up if given a choice. Indeed, being a visibly transracial family within a predominantly white community was enough of an issue to manage.

Korean Adoptee Subcultures

One way in which families encouraged ethnic exploration was by urging their children to socialize with other Asians. Two-thirds of adoptees recalled their parents making some effort to expose them to other Asians, albeit sporadically when undertaken by those who were neutral on exploration. Parents primarily accomplished this exposure by getting their children involved with some kind of Korean adoptee social network, formal or informal. That is, when parents arranged contact with Asians, it was typically with other young adoptees and their families rather than with Asian Americans or Asian immigrants.

In fact, when asked whether their families had friends who were Asian, it became clear that most did not: about one in five adoptees said that their parents had Asian friends. These friends were loosely viewed as "cultural consultants" (Carstens and Julia 2000), resources to whom families could turn to learn more about Asian culture and the Asian experience, even when the friends were of a different ethnic background than their child.

Most families did not have such resources, however. The only Asians they interacted with were their own children and other adoptees. Significantly, having Asian children of their own did not necessarily mean that parents widened their social circle to include Asians. Rather, many widened their circle to include others like themselves—white parents of Korean children.

Furthermore, we noticed that adoptees often conflated Korean culture with the subculture created by Korean adoptive families. When asked how their parents encouraged ethnic cultural exploration, adoptees mentioned attending Holt events or other adoptee events such as heritage camps, "reunion" picnics, or even simply socializing with other adoptees. By a traditional yardstick, attending an adoptee picnic would hardly be considered a Korean cultural activity, but our adoptee respondents defined it as such *when it was attended by other Korean adoptees and their families.* Like the respondents in Mia Tuan's (1998) study of later-generation Asian Americans, adoptees and their families defined culture through interaction. In this sense, the actual activity (attending a picnic, playing volleyball, singing in a choir) becomes secondary to the conscious decision to share in the activity with other self-defined members.[3]

Attitudes toward participating in adoptee social networks, both formal and informal, ran the gamut. On one end of the spectrum was forty-four-year-old Sherwin Wright, a finance manager. Recalling a Holt-sponsored picnic he attended with his family, Sherwin flatly stated, "It was like a freak show. I didn't [like it] because it was all these other Asian adopted kids and just like, 'Don't know 'em, don't want to know 'em.' " Having grown accustomed to being the only Asian around for miles, adoptees like Sherwin viewed adoptee gatherings as artificial and uncomfortable forums. In fact, experiences such as these soured Sherwin and others on ethnic exploration in later life, a topic we explore more deeply in chapters 4 and 5.

On the other end was Taylor Vogel, a twenty-nine-year-old graphic designer, who grew up in a small Oregon town. Taylor cherished the childhood friendship he had with a fellow adoptee. When his family moved into a bigger house, they chose one directly across the street from friends who had also adopted from Korea. Despite a nearly four-year age difference, the two boys were good friends.

> When I hang out with my Caucasian friends, we always BMX race and things like that, and skateboard. But when I hung out with Ron, we would always pretty much watch kung fu movies and make kung fu fights and stuff! [*laughs*]. . . . And, but it was, we almost had a routine, where I'd come over, and he'd have all these new Bruce Lee movies taped [*laughs*] or some other movies taped from Black Belt theater. We'd throw on some ramen noodles, break out some kimchi from Safeway [*laughs*]. . . . And we would just sit down there and have a little, little Korean feast and watch the fights, watch the martial arts movies, and afterwards we'd get up and duel! [*laughs*]

We were struck by Taylor's description of the activities he engaged in with Ron and the way the two boys "got down and got ethnic" with one another. He elaborated on how his friendship with Ron differed from friendships with white friends.

> TAYLOR: But, you know, we also really enjoyed eating that, as well. But, it was, it was just, it was really fun. And I guess that, I can tell you this much. It's not something we'd certainly do with our Caucasian friends, a big reason being that none of my Caucasian friends ever liked my kimchi.
>
> INTERVIEWER: Do they like kung fu movies?
>
> TAYLOR: Yeah, they do like kung fu movies. But, they would, the thing that we'd always joke about is that they weren't ever flexible at all! [*laughs*] They couldn't kick that high. . . . We'd kick them in the head, and they'd kick us in the kneecap! [*laughs*]

Taylor spent the majority of his adolescence surrounded by white people who cared deeply about him but around whom he was always a minority. The times he spent with Ron were different because they provided rare moments when he could explore what being Asian, Korean, and transracially adopted meant with someone who shared a similar story. The boys used their imaginations to create a shared ethnic experience involving martial arts movies, kimchi, ramen, and kung fu fighting. And while some might dispute just how Korean these activities actually were, the boys defined them as such because they participated in them together.

Herbert Gans's (1979) concept of symbolic ethnicity comes to mind here. Clearly, the activities that adoptees like Taylor pursued fall within the classic definition, with the emphasis on choosing only what is of interest to the individual and on pursuing leisure-time activities largely devoid of social obligation or cost. As originally conceived, the concept was meant to capture the state of ethnicity in its waning stages among later-generation ethnics, when it was perceived to be declining from "real" or more substantive ethnicity in the passage to whiteness. By contrast, Korean adoptees cannot pass for white, and their ethnic activities give content to the racial distinctiveness they continue to experience. Thus, their forays might be referred to more accurately as *improvised ethnicity*—activities assembled by individuals whose cultural ties have been disrupted and yet who are expected to be ethnically distinct. While often super-ficial or symbolic in content, these explorations are particularly meaningful for participants because they help participants respond to others' social expecta-tions of them.

LEARNING ABOUT RACE AND ETHNICITY IN WHITE FAMILIES

Up to this point, we have explored how difference was negotiated within adop-tive families. Now we shift our focus to the question of how Korean adoptees learned about their own racial and ethnic identities during adolescence given that their parents and kin were white. Our examination revealed four main avenues for racial and ethnic learning: (1) families making the effort, (2) rela-tionships with "cultural consultants" (Carstens and Julia 2000), (3) living in racially diverse communities, and (4) others' treatment of them. As discussed already, most families discouraged their children from identifying with or explor-ing their racial identity but were open to encouraging cultural identification and exploration. Only a handful of families, all acknowledgers, voluntarily brought up race and the impact it might have on their lives. Most adoptees were left to their own devices to learn about race but could count on their families to pro-vide some avenues for ethnic cultural exploration.

Families with access to "cultural consultants" relied on them to either men-tor their children's cultural learning or counsel them on parenting an Asian child. Carmen Krum and Zachary White's mothers each befriended an Asian woman they met through church, while Ryan Hilyard's parents deliber-ately hosted international students (from Japan) as a way to expose their chil-dren to other Asians. More often than not, cultural consultants were not Korean but of some other Asian ancestry.

Adoptees raised in racially diverse communities had more opportunities for racial and ethnic exploration than those raised in predominantly white com-munities.[4] From the abundance of ethnic restaurants, festivals, and shops to the opportunity to attend more diverse schools, these communities enabled adoptees to see racial and cultural diversity as a normal, everyday occurrence. With their tendency toward sizable Asian populations, these diverse commu-nities also gave adoptees the chance to interact with a wide cross-section of Asians who varied in class, ethnicity, and level of acculturation. For example, Charlene Jones, a thirty-year-old chemist, grew up in such a community in Stockton, California:

INTERVIEWER: Did [your parents] make any efforts to expose you to other Asians? Whether adoptees or Asian Americans, or anything like that?

CHARLENE: I think just, because Stockton does have so many Asians, relatively speaking. I mean, I just, you know, just, a lot of my friends are, like even my high school friends . . . were all Asians.

INTERVIEWER: So they didn't have to . . .

CHARLENE: Yeah, exactly. I mean, tons of Asians! [*laughs*]

That a Korean adoptee could be among "tons of Asians" on a regular basis was beyond comprehension for adoptees from white-dominated communities. Although they might overlook or even forget that they were racially different from their white peers, they were always the racial minority in all social situations. Being around "tons of Asians" also gave Charlene abundant opportunities to observe ethnic differences directly and to interact with Asian families—for example, through dinners at friends' houses, sleepovers, birthday celebrations, and ethnic celebrations.

And finally, adoptees learned what it meant to be Asian and Korean based on how others treated them: as foreigners, as curiosities—in sum, as outsiders. In particular, adoptees learned about race and ethnicity through their daily interactions with nonfamily members. When adoptees step outside their own doors, they encounter a world where their family composition and Asianness draw scrutiny (Dalen 2005). Even if race and ethnicity have little salience at home, this is unlikely to be the case when they leave it. Through interactions with peers and adults, both friends and strangers, adoptees learn about their place in a racially stratified society where being Asian and being Korean are meaningful to others (Adams, Tessler, and Gamache 2005; Kibria 2000). They learn about others' expectations and stereotypes of them, which may clash with their own conceptions of self.

Take, for example, Margaret Houston's experiences growing up. Margaret basked in all the positive attention she received from neighbors in her small, rural, and predominantly white community in Washington State. During our interview, she proudly showed off a local newspaper article highlighting her parents' decision to adopt a baby girl from Korea and the day of her arrival: "Yeah, they did [get excited]. We were big news. I was big news. . . . I was a big deal. I mean, I was a famous person! [*laughs*] I'm not kidding. I was." What Margaret learned from these experiences was that being Asian, Korean, and adopted made her a minor celebrity in her community.

In contrast, Jenine Peterson, a thirty-eight-year-old schoolteacher, learned that being Asian and Korean meant being subject to taunts and teasing:

> Probably the main thing that people would do a lot, and I [*pause*] . . . it was, you know, the eye thing, you know? Well, they would, you know, they would pull their eyes down, you know. . . . And then people just talked, they would try to talk, basically it was gibberish, but they were trying to be Asian, you know? That kind of stuff. And assuming that I couldn't speak their language.

Repeatedly we heard stories of adoptees coming home upset because they had been called a "chink," a "jap," "slant eyes," "Bruce Lee," "Jackie Chan," "flat nose," "ching chong chinaman," or "pancake face." Ethnic-specific slurs were used with little regard for their accuracy. As Jim Moreau, a forty-year-old automotive painter, put it, "They called me probably most anything from Bruce Lee to Jackie Chan, which didn't really bother me. I mean it, you know. It's like, 'Wait a minute. That would be great, but I'm not Japanese. I'm not Chinese.' [*laughs*] . . . I mean, I wasn't either. . . . But as far as what they perceived me, um, we all look the same." From experiences like these, adoptees learned that race, rather than ethnicity, was the salient dimension that singled them out for attention. As Amanda Quick, a twenty-eight-year-old student and mother, put it, "I never got teased because I was Korean. I got teased because I was Asian."

TO EXPLORE OR NOT TO EXPLORE

So what led adolescent adoptees to pursue identity exploration, to reject it altogether, or to feel indifferent toward it? Our data suggest that parents' attitudes toward difference, personal experiences with prejudice, and opportunities for contact with other Asians and Koreans mattered in fostering or hindering exploration. The adoptees who were most willing to explore their ethnic identity typically came from acknowledger families who had a sense of shared fate and who welcomed their children's questions about being different and created opportunities to engage in exploration. These childhood explorers were also more likely to reside in racially diverse communities that provided easy and abundant opportunities for exploration.

Frequent experiences with prejudice appeared to push adoptees in opposing directions—either toward exploration or away from it. Kerry Nowitsky was routinely harassed growing up in the 1980s in a rural and predominantly white community. Despite coming from a rejecter family without a sense of shared fate, he actively pursued racial and ethnic exploration on his own because he identified with other Asians; he went so far as to drive to a nearby community to make friends with Korean Americans and other Asian Americans and to hang out regularly with them. In contrast, Ross Green responded to similar harassment by disidentifying with and avoiding other Asians.

The adoptees who were least willing to explore came from both acknowledger and rejecter families but were united by their discomfort over feeling different from the people they cared most about. Natalie Johnson's story provides a good example. She grew up in San Jose in the 1970s at a time when immigrants from around the world were rapidly moving to the area. Having more racial diversity in her community led to more opportunities to experience different cultures, but it also led to more white resentment over the social changes taking place. As a result, Natalie experienced her share of harassment and stereotyping. She resisted her parents' efforts to encourage her to explore her ethnicity because doing so made her feel different from her white family and friends.

> They tried to share things about Korean culture with me when they came across it, which in those days was pretty rare. But I, you know, they felt like I really wasn't interested in it, especially once I turned ten or so. I really wasn't. I didn't want to be seen as different, so, and when I was younger than that, I didn't really understand.

Natalie's parents rejected racial differences but were open to cultural exploration. Still, they struggled over how much exploration to encourage and how to foster her interest (Carstens and Julia 2000; Huh and Reid 2000; D. S. Kim 1978; Lee et al. 2006; Yoon 2001). Their efforts, despite good intentions, did little to spark or sustain her interest.

Through further discussion, Natalie confided that the way her parents dealt with exploration essentially functioned to isolate her from the family rather than create a shared family experience. "I think they felt that I should be interested in it because it was something that was part of me. But I didn't feel like they thought it was that interesting *for themselves*" (emphasis ours). Going further, she added, "I mean, nobody else was really interested in it, and I think that was partly why, you know, when I told you I didn't take an interest in it, it was because nobody else was. And so it made me kind of, I kind of felt like it was weird." Parents like Natalie's acknowledged cultural differences and were will-ing to create opportunities for their children to explore, but inadvertently turned them off by making exploration an isolating experience.

Adoptees who were indifferent to exploration did not actively resist it. Rather, they saw no need for it in their adolescent lives. Stephanie Muller, a popular cheerleader during high school from a rejecter family, had no interest in explor-ing her ethnic identity because her life was filled with other activities. She felt securely attached to her family and friends and had a busy social life that left lit-tle room or incentive for ethnic exploration. Although she was a minority living in a predominantly white suburban community, she did not have any negative experiences based on her race or ethnicity. When her community experienced an influx of Vietnamese immigrants in the 1980s, she suddenly found herself attending school with other Asians. Still, their arrival had little impact on her identity given that her social world did not include unacculturated immigrants (Eckert 1989). According to Stephanie, "We didn't associate with them because they were ESL."[5] Instead, she continued to associate with other popular students, almost all of whom were white.

In sum, numerous factors led some adoptees to pursue—but most to either reject or feel indifferent about—ethnic identity exploration during their adoles-cent years. In chapter 4, we continue our examination of ethnic exploration and show that whatever their leanings in adolescence, adoptees tended to gravitate toward exploration in early adulthood, so long as they encountered opportuni-ties to do so.

CONCLUSIONS

We set out in this chapter to address three questions: How is difference (adop-tive, racial, cultural) negotiated in Korean-white families? How do adolescent adoptees learn about race and ethnicity? And what factors encourage or discour-age adoptee ethnic exploration?

In response to the first question, we found that how families negotiated dif-ference depended on the dimension of difference. We found that ethnic cul-ture was seen as an acceptable form of difference to acknowledge, while racial differences were largely avoided. Recent work by Andrea Louie (2009, 286) has shown that contemporary white parents of Chinese adoptees are eager to teach their children about their birth cultures, but often "at the expense of atten-tion to race and other issues of social inequality that permeate adoption." Our research confirms that the tendency to showcase the celebratory aspects of eth-

nic culture while ignoring the costs associated with race is a long-standing tradition within Asian adoption. Parents in our study generally did not take steps
to create a racially aware family setting or to provide their children with opportunities to explore their racial backgrounds.

This finding points to an area where adoptive parent-child relations are
vulnerable to disruption. Our data show that families who avoided discussing
uncomfortable subjects (such as the challenges of being racially different) were
less successful in creating a sense of shared fate. Furthermore, our data suggest
that once adoptees felt let down by their parents, they were less likely to seek
their counsel on difficult issues.

We stated in the preceding chapter that white parents generally assumed that
their Korean children would not need to wrestle with questions about race or
ethnicity. As a result, they were largely unprepared when their children did face
challenges. Some families supported their children and ultimately generated a
sense of shared fate, but most adoptees in our study were left to their own devices
to handle complicated situations. One implication of this finding is that adolescent adoptees need more emotional and pragmatic support to deal with racially
and culturally complex issues. If we take this one step further, it is likely that
white adoptive parents also need emotional and pragmatic support in parenting
children of color.

In response to the second and third questions, adoptees in our study learned
about race and ethnicity in a multitude of ways, both voluntary and involun-
tary, and whether or not their white parents wished them to do so. Adoptees
continuously "soaked up" information by listening, observing, and experiencing. They learned by watching how their families dealt with differences, both
within the family and beyond. They paid attention to what their parents said
as well as to what they actually did in concrete situations. They listened to how
their kin discussed other races and whether they praised or denigrated them. And
they saw how their families responded when faced with racially and ethnically
charged situations.

Outside of the family, adoptees learned based on how they were treated and
on their observations of the racial hierarchy. They observed whether racial and
ethnic diversity was a normal, everyday occurrence or a rare experience. They
listened to what others said about racial minorities and about Asians in particular. They paid attention to the media (who was considered glamorous, beautiful, dangerous, or insignificant?), and they took note of who held positions of
power in the nation. More immediately, they noticed reactions to their own

unique family composition. Some learned that being a Korean adoptee meant being a prized member of the community, while others learned that it meant being an outsider or object of ridicule. And they observed that race, rather than ethnicity, was what most people noticed about them. All of the information and experiences that adoptees soaked up, in turn, informed their willingness to explore their race and ethnicity, to reject exploration, or to ignore it altogether.

In sum, how adoptive parents dealt with differences within the family mattered in many ways. Specifically, the strategy of acknowledging differences mattered because it gave voice to, and validated, the experience of adoptees that their race, ethnicity, and adoptive status were salient to others and the broader society; because it led to a sense of shared fate with their families when acknowledging included the family response to racial incidents; and because, over time, the strategy became less a badge of moral or social status for parents and more a way to identify as a mixed family.

CHAPTER 4

Ethnic Explorations in Early Adulthood

So when I went to college, I studied Korean. I mean, I really got into it. . . . My freshman year, I studied Korean. Sophomore year I lived with two Korean, well, one was a Korean high school student and the other was kind of her, like her distant cousin who was also sort of taking care of her. And I lived with them . . . free room and board, and helped, helped them with things they needed to live in the country without their parents. And then, that summer, I went to Korea with the Holt Motherland tour. . . . Yeah, it was the first tour that they had.

—Natalie Johnson, forty-one years old

Early adulthood is an important time for Korean adoptees to pursue ethnic exploration. Far more than adolescence, this life stage initiates a higher level of personal independence and exposure to ethnic status, racial stereotypes, and opportunities for experimentation. From their childhoods, adoptees learned that race could matter in a variety of ways—from hearing their own family's comments about other racial minorities to being the recipient of comments from family, friends, and strangers. For most adoptees, these lessons were neither comprehensive nor routine; instead of being experienced as normal events, they were disruptions to be minimized at best and at worst to be endured alone. For many, early adulthood provided an opportunity to gain perspective on their childhood experiences and to pursue exploration of their ethnic identity for the first time on their own.

In this chapter, we follow our respondents into their initial years of independence from their families. Given that most adoptees do not have the "natural" opportunities of coethnic families to facilitate exploration, what opportunities do they pursue, and what conditions foster exploration for adoptees in early adulthood? We show that when adoptees encountered opportunities in early adulthood to explore whether their ethnicity might mean more to them, the majority availed themselves of those opportunities regardless of whether their families had achieved a sense of shared fate in their childhood. However, not all found opportunities for this kind of exploration in early adulthood, nor did the explorers find the same opportunities everywhere. We show that the social environment of early adulthood was critical in influencing both the conditions for and the content of exploration. In turn, opportunities in these environments depended on the historic period and the institutional setting in which adoptees spent their early adulthoods. Our comparison of adoptees with non-adopted Asian Americans also revealed a fourth factor—or more precisely, its absence in the case of adoptees: Asian and Asian American family members.

THE SIGNIFICANCE OF EXPLORATION FOR ETHNIC IDENTITY DEVELOPMENT

Ethnic exploration is important to psychologists and sociologists who study ethnicity because it transforms ethnic identities. For psychologists, exploration moves individuals from having a diffuse identity defined by others to an achieved identity defined by themselves. For sociologists, exploration changes the meaning of identity from a descriptive membership to a complex sense of belonging. For both, ethnic identity is not simply given by ancestry; instead, it must be developed, and ethnic exploration is the engine in the process by which individuals develop some form of identification with their ancestry. To extend the metaphor, if exploring is the engine, what is the fuel, and where does the engine "go"? In other words, what are the motivations that shift individuals from diffuse identity to exploration, and what effects does exploration have on identity?

With respect to motivations, researchers point either to crisis events that overwhelm individuals' beliefs about social belonging (Cross 1978; Tatum 1992) or, less dramatically, to their growing awareness of group membership and a tension between societal stereotypes and personal identification (Phinney 1989). In either case, racial visibility is a factor that compels nonwhites to explore their ethnicity.[1]

With respect to the effects of exploration, researchers point to either explorers' reflections on the new activities they deliberately chose for exploring ethnicity or their internalization of the norms and perspectives arising from their participation in new ethnic networks. In the first version, which tends to be associated with motivations stemming from gradual interest, exploration is marked by *personal intent.* By focusing on exploratory intent, this distinction removes nominal explorers who actually make little or no effort at exploration despite immersion in the social life and cultural practices of their ethnic group. Without attention to exploratory content, however, this research lumps solely personal exploration, such as reading books, with interactive exploration through ethnic involvement whether past or present.

In the second version, which tends to be associated with motivations stemming from dramatic interest, exploration involves *social immersion* in peer groups insulated from majority-group attitudes. This is less a psychological stage for resolving a developmental conflict than an emergent strategy for social belonging. Ethnographers, for example, often compare multiple subcultures within an ethnic group for their alternative norms, perspectives on society, and consequences for social engagement (Lee 1996; Waters 1999).[2]

Both psychological and sociological conceptions of exploration assume that local environments provide opportunities for ethnic identity development (Goossens and Phinney 1996; Wijeyesinghe and Jackson 2001). This common assumption implies that the range of available activities shapes both the magnitude and the direction of ethnic exploration. In the personal version, explorers have access to modest social resources, such as information about group history, traditions, and customs and opportunities for conversation about the ethnic group (Phinney 1992). These resemble the resources that are more easily available in school settings, public libraries, and bookstores. In the immersive version, the social environment includes sufficient numbers of coethnic or nonwhite peers among whom explorers can immerse themselves and renegotiate the meaning of group membership in relative autonomy from the gaze of the majority group (Tatum 1997). Whereas personal explorers can practice reified ethnicity in the form of cultural "artifacts," social explorers require "living" culture, whether traditional or emergent in form.[3]

A third type of exploration is the *transnational homeland visit* in which individuals travel to a social context removed from their childhood social geography. The importance of social context is further underlined by the institutional assistance typically needed to enable this type of travel. Second-generation young adults, who tend to pursue these opportunities, generally lack the social, cultural, and linguistic competence to navigate or arrange these trips (Kibria 2002b; N. Kim 2007a; Louie 2002, 2004). Assistance often takes the form of government sponsorship by an Asian nation combined with help with trip preparation from first-generation families or community-based ethnic organizations.[4]

Higher education is yet another salient institution for ethnic exploration; indeed, the social immersion research focuses on college students to the near exclusion of any other postsecondary population (Kibria 1999, 2002a). Absent comparisons to young adults outside of college, however, researchers have not confirmed whether colleges are merely natural settings for exploration or also institutions that influence the scope and type of ethnic exploration (Bloom 1987; D'Souza 1991; Glazer 1997; Schlesinger 1992).[5] On the one hand, changes in the ideological climate have both encouraged ethnic exploration and made it less necessary. On the other hand, it is clear that certain resources for exploration have become available only in recent decades, especially in higher education.

In sum, we suggest that *the motivation to explore* depends on both the salience of racial visibility and the conditions for exploration at particular life stages. When adoptees leave home in early adulthood, they also leave an important anchor of their status as honorary whites while their status as nonwhites remains unchanged. However, whether they choose to explore also depends on the availability of resources for exploration. If they explore, *the effect of exploration on identity* depends on both its intentionality as distinct from preexisting ethnic activities and the content of the available activities. Adoptees gain more discretion to initiate new activities when they leave home, and we expect that what they choose to explore depends on an institutionally conditioned menu of options. Lastly, we anticipate *historical variations in both the motivations and effects of explorations,* especially a greater availability of opportunities and a wider range of options for more recent cohorts.

AN OVERVIEW OF EARLY ADULTHOOD EXPERIENCES

So what did we find? First, we found that Korean adoptees and their non-adopted coethnics varied in the magnitude of their ethnic explorations in early adulthood, and we divided them accordingly into non-explorers, modest explorers, and substantial explorers (see table 4.1). *Non-explorers* included adoptees who experienced a measure of contact with Asians and other Asian Americans during early adulthood but refrained from taking the opportunity to intensify that contact. Most

Table 4.1   Variations in Non-Exploration and Ethnic Exploration Among Adoptees

Reasons for Non-Exploration (*n* = 26)	Specific Conditions
Absence of opportunity	College attendance during earlier decades (n = 3)
	Racially homogeneous workplaces and communities (n = 8)
	Substantial family or life responsibilities (n = 5)
	Dysfunctional personal situations (n = 5)[a]
Lack of interest	Nonsalience of race (n = 5)
	Aversion to Asians and Asian Americans (n = 5)

Types of Ethnic Exploration (*n* = 32)	Specific Content
Nominal	Preexisting social immersion (n = 2)
Personal	Open-ended school assignments (n = 2)
Interactive (tracks)	
Social exposure track	College-related programs and activities, including ethnic student associations (n = 13)[b]
	Nonpeer social interactions (n = 3)
	Asian-business employment and Asian-coworker friendships (n = 3)
Cultural heritage track	College-related programs and activities, including study abroad in Asia (n = 9)[b]
	Military service in Asia or the Pacific (n = 3)

Source: Shiao and Tuan (2008b). © 2008 by The University of Chicago.
[a]The dysfunctional cases are also counted among the other "absence of opportunity" categories.
[b]The college-related cases include duplicate counts of three adoptees who reported a balance of activities on both tracks.

non-explorers, however, simply had little opportunity for direct contact. *Modest explorers* included adoptees who experienced their contacts as positive opportunities even if they did not choose to pursue them and adoptees who pursued opportunities but limited their participation in some way. *Substantial explorers* went further by, for example, taking more than one course in Asian or Asian American studies, regularly attending the social events of Asian American organizations, immersing themselves in informal Asian or Asian American social networks, making a trip to Asia, or living in parts of the country where Asians are a majority of the population. We also further validated the modest and substantial explorer categories by examining whether they were simply *nominal explorers* or *personal explorers*. We discuss these cases separately from the vast majority who explored through activities that were both new and interactive.[6]

Notwithstanding individual temperaments and circumstances, we found that adoptees typically chose one of two types of ethnic exploration, social exposure or cultural heritage. While three adoptees pursued a balance of both types, most pursued either (1) exposure to others "like themselves," that is, coethnics and other Asian Americans, or (2) knowledge of their "origins" in the sense of becoming familiar with the culture and history of Asia—mainly of South Korea but also Japan, China, and other nations. The activities within each type of exploration formed "tracks," or sequences of opportunities, though not every explorer followed a track to its final destination. Each track provided explorers with a distinct set of experiences, although their exploration along one track also raised aspects of the other. On the *social exposure* track, modest explorers tried out Asian American organizations and made Asian acquaintances and friendships. Meanwhile, substantial explorers deepened their involvements, immersing themselves in ethnic networks in which being Asian American was the norm. On the *cultural heritage* track, exploration typically started with language classes or other college courses about Asian societies and continued toward travel abroad, which led to the shocking experience of being in the racial majority, often for the first time in their lives. Despite these experiential parallels, these types of activities remained mutually exclusive tracks for most adoptees (see table 4.1).

The *historical period* during which early adulthood took place significantly shaped adoptees' involvement in different tracks of ethnic exploration.[7] During the 1970s, the majority of adoptees who were in early adulthood were non-explorers, but from the 1980s into the 1990s, only a minority of adoptees in early adulthood remained non-explorers.[8] Focusing on the substantial explorers, we saw a similar trend: substantial explorers shifted (1) in size, from making up a minority of their early adulthood cohort in the 1970s to a plurality in the 1980s, and eventually a majority in the 1990s, and (2) in focus, from social exposure alone to a combination of social exposure and cultural fluency by the 1990s. Among non-adoptees, non-exploration had vanished entirely by the 1990s, during which time a majority among both adoptees and non-adoptees pursued substantial exploration. Whereas both adoptees and non-adoptees mainly pursued social exposure during the 1970s, cultural heritage gained ground in the 1980s and for adoptees became a major track by the 1990s, whereas non-adoptees remained overwhelmingly engaged in social exposure.

We also found variations in adoptees' *institutional environments,* which was consequential for whether and how they explored their ethnicity. College-only adoptees were traditional college students who spent their years immediately after high school (or soon after) attending a bachelor's degree–granting institution, including those who transferred from a community college. We categorized adoptees as "college and other" if they had another significant work or life commitment that they reported as competing with or being equal in importance to their investment in higher education. This included traditional students who quit school before finishing their degree, students who completed an associate's degree while being employed and/or raising children, and students who worked jobs with considerable hours in order to finance their coursework, sometimes full-time. College "dabblers" were those for whom higher education only supplemented a primary work or life commitment. They included respondents who pursued vocational training to begin a trade, intermittently took college courses—for example, between military tours—or developed more important commitments but finished their degree simply for the sake of closure. Fourth, we classified as "no school" those respondents who did not participate in any form of higher education. These variations during early adulthood are important because whether and how adoptees pursued ethnic exploration depended more on their institutional settings, the available types of exploration, and the surrounding historical period than on any factors that had separated them during their childhood and adolescent years.

NON-EXPLORATION IN EARLY ADULTHOOD

Our examination revealed that adoptee non-exploration depended on four factors: (1) lack of opportunities, (2) competing life responsibilities, (3) lack of personal interest, and (4) dysfunctional circumstances in early adulthood.

Lack of Opportunities

Adoptees who had no opportunities for exploration in early adulthood included those who were traditional college students during the 1970s and early 1980s and those who lived and worked in racially homogeneous workplaces and communities with few other Asians. For example, Marianne Townsend, a forty-five-year-old accountant, had a long-standing interest in exploring what it means to be Asian that preceded even her college years. However, she was unable to act on that interest until her thirties, when she participated in a Holt-sponsored trip to Korea. She exemplifies the relative lack of opportunities for ethnic exploration confronting adoptees who attended college during the 1970s. Even by the 1980s, Jenine Peterson, now a thirty-eight-year-old elementary school teacher, found that her small, homogeneously white, Christian college in the Midwest had developed only modestly greater opportunities. In this setting, opportunities were scarce for her to engage in any type of exploration.

Other adoptees spent their early adulthoods in the same homogeneous settings in which they had been raised, demographically and culturally dominated in most cases by whites. Especially for working-class adoptees like Jim Moreau, a forty-year-old automotive painter, their social networks did not change much because they still lived in the same predominantly white communities in which they grew up. As a result, almost no basis for ethnic identity was available to these adoptees, because there were few resources in their communities to stimulate its development.

Competing Life and Family Responsibilities

For somewhat different reasons, adoptees who started bearing significant life responsibilities during early adulthood also reported little exploration of their ethnic identity because school, work, marriage, and parenting responsibilities left them little free time. Instead, meeting and marrying their significant other and finding full-time employment had been far more crucial events in early adulthood than ethnic exploration. Thomas Ryan, a twenty-six-year-old probation officer, began early adulthood as a traditional college student but soon married and went to work as a corrections officer.

> INTERVIEWER: Some folks say that college is a time for exploring their racial or ethnic identity. Was that the case for you?
>
> THOMAS: Oh, not really. I think I was pretty much determined to get my degree. I was kind of focusing on my major and things like that. . . . Actually, we got pregnant before we got married, so pretty much I had to hurry up and get my life on track.

With a baby on the way, Thomas had more pressing things on his mind than exploring his ethnicity. Ultimately, by persevering to a degree that precluded much consideration of his ethnic background, Thomas earned his bachelor's degree. The early onset of significant family responsibilities was sufficient to distract adoptees like Thomas from personal ethnic exploration.

Lack of Interest

Among non-explorers who claimed to be uninterested in exploration, two groups emerged: adoptees for whom race and ethnicity were *not salient enough* to warrant more than a casual curiosity, and adoptees who did not explore their ethnicity because they were *averse* to other Asians and Asian Americans. In their minds, Asians were "the other"—associated with negative characteristics; these were people to be avoided when encountered. Revealingly, non-explorers who voiced this sentiment were all in their forties, had grown up in the 1950s and 1960s, and had experienced their early adulthood in the 1970s.

Several adoptees reported that they had more important life commitments that overrode any interest in exploration. In short, they were "on a mission" from which they could not be dissuaded. Jennifer Welch, a forty-one-year-old corporate manager, provides a good example. She attended an elite Ivy League school and saw that opportunity as her ticket to upward mobility.

> [College] was definitely not a social outing for me. It had a part in my future that I was serious about and didn't want to mess up on. Um, and I was definitely not—I remember being told, you know, "You should have more fun while you're in college. It's your college years, for God's sake. Pretty soon you'll be in the working world." And I said, "You know, I don't care," you know? [*laughs*] "I'm here to do what I need to do." So I took challenging classes, and I worked really hard. . . . [I didn't] goof around at all in college.

Hewing to a strict academic path with no room for ethnic exploration, adoptees like Jennifer pursued objectives that made ethnic exploration a very low priority. The reason other adoptees cited for their lack of interest in exploration was not so much an alternative mission as a secure sense of community among whites. In college, Sherwin Wright, a forty-four-year-old finance manager, was brought into contact with non-adopted Asian Americans whose affinity for coethnics surprised him.

> In college I started having more contact with [other Asians] and kind of started becoming aware, you know? So I guess I always thought of myself as a white

guy, more or less. Now I sort of became aware, like, "Oh yeah." And then I got new friends, and they would even, you know, they would say stuff to me like, "Oh yeah, so what are you? Are you Japanese or . . . what are you?" You know? And stuff like that. So I became much more aware of my cultural background. . . . And I got to know some more Asian people and, you know, saw how they actually were kind of, you know, drawn to me just 'cause I was Asian. I just never experienced that in my life.

However, neither this discovery nor his realization of not actually being white threatened his sense of self. Non-explorers like Sherwin had found an exceptional level of acceptance in a predominantly white community that simply made ethnic exploration unnecessary.

In contrast, adoptee non-explorers like Ross Green actively distanced themselves from ethnic exploration. The forty-two-year-old construction foreman reflected on how childhood experiences with racism led him to avoid exploration in early adulthood.

> **INTERVIEWER:** And did you have any interest in exploring your ethnic or racial identity during that time?
>
> **ROSS:** No. I was, you know, ashamed to be Asian at that point.
>
> **INTERVIEWER:** Did you avoid Asians during that time? After high school?
>
> **ROSS:** You know, probably if I saw them, I probably would steer away from them.
>
> **INTERVIEWER:** Did you have any particular feelings about seeing other Asians around?
>
> **ROSS:** Yeah. It probably made me uncomfortable.

Ironically, Ross's aversion to other Asian Americans coincided with his entry into military service, which he describes as more welcoming or at least more tolerant of Asians than his childhood community. Although he had less reason in the military to dissociate from other Asians, his brief stint in the Navy also gave him the freedom to define himself apart from the negative connotations of Asianness, internalized from his childhood during the 1960s and 1970s.

Dysfunctional Circumstances

And finally, we encountered a small group of non-explorers whose early adulthoods we cautiously characterize as *dysfunctional*. For them, unusual personal problems and circumstances minimized the possibility of ethnic exploration during this life stage. Included in this group were adoptees Mary Klein, a forty-six-year-old accountant, and Caleb Littell, a twenty-eight-year-old producer of extreme sports videos.

By her own account, Mary had a "different" childhood characterized by problematic family relations. She believes that her parents adopted her and another Korean, her brother, to help with the family's janitorial business. Adopted in the late 1950s, she painted a grim story of a family without much happiness or warmth. Mary was paid $75 a month to work after school and on weekends, with half taken back as "rent."

> At this time I'm about in sixth grade, and my brother is in ninth, well, junior high. So anyway, my parents started getting more contracts for cleaning banks, credit unions, and that type of thing. And they had us working at night cleaning the, you know, the banks, and emptying garbage, cleaning toilets and urinals, and all that kind of stuff. . . . I kind of had a different childhood because I felt my parents brought me over here to work me. That's the feeling I get.

Mary's businesslike relationship with her parents continued through college, with her mother picking her up every day after school to take her to a job site. In short, there was no time for extracurricular activities of any sort. A more normal context for attending college might have provided her with earlier opportunities for exploration, though it must be noted that she attended during the 1970s when opportunities were fewer even in colleges.

In Caleb's case, an emotionally intense early adulthood characterized by drug and alcohol addiction and run-ins with the law precluded any ethnic exploration. As Caleb put it, "Right after I got out of high school, I moved into north Seattle . . . and dealt drugs and partied [*laughs*] . . . for a good four or five years in my life." Exploration, in short, was far from his mind as he pursued an increasingly chaotic and dangerous trajectory at this stage in his life.

Conditions for Non-Exploration
Among Non-Adoptees

The conditions for ethnic exploration for non-adoptees paralleled those of adoptees, albeit with important differences. First, the early onset of significant family responsibilities sufficed to distract them from exploration, but we found no evidence among this group of the dysfunctional personal situations that had distracted adoptees like Mary and Caleb. Second, the absence of opportunities in colleges during the 1970s also precluded non-adoptee explorations, but we did not find ethnically homogeneous workplaces playing the same role as they did for adoptees. Third, a lack of interest also inhibited non-adoptees from availing themselves of existing opportunities for exploration, and in these cases we found that disinterest had similar roots—either the nonsalience of race and ethnicity or an aversion to other Asians. Non-adoptees Courtney Perry and Peggy Chang gave accounts of not having time for ethnic exploration. Courtney, a thirty-one-year-old underwriter, quit college at the age of nineteen when she became pregnant, and Peggy, a thirty-four-year-old senior accounting technician, attempted to attend school full-time while also working full-time. Laughing at her youthful ambition, Peggy recounted, "And so what gave way? School gave way, of course." Their cases suggest an association between ethnic exploration and the more leisurely early adulthoods that are characteristic of middle-class American families.

In sum, non-adoptees voiced the same reasons for non-exploration as adoptees, though they mentioned specific conditions that were narrower with respect to personal freedom and institutional opportunities but not racial salience.

EXPLORATION IN EARLY ADULTHOOD

Across historical cohorts, higher education was the most important institutional context for ethnic exploration. Half of both "college only" and "college and other" adoptees engaged in substantial exploration during early adulthood, in comparison with fewer than one-fifth of "no school" and "college dabbler" respondents.[9] Being primarily in school quintupled the odds of any ethnic exploration in comparison with being primarily involved in non-school contexts.[10] As suggested in the preceding section, the availability of opportunities for ethnic exploration was simply greater in school than in non-school settings.

Although the centrality of higher education persisted across time, there was a shift in the institutional options for ethnic exploration pursued outside of school. For the 1970s and 1980s cohorts, military service in Asia was the alternative context experienced most frequently, but that option had disappeared by the 1990s. Meanwhile, employment in an Asian business was rarely available during the 1970s, but by the 1990s it had replaced military service as the main nonschool source of opportunities. Accordingly, opportunities for social exposure were almost exclusively college-based in the 1970s and expanded slightly to include Asian employment by the 1990s, whereas opportunities for exploring cultural heritage were equally military- and college-based before the 1990s, when higher education became the exclusive source of opportunities.

Nominal and Personal Exploration

The significance of historical cohort and institutional opportunities becomes clear from a closer analysis of *how* nominal explorers were already immersed in ethnic involvement and *where* personal explorers found their opportunities. Although the activities of nominal explorers resembled exploration, these adoptees had actually grown up with Asian American friends, often in racially diverse communities, and they simply continued their social involvements into their college years. Not surprisingly, they were young adults during the 1990s, when the Asian American population, especially its second generation, was larger than in earlier decades. One of these was Karen Granger, a twenty-six-year-old bookkeeper whose friends after high school included many Asian Americans. During her interview, she laughed at our inventory of formal ethnic explorations as unnecessary activities.

> INTERVIEWER: Have you ever attended a special program or event on ethnic or minority issues?
>
> KAREN: No. [*laughs*]
>
> INTERVIEWER: Have you ever been to Korea?
>
> KAREN: No. [*laughs*]
>
> INTERVIEWER: Let's see. You've obviously been in kind of predominantly Asian American places before. Have you been to Koreatown?
>
> KAREN: Oh yeah.
>
> INTERVIEWER: What was it like to be in a place that was predominantly—
>
> KAREN: I liked it.
>
> INTERVIEWER: —Asian American.

KAREN: Yeah. It's just, you can just do whatever you want, and it's, I don't know, I just liked it. I like the environment. I like everything, you know?

Karen's affection for Asian American environments and the sense of freedom they afforded her is unusual because she was specifically referring to Korean-centered situations dominated by adult immigrants, whose cultural expectations typically make many adoptees uncomfortable. Her experiences cast in relief the narratives of most other explorers who pursued formally organized ethnic exploration precisely because comparable opportunities for informal exploration were absent from their childhood communities.

Adoptees who were personal explorers reported taking college courses that may not have been centrally focused on Asians or Asian Americans but that gave them opportunities to focus an assignment on the Asian adoptee experience. Such activities resembled ethnic exploration but actually were focused on their adoption. Gabrielle Anderson, a forty-three-year-old notary public, used a college assignment to examine her personal documents.

> In college, um, in my speech class I did a paper on this, on my passport. What it meant to me. And it kind of made me dig up feelings and everything. It's like, it kind of proved to me that that's who I am. It kind of reaffirmed that I was adopted, I guess.

As a result of this assignment, Gabrielle's identity as an international adoptee was privately affirmed. Like the nominal explorers, however, personal explorers like Gabrielle were exceptions. The majority of explorers participated in the more interactive activities of the social exposure and cultural heritage tracks.

Pursuing Social Exposure in College, Unequal Interactions, and Employment

Among adoptees who pursued social exposure, one-third stopped at a modest level and the remainder continued to a more substantial level. Of special significance was their institutional membership, which distinguished their opportunities for intensifying their explorations. Many modest explorers and substantial explorers found their opportunities in college.

Modest explorers pursued one or two of the following options: taking a single course in Asian American studies, writing a paper on a Korean adoptee-related topic in a non-Asian-specific course, or participating in student networks that were unusually diverse but not predominantly Asian. Carrie Bennett, a thirty-one-year-old counseling manager, had thoughtful reasons for taking an Asian American history class.

> **INTERVIEWER:** What was your motivation for taking that class [on Asian American history]?

> **CARRIE:** It almost seemed like part of me really wants to know, and part of me, even now. . . . I feel like I need to understand, um, historically, how Koreans have been treated, or what's happened to them in this country . . . and other Asian groups. And at the same time, I feel like, I don't, I don't know [if] any of my ancestors went through that.

Despite not having immigrant parents, much less Korean ancestors in the United States, Carrie felt drawn to learning about how the United States had treated Korean Americans and other Asian Americans. However, her perceived connection with other Asians had limits. Like other modest explorers, she was ambivalent in her interactions with other Asians, especially within the context of the ethnic organizations on campus. Although Carrie found a greater comfort in the higher representation of Asian Americans around her, she saw joining the available Asian student organization as a whole other step. In brief, modest explorers appreciated their new proximity to non-adopted Asian Americans but also kept them at a friendly distance. By contrast, substantial explorers moved past an initial sense of discomfort and even bonded with other Asians over common experiences with racial issues.

When adoptees pursued deeper connections with other Asian Americans, they continued coursework in Asian American studies, added coursework in Asian studies, participated in predominantly Asian American social networks, and even joined Asian American student organizations. Their explorations often led to shifts in self-perception that involved the redefinition of their American identity and a greater recognition of its racialization. Natalie Johnson, a forty-one-year-old business executive turned homemaker, recalled her college opportunities for exploration as a transformative time in her life. Despite an early curiosity about her Korean roots, by adolescence she felt ashamed of looking different from her white family and peers. Her attitude changed immensely, however, after she started college at the University of

California–Berkeley and encountered many non-adopted Koreans and other Asian Americans.

> So, yeah, I totally, I really got into it freshman and sophomore year. . . . I had a Korean boyfriend. I met a lot of Asian Americans, in my classes and stuff. And it's funny—it happened in almost every class—Asian Americans would just sort of gravitate together. It wasn't, it wasn't so much Korean to Korean, but, you know, a lot of the friends I made were Asians in college.

Elaborating further, Natalie reflected on this period as a counterweight to earlier negative experiences that she once accepted as normal.

> **INTERVIEWER:** What do you think was the spark behind that [exploration]?
>
> **NATALIE:** I mean, it sort of came about in high school and coll— probably college. I mean, Berkeley was a tremendous influence on me. And I took Asian American studies and . . . I think that's where I really developed pride in being Asian. . . . It's partly in numbers, you know, there's strength in numbers. And meeting so many people who were, you know, they were never ashamed of it, and I don't know if they were teased or not, but it just gave me a lot of pride.

On the one hand, the scope of Natalie's involvement suggests the self-segregation observed by critics of campus balkanization. On the other hand, she showed no evidence that an explicit ideology, nationalist or otherwise, lay behind her explorations. Instead, her narrative and those of similar explorers from every cohort suggest the defining condition to which ethnic immersion (Tatum 1992; Tuan 1998) was an answer: a preexisting shame for not being considered a real, or full, American.

Although Natalie associated her lack of racial self-esteem with being adopted and raised in a predominantly white environment, non-adoptees in our study reported feeling a similar sense of shame. Sandra Chan, a thirty-one-year-old university academic adviser, described her ethnic exploration as having given her a new sense of racial belonging. She recounted her first impressions of college life:

> I was actually afraid of all the other Asians because there were so many of them. [*laughs*] I was overwhelmed. . . . As a freshman student coming from [her small

town], coming to [her college] was like, "Oh, my God, [there are] so many people of color. It's so amazing." [*laughs*] But—at the same time, not knowing how to approach other Asian Americans, because I mean, like I, you know, in high school anytime we [Asians] were in a group, we would want to disperse because you didn't want to be clumped as "those Asians." And so, like when I lived in the residence halls . . . most of my friends were white. . . . My junior year was when I was in the, in the whole yellow power thing. I was all about yellow power. [*laughs*] And I was like, "I'm not going to have any friend who's not Asian because . . . they just won't understand."

Sandra's experience demonstrates the extreme extent to which exploration could be transformative for the ethnic identities of these young adults. Like Natalie, Sandra experienced a contrast between her early adulthood and her childhood experience of being stigmatized for being Asian.

The remaining modest explorers and substantial explorers found their opportunities outside of college. Peer interaction was noticeably absent among modest explorers: for example, they explored their ethnic background with small children, who were in no position to judge the adult adoptees' lack of familiarity with Korean culture or the Asian American experience. For Susette Morgan, a twenty-nine-year-old homemaker and administrative assistant, the child in question was her own son when he began asking questions about his father's mixed Peruvian and Chinese parentage. However, she set the same ground rules for her son that her adoptive parents had set for her with respect to her childhood curiosity.

> **INTERVIEWER:** Since high school, have you . . . started to explore your ethnic heritage . . . ? Or your adoptee identity?
>
> **SUSETTE:** I didn't. But I did explain to Tim, my son, about his background. And he has some interest, especially with the Chinese side. Because he has three different cultural, you know, he has the Peruvian, he has the Chinese, and he has the Korean. And the Chinese is more what he wants to do. And you know, and the same thing as my parents said for me, or explained to me that, you know, "You do what you want to do," you know? But you also have, *"If you really want something, then you have to go get it yourself."* [emphasis ours] So he asked questions about, you know, "What do the Chinese do," and I try to answer them the best I can. But, um, but he and I talk. And actually, he and I talked about adoption too.

Susette's rules reflect a peculiarly American mix of freedom and responsibility that conveniently defines parents' orientations to ethnic exploration (Waters 1990). They also resemble a cultural socialization strategy that Richard Lee (2003a) terms "child choice," which keeps lines of communication open within the family but also places the burden on the child. Like Susette when she was a child, Tim was free to raise questions, but he would have to find deeper answers for himself.

Substantial explorers found opportunities during the 1980s and 1990s through employment at Asian-themed and Asian American–owned businesses where employers or coworkers took them "under their wing." Kerry Nowitsky, a twenty-five-year-old computer support technician and student, spent his early adulthood playing professional baseball in Japan before returning to the United States, where working at a pan-Asian supermarket connected him to the local Korean American community. His experience abroad reinforced his consciousness of not racially "blending in" in the United States; however, it was not until he returned to the United States and started working at the supermarket that he encountered Korean Americans.

> I met a couple of Korean kids out there, and just one day they were like, "Hey, why don't you come with us to X," and [this city is] not a very big town, you know, so the Korean community is pretty tight-knit. And, you know, I was so surprised in how accepting they were. . . . I wasn't really expecting that. I was kind of thinking, you know, they'll just be like any other people that I've ever met before, but anytime I've run into a Korean person in this town they're always like, "Hey, are you Korean? Come on in my house."

Kerry met friendly coethnics at a point in his life when he was an outsider in a new social milieu and perhaps also particularly open to new friendships. Like others who pursued substantial social exposure, he developed an appreciation and affection for coethnic and panethnic communities.

Exploring Cultural Heritage in College, During Study Abroad, and Through Military Service

Among adoptees who explored their cultural heritage, only one stopped at a modest level; the rest continued to a more substantial level, including several who also pursued social exposure. As with the pursuit of social exposure, institutional membership distinguished opportunities for intensifying the exploration of cultural heritage. Substantial explorers across all cohorts found their opportunities in college, but especially in the 1990s. They studied Asian languages and the history of Asian nations and participated in other internationally oriented university programs, which in turn led most to travel to Asia, typically through a college study-abroad program.

When adoptees traveled to Asia, they experienced some combination of culture shock, reflection on their own identity and that of their adopted nation, and a welcome sense of "blending in" for the first time in their lives. None traveled under the auspices of the homeland return programs designed by Asian governments and Asian American community organizations for second-generation Asian Americans. As a result, all traveled in the company of non-Asians—primarily white fellow students or fellow soldiers—not other Asian Americans, much less coethnics. Nevertheless, their narratives included themes that were very similar to the documented experiences of non-adoptee travelers: substantial contrasts between traveler expectations and trip experiences, encounters with cultural censure, renewed identification with American nationality, renewed ethnic identification, and the pervasive influence of institutional mediation (Kibria 2002a; N. Kim 2007a; Louie 2002, 2004).

Brandon Luebke, a twenty-eight-year-old river-rafting guide, discovered Japan through language studies and international studies coursework that ultimately led to a second major in international business. Despite extensive preparation, he experienced a shock that was not only cultural but also racial. In fact, academic study fostered a confidence in him that proved quite mistaken. Upon returning, his primary community did not shift to an Asian or Asian American network; however, he regularly injected his racial experience abroad into discussions within the international studies community. Brandon's new experience of invisibility abroad ultimately prompted a realization of difference at home. In brief, his racial visibility became more salient as a result of his exploration experiences.

Exploring Asia but Not Korea

Notwithstanding the salience of race, Brandon's study abroad in Japan raises the question of why he and other adoptees pursued non-Korean explorations in Asia. One reason was simply that Korean language study and study abroad in South Korea were not options at many universities, whereas studying Japanese was a more popular program given Japan's stature as the leading Asian economy at the end of the twentieth century. The ironic consequence of this geopolitical reality was that many adoptees became more familiar with Japan than Korea. When we asked Brandon where he felt more comfortable, Korea or Japan, his response hinged on his greater academic exposure to Japan.

Another, less institutional reason was that Korea was not merely the nation of his birth but also the place where he had been orphaned and "given up" for adoption. A brief family trip to Korea left him shaken.

> I don't know if it affected my sister as much as me, but I was weirded out by it. I was, like, I can't speak anything in this country. I don't know anything, but I look—and I'm from here, but I don't know anything about it. So it never, like, forced me to want to say, "Oh, I'm going to learn a whole bunch about it," but in fact I think it kind of had the opposite effect a little bit, as it kind of freaked me out enough where I was just kind of like, "Whoa, get out of here!" [*laughs*]

Brandon wanted to return to Korea after achieving sufficient emotional distance because at the time of his first visit he felt only fear and dislocation. By contrast, Japan provided cultural exploration and racial immersion, but also a buffer against personal stigma and thus did not demand deep personal reflection. In short, visiting Korea came with significant baggage that Japan did not.

Even so, upon arrival in Japan, Brandon found that his adoptive history remained unavoidable because his ability to blend into the crowd depended not only on his appearance but also on his performance of its associated cultural expectations. His obvious lack of linguistic fluency prompted questions from locals, which typically led him to explain his adoption. We learned of this routine experience when we asked him about his relative consciousness of being Korean versus being Asian.

> **BRANDON:** Uh. [*pause*] . . . That's a good question. I've never really thought of that before. Like, do I consider myself Asian sometimes and then Korean at different times?
>
> **INTERVIEWER:** Right. . . . Does that differ, or is it basically just one thing for you?
>
> **BRANDON:** Growing up, it was definitely just one thing. But . . . when I went over [to Japan], they thought I was Japanese. And then I opened my mouth, and they knew that I wasn't Japanese, and I'd say I was from America, and they were like, "No, you're not from America." [*laughs*] . . .

And so I had to go, like, every time I met somebody new, I'd have to go into this, like, ten-minute elaborate story of question and answer on what my background was. And then, I [had] always considered myself just Asian. It didn't really matter to me. You know, I was always considered, or I always considered myself, just kind of one big lump along with my Vietnamese and Chinese friends. But when I went to Japan, I was very— I was labeled Korean more often than I was American, right, so I thought of myself as being Korean for the first time in my life.

In brief, Brandon's identity became more complex in an environment that did not casually lump Koreans with Japanese and where adoption by nonrelatives was considered unusual.

Blending In

In reporting on their experiences abroad, adoptees touched on similar themes—above all the surprising privilege of racially "blending in." Diane Genovese, a thirty-one-year-old director of an international visitor program, went to Japan to teach English immediately after college graduation. She spent two years there in the popular Japan Exchange and Teaching (JET) program, which she remembered fondly.

> Yeah. I went to Japan. I lived there [in the 1990s]. Lived in a tiny town, seven thousand people in the entire village, and I was the English teacher. I taught kids from age one to fifteen, plus an adult class. And that was great, so interesting really. And interestingly, I felt more at home in Japan than [I have] just about anywhere else. And part of that, I think, is sort of the novelty of being in a place where people looked basically like me, which I've never really had. When I traveled, yes, but not to actually live.

The upside to blending in for adoptees like Diana was the sensation of being indiscernible in a crowd, of being part of the majority, of feeling "at home."

Not everybody appreciated being viewed as an insider, however, especially when it included the experience of being judged for falling short of expectations. We heard an earful from Stephanie Muller, a twenty-seven-year-old financial consultant, regarding her trip to Korea and the gendered assumptions she encountered as well as the negative judgments about her birth mother's social background and moral character when local Koreans learned of her adopted status. Challenged to negotiate a status that would preserve her dignity, Stephanie characterized herself as the best of both Koreans and Americans, endowed with a genetic drive for excellence but raised with cultural independence and rationality.

> I can see how [genetics] play such a . . . much bigger role than I previously thought, you know. . . . These people have these traits and these attributes, and you know . . . but I could see how my environment had changed that. . . . And being raised to be so independent, because they're very conformist. They're like sheep. And it used to drive me crazy, but you know, that's just the way they are. . . . But for a whole culture to be like that, I just thought it was real funny. It's like, I could see how my environment has changed me to be this free-spirited and independent and . . . not to be, um, held back by any social norms, and feel that kind of pressure. But at the same time I can see where my drive comes from. Where I had to get straight As, where I had to be smart. Because everybody . . . I mean everybody there's literate. They're very intelligent people. They just are afraid to be different.

In light of the South Korean attitudes she faced, we suggest that Stephanie's claims about Korean culture and genetics were defensive efforts to use Western stereotypes of the East to parry the Korean association of adoption with low status and degradation. Although her narrative bore similarities to those of non-adopted returnees in the literature, her adoptive status was uniquely salient to her experience and response. Non-adopted returnees also face cultural censure, but they tend to reject only parts of their homeland's culture—such as a perceived preoccupation with status distinctions—to evaluate their immigrant family culture as a positive hybrid, and to develop affection for an ethnic-American identity (Kibria 2002a; Louie 2002, 2004). By contrast, Stephanie repudiated Korean culture in toto for a "superior" American culture while finding ethnic pride in the one thing that South Korean prejudices did not denigrate—their shared genetic ancestry.

Whereas some female adoptees encountered gendered expectations that they experienced as constraining, Christopher Hurley, a fifty-one-year-old train engineer, encountered a flattering form of attention when he traveled through Asia.

> The very first time I went to Asia, I was, like, twenty-four years old. It's, like, prime of my age; I was really big and stocky. Everywhere I went I drew a lot of

attention, you know. The—like when I went to Hong Kong, they just stare at you. And then when I went to, like, like, one of the guys I met at the college there, I was, you know, using their weight room, he said, "You know what? You're the biggest Chinese I've seen." I said, "Well, I'm not Chinese. I'm Korean." And then, when I went to Tokyo, and these cops, you know? They saw me walking, they stopped and they asked me some questions. And I said, "Oh, I'm trying to go here." And so they gave me a ride. They say, "You're a big Japanese." "I'm not Japanese. I'm Korean." Then when I go to Korea, these guys I met, they all want to arm-wrestle me and everything, you know?

In this new context, Christopher's size and muscularity became assets, drawing attention that he enjoyed and found refreshing. Because his distinctiveness made him more of a celebrity than an outcast, the attention actually accented his feeling of belonging. In short, his "value" as an idealized male type rose in this new context.

In sum, among adoptees exploring their cultural heritage, Brandon Luebke was an exception for his reflections on the domestic implications of his experiences abroad. While his counterparts enjoyed the racial comfort of being in the majority for once, most responded by occupying themselves with the cultural differences that set them apart from other Asians and the commonalties that strengthened their sense of belonging with the Americans who populated their families and social networks.

And finally, military service provided adoptees with an alternative outside of college for pursuing cultural heritage exploration. Service with the U.S. Air Force, Marines, or Navy in the Pacific in or near South Korea in the 1970s and 1980s provided several adoptees with experiences highly similar to those reported by adoptees who studied abroad. Samantha "Sam" Cawthorne, a forty-one-year-old air traffic controller, gave an account that echoed the themes of "blending in" racially, standing out linguistically and culturally, and negotiating social acceptance.

INTERVIEWER: So people tried to speak to you.

SAM: Yeah. Oh yeah. I mean, they'd see me, and then they'd speak, and I couldn't answer them back. And then they would get really mad, and I tried to explain to them that I was adopted, you know . . . and it was like, uhh [*exasperated*]. It was really horrible. But then, as people, as they got to know me, and then they, they realized that I, you know, was a GI [*laughs*] . . . and I had lots of stripes, and that I must be smart, because . . . I had lots of stripes. [*laughs*] That's what they said. And then they began to like me. . . .

INTERVIEWER: You blended in.

SAM: Yeah. It was just like, it was amazing. I'd go to the school rallies, you know, and, if I didn't open my mouth, it, I didn't get stared at [*laughs*].

INTERVIEWER: Whereas that wasn't the case in the U.S.

SAM: Oh! Oh! Of course not! [*laughs*]

Despite sharing with study-abroad participants some similarities in their travel experiences, military adoptees like Sam experienced Asia through the distinct lens of their institutional membership. Sam's military rank gave South Korean locals a reason to take pride in her despite the stigma attached to her adoption. South Koreans may not have associated every adoptee with the U.S. military, but the visibility of the U.S. military in Korea was a reminder of the Korean War and the country's subsequent inability to take care of its orphans without sending them abroad. In other words, while the military had a direct impact on the experience in Korea of adoptee officers and servicemen, it also indirectly influenced the reception of adoptees who visited South Korea as participants in study-abroad programs.

Context and Content for Exploration
Among Non-Adoptees

College was a critical context for non-adoptees to experience opportunities for ethnic exploration. In fact, for non-adoptees, it was the only context that mattered.[11] Given the greater opportunities for exploration to be found in higher education, we believe that the higher level of educational attainment among non-adoptees explains their higher propensity for ethnic exploration. Whereas slightly fewer than half of adoptees in our study were traditional college students during early adulthood, almost nine out of ten non-adoptees had traditional college experiences.

Although a few non-adoptees pursued social exposure in nonschool settings, none reported exploring their cultural heritage outside of college-related activities. Within the context of higher education, non-adoptees found opportunities very similar to those found by adoptees, though more non-adoptees tried ethnic student organizations, fewer non-adoptees pursued any cultural heritage exploration, and they were especially unlikely to pursue it to substantial levels. A more important difference was that having an Asian family proved to be uniquely salient for non-adoptee ethnic exploration.

Social Exposure Exploration

For non-adoptees in college, *modest exploration* took a parallel but distinct form. Whereas adoptees explored academic courses on ethnic subjects but avoided ethnic organizations, their non-adoptee counterparts took the additional step of "trying out" those organizations before deciding to end any further ethnic explorations.

Like their adoptee counterparts, *substantial explorers* found community both within ethnic student organizations and outside of them in informal networks, or they pursued friendships with other Asian Americans more to their liking. Sandra Chan experienced a similar shift from shame to pride about being Asian. However, her experience also illustrates some differences from the adoptee experience.

> My friend Jerry, who was a codirector of the [Asian student union] back then, he happened to be in my journalism class. And we were sitting together commiserating about some awful homework assignment, and we were going to go study together. And he said, "Well, I can't go study right now. I have a [club] function to go to." And I'm like, "What's that?" And I'd been on the campus for two years. And he said, "Why don't you just come? We're having our fall term get-together." And I get there, and there are, like, other Asian Americans. We're not talking Asian international students, who I'd been meeting in the residence halls. And I felt so much at home. . . . It was the first time I felt really at home.

Whereas academic courses were key points of entry for adoptees, informal interaction was a more common starting point in the accounts of non-adoptees, from first-year placements in exceptionally Asian dorms to encouragement from siblings or cousins to become involved in ethnic organizations or to join their mostly Asian social networks. We suggest that residential life staff at some institutions might have used recognizably Asian family names to shape the composition of first-year units, a practice that would have missed adoptees, whose surnames were largely indistinguishable from culturally white names.

No adoptees had Asian family members already attending their institution, nor did we hear any accounts of white family members connecting them with Asian American organizations or social networks. By contrast, non-adoptee Lindsay Yang, a thirty-year-old college bookstore supervisor, mentioned that family connections led to her gaining, albeit somewhat reluctantly, a circle of Asian American friends.

> **INTERVIEWER:** You still found yourself in a circle of largely Asian [friends]? How did that happen?
>
> **LINDSAY:** I think it was due to my friend Diana. [*laughs*] . . . Her grandfather went to school with my grandfather. . . . Her parents went to school with my parents. . . . So we're going to school [*laughs*]. We were like the third generation of school friends, I guess. . . . She was more connected to other Asians. And I think she kind of helped . . . she kind of did my social networking for me. . . . I just [hopped] on. [*laughs*]

Although non-adoptees were more open to trying ethnic student organizations, these organizations also played a divisive role. Even among substantial explorers, some continued their explorations but skirted organizational participation in favor of informal social interactions. These networks could become substantial involvements, even as our respondents continued to distance themselves from becoming organization joiners. Whereas these non-adoptees saw organizational membership as redundant with their already Asian social networks, others found fulfillment in ethnic organizations and felt no reluctance about joining Asian social networks outside of their organizational activities. Indeed, some like Sandra Chan regarded organizational membership as crucial to their ethnic explorations: it functioned either from the beginning as the anchor for their networks or alternatively as the culmination of their informal efforts at ethnic exploration.

An important distinction between these groups of substantial explorers was the degree to which they perceived themselves as "typical" for the organization's membership. Non-adoptee Jessica Ho, a thirty-four-year-old mother and homemaker, was surprised by the large number of Asian American students in college; she tried to participate in an Asian organization but found that "there wasn't a real strong affinity there." Nevertheless, through informal channels she met other Asian American students with whom she developed close friendships despite significant gaps between her experience and theirs.

INTERVIEWER: You were saying you were struck by the number of Asians who were present?

JESSICA: Yes. And I was also struck by the myriad types of Asians that were present. And for the first time, I had a lot of long, intense late-night conversations with friends about race that I was completely oblivious of, basically. A lot of my friends that had grown up in the, in an urban setting had very different experiences with growing up Asian. And I was just fascinated. I was stunned, and it was all new to me.

INTERVIEWER: What kind of experiences did they recount?

JESSICA: They recounted more racism. And basically more tension about identity. And I [thought], "This must be an urban thing." [*laughs*] It must be an issue because [in an] urban setting, you know, people are closer in proximity, and there must be more tension. I don't know. But it was very foreign to me. . . . I felt a [real] deficiency as far as me understanding this whole Asian American experience. . . . And people would talk about it, and then they would relate it, and I'd say, "How come I don't understand what—how, I mean, I understand what you're talking about, but I don't identify with what you're talking about." . . . So, probably my junior, sophomore year is when I made a choice: "Okay, I'm going to try to explore this Asian American thing and try to figure out what it means."

The different associations that Jessica and others made between ethnicity, religion, race, and discrimination point to the differing ways in which propinquity shaped whether our respondents experienced any affinity with other Asian Americans during early adulthood, whether through organizations, informal networks, both, or neither.

Cultural Heritage Exploration

Non-adoptees explored their cultural heritage primarily through college opportunities. Unlike their adoptee counterparts, who overwhelmingly explored to substantial levels, fewer than half of non-adoptees continued exploring to substantial levels. Substantial explorers who traveled to Asia did so with motivations similar to those of their adoptee counterparts, participated in study-abroad programs that provided similar institutional opportunities, and connected with a similar milieu of white explorers.

Curiously, however, they also reported experiences that set them apart not only from their adoptee counterparts but also from the homeland visit literature that mostly focuses on non-adopted returnees. Deborah Kuohung, a thirty-four-year-old investment banker, encountered a situation abroad that was similar to what adoptees reported. However, she also experienced her arrival in Asia with a shock that was less directly cultural and more directly familial.

> My relatives in Hong Kong were all excited to hear that I was going to Hong Kong. And at the airport, what happens is, you have the program, the [university] people there meet you and take you to the dorms and so forth. Well, my relatives arrived en masse at the airport. [*laughs*] And I just, my first transpacific flight, you know. . . . I'd been on the plane for hours on end. . . . And then all of a sudden there's a mass of people who I don't know. [*laughs*] All greeting me. And then there's the university people as well. And I'm just like, "Oh, my God," you know? [*laughs*] What do I do? And then, you know, it's nighttime. And they want to take me home to their place, and they want to feed me, as usual. And I probably did the thing that was the biggest slap in their face, though. I said, "No, I'm going with the university." [*laughs*]

Although Deborah's extended kin in Hong Kong would later prove to be important resources for her visit, she initially experienced them as a challenge to her intended explorations and perhaps a bit of an embarrassment. Her reaction to them implies another element that distinguished non-adoptees—a greater familiarity with cultural difference as revealed in their anticipation of breaching specific cultural expectations.

Unlike adoptees' reports and the narratives reported in the literature, Deborah's account of her study-abroad experience lacks a certain intensity. In particular, she voiced no surprise about "blending in" with the local population, much less having a renewed sense of ethnicity as a result, and she also did not experience much, if any, cultural censure that might have made her question her ethnic authenticity and confirm her sense of nationality. We suggest that having a coethnic family may have *inoculated* some non-adoptee travelers from the more extreme impacts of cultural heritage exploration as reported by their adoptee counterparts. Having an Asian family lent nuance in multiple ways to the ethnic explorations of Lindsay Yang, beyond connecting her to a circle of Asian American friends:

Well, I thought it was really neat, you know, going to China and looking at all the different stuff. And I think it pointed out to me, you know, the differences between the cultures, which made it kind of interesting. It wasn't like I didn't like going to China. It was just different. That part of China. And so, I mean, I think it was interesting, you know, and I liked traveling. It was kind of fun, you know, you get to visit all these places. Trying these different foods, you know? Different people. That was interesting. . . . I mean, in a way it did feel kind of like home. . . . I spent a lot of time, like, asking, because I was really curious to see why my parents came here . . . asking questions all the time. "How was it like when you went to school?" You know? "Did you do this, did you do this?" And so I think I was more interested in my family situation.

First, having been raised in an immigrant family, Lindsay was already prepared to negotiate cultural differences—indeed, often in the direction of hiding her personal deviations from Chinese cultural norms. Second, this was not Lindsay's first trip to China: her parents had taken the family back to China as children for multiple trips with both kin and family friends. Last but not least, Lindsay's focus on her parents' lives before immigration suggests that her goals for ethnic exploration centered less on coming to terms with the social status of her ethnic group and more directly on understanding the cultural factors in her family history.

CONCLUSIONS

Whether Korean adoptees pursue exploration in early adulthood, reject exploration altogether, or feel indifferent toward exploration is determined by numerous factors. Our research suggests that the conditions necessary for ethnic exploration are a moderate but not excessive level of racial stigma, the historical and institutional availability of opportunities, and a sufficient measure of personal freedom associated with a "normal" early adulthood. In brief, when given the resources, most adoptees pursued ethnic exploration in early adulthood if they also had the freedom to use those resources, regardless of whether their families had sought to acknowledge differences or achieved a sense of shared fate during their childhoods.

Four key findings stand out in this chapter. First, both exploratory intent and available options mediate the content of ethnic activities in early adulthood. Furthermore, the content of exploration depends on the institutional context and historical availability of particular opportunities within that context. We identified two types of activities—social exposure and cultural heritage—and found, as expected, that involvement with either type is more likely in school than in nonschool contexts. Our analysis indicates that college has been a critical context for adoptees to experience opportunities for ethnic exploration. Although they reported explorations in both college and noncollege settings, those in primarily nonschool settings had to work harder to pursue substantial exploration to the point of social or cultural immersion.

Second, we found evidence that historical context also matters for the salience of race and for the nature of nonschool opportunities. It was solely the 1970s cohort that reported an aversion to other Asians strong enough to preclude any exploration. Service in the U.S. armed forces was the primary source of opportunities outside of college during the 1970s and 1980s, after which employment in Asian American businesses predominated.

Third, the experience of exploration shapes ethnic identity by reinforcing and complicating the initial salience of being socially different. Modest explorers of social exposure turned back from further activity often because they experienced discomfort in their interactions with other Asian Americans. Their efforts to find racial belonging raised unwanted anxieties about escalating their racial visibility and, for adoptees, meeting unfamiliar cultural expectations. Any anxieties of the respondents who continued to a substantial level of social exposure were overshadowed by an increased salience of race, which led to greater solidarity with other Asian Americans. Although the experience of social exposure tended to reinforce the salience of race and thereby also ethnic identity, the experience of exploring cultural heritage tended to raise the salience of adoption or, for non-adoptees, family history over that of racial visibility and to render ethnic identity largely symbolic.

And finally, the presence of Asian families was uniquely salient for non-adoptees. Asian family members did not add much to the institutional opportunities available to non-adoptees but instead tended to strengthen the connection of non-adoptees to their formal opportunities. Not surprisingly, however, Asian kin were also salient as bearers of burdensome expectations, to the point of becoming a reason for avoiding ethnic exploration, if not also any interaction with other Asian Americans.

CHAPTER 5

Ethnic Explorations in Later Adulthood

Years before, I was in an elevator, and the flight crew from [a] Korean airline got on. And [then] these two white guys got on. And they started talking. They were very rude. All of a sudden, I realized that they thought I couldn't understand [them] because they figured I was Korean. And I thought, "This is the first time I have ever felt like I was a majority in my whole life." I just stood there going, "This is the weirdest feeling I've ever had in my life." [*laughs*] I felt so much like going, "Excuse me! [*laughs*] I'm as American as the rest of you guys. Knock it off!" [*laughs*] So, going to the Gathering[1] and realizing [again that] I was the majority and that there [were] no rude people there, was the weirdest thing of my life. My husband had encouraged me to go, and I said, "Oh, I don't know," you know? But to go and be the majority was just phenomenal. [*laughs*] I've never been, like I said, I've always been with [adoptees who were] little kids. [But] to be with people my age! [*laughs*]

—Margaret Houston, forty-three years old

In chapter 4, we showed that ethnic exploration occurs not only during adolescence but also in early adulthood, when most Korean adoptees become independent from their adoptive families. If we were to stop our examination there, we might assume that those explorations established adoptees on particular ethnic paths through their later adulthood and into their present circumstances.

And yet, cases such as Margaret Houston's call that assumption into question. Prior to attending the Gathering, Margaret had only a modest interest in ethnic exploration. Although she was initially hesitant to attend, the experience shifted Margaret's attitude toward learning about her roots and set her on a course for further exploration.

By following our respondents into later adulthood, we are able to examine several questions about the continuing salience of ethnicity. To what extent do the non-explorers of early adulthood remain in their culturally and socially white worlds? How long do social exposure explorers remain in the company of non-adopted Asian Americans? How do former cultural heritage explorers continue to balance their cosmopolitan travel experiences and white social worlds? In brief, when do adoptees continue their ethnic explorations into later adulthood, what life events facilitate or inhibit exploration, and what are their ethnic practices, if any, in later adulthood?

In this chapter, we examine whether and how adoptees and non-adoptees in our study have explored their ethnicity since early adulthood. Overall, we found that Korean adoptees and non-adopted Asian Americans varied in whether they explored their ethnicity in later adulthood. While seven out of ten non-adoptees pursued exploration, fewer than half of adoptees did so. Part of the difference originates from the smaller fraction of adoptees who had explored in early adulthood; individuals who explored in early adulthood were more likely to continue exploration in later adulthood. Adoptees were also more likely to remain non-explorers or to discontinue exploration after early adulthood. Nevertheless, more than one-third of adoptees who had been non-explorers after adolescence began exploring their ethnicity during later adulthood, and fully half of adoptees who had been explorers continued to examine their ethnicity in later years.

NON-EXPLORATION IN LATER ADULTHOOD

Adoptee non-explorers voiced four reasons for not exploring their ethnicity in later adulthood: (1) they felt an aversion to the prospect of ethnic exploration; (2) race, ethnicity, and adoption were no longer salient in their adult lives; (3) they were already immersed in ethnic networks and activities; and (4) they were interested but lacked the opportunity to act on their interest.

The early adulthood experiences of the adoptees who cited one of these four reasons reveal how later exploration is channeled by earlier experience. Almost all of those who were averse to ethnic exploration in later adulthood had been averse in early adulthood. Almost half of those who lacked opportunities for ethnic exploration in later adulthood had also lacked such opportunities in early adulthood. Most of those who were immersed in ethnic networks and activities in later adulthood had been explorers in college settings. We did not find a clear pattern among the earlier experiences of those who perceived race, ethnicity, or adoption to have become nonsalient in later adulthood.

Apart from the averse group, every group of non-explorers included former cultural heritage explorers. This fact is significant because most adoptees who explored their cultural heritage in early adulthood became non-explorers, whereas most of their social exposure counterparts remained explorers in later adulthood. In sum, apart from those who were already immersed in ethnic activities, non-explorers were mostly those who had not explored their ethnicity in early adulthood plus those who had largely retreated from ethnicity after exploring their cultural heritage.

A Continuing Aversion to Exploration

Judy Hudson, a forty-two-year-old surgical dental assistant, had never explored her ethnic identity and attributed that fact to her early and long-standing disinterest in associating with others like herself.

> Okay, this is just so funny, because I think I disappointed my parents more than anyone! [*laughs*] You know, now that I think of all this, I think that I probably just never had an interest in seeking any of that out because, you know, when the kids would point this out to me that I was different, then it made me feel not only separate from everyone else, but it make me feel, um, like different was a bad thing. "Because I'm different from you all, I'm not as good as you. I don't measure up to you." So because of that I've just thought, well, why would I want to seek that out when that makes me all that much more of what they're saying I am?

As Judy's narrative reveals, her parents raised their family to acknowledge the differences arising from adoption. They were eager to support Judy in pursuing ethnic exploration but waited for her to show interest, which she never did. Judy's present humor about these experiences notwithstanding, for her exploration would have been tantamount to capitulating to the social stigma of being different; by the time of our interview she had not even tried Korean food. That said, she also claimed that getting older had mellowed her aversion to ethnic exploration, though she predicted that any steps she took toward exploration would probably be at the encouragement of her white in-laws, who had a greater appreciation of ethnic food than she did. In brief, adoptees like Judy who tended to avoid ethnic activities were even less likely to engage in exploration, and for most of them, their avoidance had a long history.

Insufficient Salience

Mary Klein, a mixed-race forty-six-year-old accountant, confided that exploring her identity has not been a priority because racial and ethnic differences had lost their significance in her current life.

> INTERVIEWER: What about trying to explore what it means to be Korean American, or Korean, or Asian American? Is that something that's important to you?

> MARY: Well, as far as exploring, I don't really explore it because I'm having fun in the life that I have now.

> INTERVIEWER: It's not relevant?

> MARY: Yes, it's irrelevant. And the people that, like I mentioned earlier, that I worked with at the medical center were from all kinds of cultural backgrounds, ethnicity, and every—there was one woman there, she's Filipino, and she and I just got along great. We had offices across from each other, and we were both accountants and collectors with UC Davis Medical Center. And we just got along great. We identified with all kinds of stuff. People there from Japanese and Indian descent. Just all kinds of [pause] . . . it didn't matter anymore.

Simply put, exploration was not salient for Mary because the magnitude of diversity at her workplace made being different (different from white) simply normal. Moreover, recall from chapter 4 that Mary's childhood was particularly unhappy—she believed that her parents adopted her partly to assist them with their janitorial business. Although Mary had many questions about racial and cultural differences when she was younger, her family did not create an environment in which she could ask them. Her adult lack of interest in ethnic exploration was tied to the fact that she was enjoying the current period in her life. Although she remained open to ethnic exploration, she felt no pressing need for it at that time and in fact just wanted to live her life.

Curiously, adoptees like Mary did not report that race, ethnicity, and adoption had never been salient in their lives. Unlike those who were averse to exploration in both early and later adulthood, the adoptees who mentioned the nonsalience of ethnic exploration in later adulthood were not the same individuals who had mentioned nonsalience in early adulthood. Most of the latter adoptees remained non-explorers but also became interested in exploration in later adulthood, though they reported having no avenues in their current communities for pursuing their emerging interests.

Already Immersed in Ethnic Networks

Brian Packard, a twenty-seven-year-old technical writer for an engineering firm, was curious about his ethnicity and interested in visiting South Korea, but he was comfortable with deferring that interest into the indefinite future, noting that he had a similar interest in visiting Spain and Egypt. Exploration was not salient for Brian because his friends and girlfriend were already all Asian. Furthermore, he grew up in the San Francisco Bay Area, was raised by a mother who actively supported his ethnic exploration, and had been surrounded by a diverse network of Asian Americans since adolescence. Since his college years, when he formally explored his ethnicity through coursework and club membership, he had been immersed in ethnic social networks and simply felt very little urge to do more.

Similarly, the all-Asian network of friends of non-adoptee Viet Thai, a twenty-nine-year-old software engineer, more than satisfied any interest he had in exploring his Vietnamese ethnicity. Despite having moved to a predominantly white area for his career, he ate ethnic food "four or five times a week" and celebrated ethnic holidays when he visited his hometown, which had a sizable Asian American community. As a result perhaps of his chosen activities, he observed, with respect to understanding Vietnamese culture, "I don't think I've learned anything new in the past five or six years. At one time, like, I wanted to speak Vietnamese. But now I don't really care about it too much. It was just too hard." In brief, some individuals, adoptees and non-adoptees alike, were immersed enough in ethnic exploration and involvements in early adulthood to the point of feeling little desire for further exploration in their later lives.

No Opportunities

Members of the largest group of non-explorers were those who were interested in exploration but lacked opportunities to act on their specific interests. Half of this group consisted of adoptees like Stephen Pratt, a police training supervisor who, at forty-eight, had still not found opportunities to explore his ethnicity since adolescence. His parents were among the earliest families to adopt from Korea, and they personally knew the Holts.[2] Like many families who adopted in the early days, Stephen's parents discouraged discussions about difference and raised their two Korean sons to handle situations for themselves.

In later years, Stephen made plans to visit South Korea on a Holt motherland tour subsidized by the Korean government, but his specific tour group was canceled for insufficient enrollment. Since then, no new opportunities for exploration had surfaced, but recent events had revived his interest: "We've had a couple friends that have adopted in the last fifteen years, and they've gone over there and gotten to pick up their child in Korea. And I've seen their home videos and everything. Yes, there's still interest. I'd still like to, just because." That said, Stephen's interest in exploration was narrowly focused on international travel. He noted that there were large Korean churches in his area but dismissed the possibility of visiting them as "artificial," because he did not speak Korean. In other words, going to a Korean church would not have provided the specific opportunity that was of interest to him. By comparison, he found the prospect of visiting Korea, despite the expense and distance, more compelling.

Conditions for Non-Exploration
Among Non-Adoptees

Non-adoptees who did not pursue ethnic exploration voiced three of the same reasons mentioned by their adoptee counterparts. Michael Shin, a forty-one-year-old Air Force program manager, was actively *averse* to exploration. Michael resisted his family's efforts to increase his interest in his ethnicity and regarded their encouragement for him to visit South Korea as unconvincing and superficial. Because Michael's family left South Korea after he had already started going to school, he also had memories of growing up in Korea, which he recalled in rather negative terms: "Growing up in Korea was not a good time. They have corporal punishment in the schools, and they beat you for missing questions on a test, okay? So it's a sick system as far as I can tell." Like his adoptee counterparts, Michael had not pursued exploration as an adult. Unlike adoptees, his aversion was grounded in personal experiences that had left a bad enough impression to create a firm boundary against any exploration at that time in his life.

The remaining non-adoptees felt that exploration was not salient largely because they were *already immersed* in ethnic networks and activities or were *interested but lacked the opportunity* to act on their interest. None voiced the fourth reason mentioned by adoptees—that *race and ethnicity were no longer salient* in their adult lives. For the most part, however, the differences between adoptees and non-adoptees with respect to ethnic exploration were differences in degree rather than in kind.

EXPLORATION IN LATER ADULTHOOD

Adoptee explorers reported three types of ethnic exploration that were similar to the range of early adulthood activities: personal exploration, social exposure, and cultural heritage. Their earlier experiences channeled later explorations in a myriad of ways; however, we found that almost none of the later explorers had explored their cultural heritage earlier in life. In fact, the later adulthood explorers were exclusively those who had pursued some level of social exposure exploration or had not explored at all during early adulthood.

Personal Exploration

Some personal explorers explored by reading Asian American literature and occasionally nonfiction by or about Korean adoptees. Reading such non-fiction was very difficult for Natalie Johnson, a forty-one-year-old homemaker with an MBA, because, as she put it, "honestly, it's painful for me." By contrast, she enjoyed Asian American literature, which she had continued to collect since her college years spent exploring her ethnicity, primarily through social exposure activities. Presently living in a predominantly white area, she felt at a loss for ethnic activities, much less opportunities for exploration. Particularly with respect to raising her daughter, Natalie confided, "I really wish we were in the [San Francisco] Bay Area, because I really miss . . . the natural diversity of people. So I tried to, well, I started an international playtime once a month. . . . I did [China and Japan,] and I got some other moms to do India and France." Unlike personal exploration in early adulthood, which focused on personal adoption history, exploration in later adulthood was largely pursued by former explorers trying to maintain some level of ethnicity in their lives while living in ethnically homogeneous communities.

Social Exposure

Other adoptees pursued social exposure through opportunities that they stumbled across at their workplaces. Typically, they were also adoptees who had lacked opportunities for exploration in early adulthood. Over the years, Linus Hobart, a forty-six-year-old engineer and mixed-race adoptee, had met an increasing number of Asian Americans in his industry, as both coworkers and clients. Although he grew up in a family that rejected differences and he had few opportunities to interact with Asian Americans during adolescence, college, or the first decades of his career, he now regularly found himself in professional situations where other Asians were present and whites were not in the majority. Although his personal networks remained predominantly white, Linus had taken the opportunity to learn more about his ethnicity through work. In particular, he remembered meeting a Korean American client with whom he compared childhoods and discussed the receptivity of non-adopted Koreans to racially mixed individuals such as himself.

> LINUS: She was definitely full Korean. You could tell. And I think she spoke it. And she talked to me some and said, "I wish you had more experience with the Korean culture," and stuff, 'cause it's very family-oriented and it's real tight. And you know, I brought up the fact that, you know, I'm only half, and I would feel an outcast more or less, and I don't think I could try and fit into a, you know, full Korean environment.
>
> INTERVIEWER: And what did she say to that?
>
> LINUS: She said, "Yeah, I can understand your feelings. But," she said, "I don't think, you know, nowadays they don't feel that [sentiment] that much toward mixed, um, people," at least in her environment, the people that she deals with.

Although encouraged by this younger coethnic's belief that prejudice against multiracials had significantly declined for her generation, Linus had continued to defer any deeper ethnic exploration for his retirement. In brief, adoptees sometimes found opportunities for exploration through work or work-related contacts, either through serendipity or as the number of Asian Americans increased in their occupations, and appreciated the exposure that these contacts provided. However, they were generally not ready to deepen these explorations, nor even interested in doing so.

Still others pursued social exposure exploration through social networks. These were mostly adoptees who were continuing social exposure explorations begun in early adulthood. Kerry Nowitsky, a twenty-five-year-old computer support technician and student, lived briefly in Japan in early adulthood; upon returning to the United States, he befriended a circle of Asian Americans. He had continued to explore his ethnicity through this social network and had even made plans to travel to South Korea with some of them. Through social exposure exploration, Kerry had gained access to Asian families as resources and even hosts during his group's trip.

Margaret Houston is the forty-three-year-old small business owner whose experiences at the Gathering began this chapter. During the Korean adoptee conference, she and other attendees recognized certain similarities in their experiences as the earliest generations of Korean adoptees raised in families that largely rejected differences. But she also enjoyed learning about the variety of experiences among adoptees.

> I guess I didn't expect to enjoy [the Gathering] as much as I did. I just really thought I'd just go, and it would be fun. I didn't expect to really have it mean something deep inside. I didn't expect it to change my attitude as much as what it did. I didn't think it would start a new chapter, and now I'm ready to kind of say, "Okay, now I'm Korean. Let's see where it's going from there." You know?

The camaraderie and sense of community that Margaret experienced while attending the Gathering inspired her to take further steps. Currently, she was planning to start a local adoptee organization with friends she made at the conference, learn more about Asian American history, and explore community activities in her area.

Margaret's narrative shows that informal contacts can lead to friendships and substantial exploration even late in life, as further illustrated by the experience of Gwen Owens, the forty-one-year-old office manager of a real estate development office. Just five years before our interview, a coworker of Gwen's had informed her that the Asian man working in the café below their office was Korean. Since she had met only two Korean men before then, Gwen introduced herself to Michael, with whom she became friends. In addition to taking Gwen to Korean restaurants and community events, Michael introduced her to his family, who "unofficially adopted" her into the family a few years later. In fact, she and her boyfriend John now lived with Michael's sister, Ji-Yeon, whom Gwen regarded as a sister.

> When I met Michael, I hadn't really gone to Korean restaurants, you know? I didn't really know anything about Korean culture other than some things that I had read. And even that's real limited, you know, about what you can read and stuff that's available. I mean, to really live it and see it, so he started taking me to the Korean festivals, both in L.A. and in Garden Grove. He's taken me to, he loves to eat, we've gone to just about every Korean restaurant he knows.

With Michael and his family acting as "cultural consultants" (Carstens and Julia 2000), Gwen had deepened her understanding of Korean culture and was excited about the prospect of traveling to Korea with her unofficial Korean family.

Asian American social networks were also very important for non-adoptees. Patricia Song, a twenty-four-year-old working in corporate public relations, lent her professional skills to volunteering as a fundraiser for Asian American nonprofit organizations.

> I'm currently helping a domestic violence shelter, an Asian–Pacific American domestic violence type thing, with their fund-raisers. I worked with a local chapter of a national organization for Asian women's rights. They did Asian American voter registration, stuff like that.

As someone who intensively explored her ethnicity through activism in college, Patricia felt guilty that her current level of involvement, while high compared to most respondents, was not greater. Not surprisingly, she had moved to her current city after college because it was "a more Asian American type [of] place." She also planned to visit Hong Kong, though her motivation was as much to meet her boyfriend's grandparents as it was to further explore her ethnicity.

Cultural Heritage Exploration Through Travel

Marianne Townsend, a forty-five-year-old accountant, finally had the opportunity to act on her interest in ethnic exploration during her early thirties, when she took a Holt-sponsored trip to South Korea during the Olympics. Although lack of opportunities had been an important factor delaying her exploration, another had been concern over hurting her adoptive parents' feelings by examining her roots. Marianne was raised in a rejecter family that was not comfortable talking about difference. Even as she prepared to depart, her brother railed against what he considered to be her glaring insensitivity.

> He was mad at me for going. "I don't see why you think you have to go. . . ." Blah-blah-blah. I said, "Well, Sam, you know, I want to see where I came from. I have to see. I don't know my birth date, I don't know my mom, I don't know what I'm going to look like when I get old." You know? He didn't care. It's like, "Well, I don't see how you can do that to Mom and Dad."

Nevertheless, Marianne enjoyed her trip and observed that she would love to return and bring her mother with her.[3]

> INTERVIEWER: Have you ever been able to talk to your parents about, as you put it, that [you feel that] there's this hole . . . ?
>
> MARIANNE: No, I don't want to hurt their feelings. You know, it's like, I'm just afraid that I would hurt Mom's feelings. And I would never do that. You know, when I was getting ready to go back to Korea, she was very happy for me. And in fact, she, she would love to go back with me. And I would love to take her back. I would love to do that for her. I told [her,] "You would love it back there too, Mom. It is so cool. It is so neat."

Notwithstanding the level of her interest in returning to South Korea, her primary interaction with other Asians involved visiting a local Chinese restaurant that stocked kimchi primarily for her and sporadically hosting Japanese and Korean exchange students. In her daily life, therefore, Marianne remained quite isolated from other Asian Americans. Interestingly, she was representative of adoptees who explored their cultural heritage through travel intended primarily for exploration: they did not explore their ethnicity in early adulthood, or did so only modestly; they had few expectations of what they would encounter in their travels; and they were highly satisfied with their travel experiences.

In contrast, Marsha Nelson, a forty-five-year-old retired computer network salesperson, realized that more deliberate travel might have been more satisfying than the side trips to Korea she made while traveling in Asia for business. Admitting that "I didn't have a good experience there," she described her encounters with language barriers, culture shock, and, worst of all, painful stereotypes about adoptees.

> I've been [to Korea] twice. I went on business. I never went with a returning adoptee tour. I think it would have been nice to do that, because it would be arranged, you know, around that. I didn't have a good experience there. It's hard because you don't speak Korean, you look different, people are staring at you. . . . And I had a customs [official] tell me on my second trip, when I gave them my name, he said—he basically wanted to know why [my name] was "Nelson," and I said, "I'm adopted." And he goes, "Oh, you no father." And I'm looking at him and going, "First of all, that's out of line. This is not part of your job, and you're not a social worker. And the second thing is"— you know—"it's just rude." Because he kept saying, "You no father." And I said, "But I do have a father, he's an adopted father, but he's a father." And I was trying to correct the guy, and of course he wasn't listening. So I was offended by that. It hurt actually. It just hurt.

We found that adoptees like Marsha who had been explorers actually had a rougher time with their trips. We suggest that their previous exploration diminished their experience by raising their expectation that they would feel some sense of belonging, thereby lulling them into assuming that they would not "need" the institutional mediation of a more organized tour. To be clear, their previous exploration in early adulthood was primarily through social exposure with other, albeit non-adopted, Asian Americans. In other words, none of our respondents who had been solely cultural heritage explorers in early adulthood continued to explore their cultural heritage in later adulthood.

Similarly, non-adoptee Alice Root, a forty-three-year-old mother, substitute teacher, and former accountant, expressed that until recently she had felt little interest in exploring her ethnicity and had few opportunities to do so. Her attitude changed, however, when she and her husband decided to adopt from China and she began asking her father about "a lot of things in my background"—such as why her parents came to the United States—in addition to reading more about China. Nevertheless, it was not until she crossed the Pacific to adopt her daughter that she found herself feeling pride in being Chinese.

> My father went with me to China when we got our baby. It was very, I don't know, for probably the first time in my life I was glad I was Chinese. For one

thing, I looked at all these Caucasian mothers, and I'm sure that they all worry about the fact that they don't look like their daughters. And I don't have to worry about that.

Revealingly, her new sense of pride was not rooted in Chinese history or society but in the similarities in appearance between her and her daughter, a comparison made salient by their contrast with the largely white adoptive parents who made the trip with her. Nevertheless, Alice's new interest in her ethnicity was a largely personal interest rather than a desire for Chinese American or Asian American community.

The Context of and Content for Exploration Among Non-Adoptees

Non-adoptees in our study had a greater propensity for exploration in later adulthood regardless of whether they had explored in early adulthood. Whereas fewer than half of adoptee non-explorers took up exploration in later years, most of their non-adoptee counterparts did the same. Whereas only half of adoptee explorers continued exploration, nearly all non-adoptee explorers did so. We suggest that a major factor behind the greater tendency among non-adoptees was the presence and varied roles of their Asian American families even into later adulthood.

Apart from those who were already immersed in ethnic activities, non-explorers combined two early adulthood streams: non-explorers and modest explorers. Those who pursued social exposure or who were already immersed in ethnic activity came from a single early adulthood stream: social exposure explorers. Lastly, those who explored their cultural heritage in later adulthood came from the broadest range of early adulthood tributaries: non-explorers, social exposure explorers, and also—unlike adoptees—cultural heritage explorers.

Among non-adoptees, Asian birth families played a unique range of roles in ethnic exploration. For some, parents played a *minimal role* in their explorations as, at most, the bearers of traditional expectations or as the source of complaints about their relative acculturation. For others, family constituted the *scope* of their explorations, whether because exploration was only a modest priority, family was their exclusive vehicle for international exploration, or they had "burned out" in early adulthood on nonfamily domestic exploration. For another subgroup, family provided a *channel* to other explorations or otherwise facilitated them, such as participating in Asian social networks, keeping up on ethnic traditions, developing pride in their ethnic background, and providing opportunities for their children to learn about their ethnic background. For most non-adoptees, however, family, though an important resource, was ultimately *only one of many opportunities* for ethnic exploration and involvement in adulthood.

Kenneth Maxime, a forty-four-year-old, biracial parcel delivery driver, lives in a city that is "95 percent white" and provides few opportunities for social exposure to other Asian Americans. He remains connected to ethnic activities and interested in cultural heritage exploration, however, mostly because of his children, his wife, and his parents, especially his Japanese mother. Like adoptees, non-adoptees like Kenneth found themselves pushed to explore their ethnicity by the interest of their children and the encouragement and accommodation of their spouses. Unlike adoptees, Kenneth's mother was a critical resource for both his wife, who is white, and their son. Beyond his mother, his extended family was also a potential resource, as revealed when Kenneth mentioned visiting Japan. "It was great! I'd love to go back. I mean, the kids would love to go. I'd love to take them. I know they'd have a ball. The neat thing about us is all we need is airfare because we can stay with family and friends."

Many cultural heritage explorers were like Kenneth in that their explorations did not extend far beyond their kin. By contrast, for many non-adoptees who pursued social exposure, other activities were as salient as family resources in their exploration. This combination encouraged not only a sense of ethnicity rooted in family ties but also a strong identification with coethnics as a group.

Sandra Chan, a thirty-one-year-old college academic adviser, explored her ethnicity during early adulthood through social exposure activities, which in turn led her to become part of Asian American and people-of-color social networks, both personally and professionally. She remained interested in exploring her ethnicity, especially because she and her husband were considering having children. In fact, she worked with young adults who were grappling with the same issues that had driven her own explorations earlier in life.

> The reason I'm really interested in multicultural counseling and just being involved is because I remember what it was like for me when I was growing up and not having role models or being really confused about who I was. I mean, "Why did I hate being Asian or being Chinese?" "Why did I so want to be white?"

Although her parents had not been a resource for her as she coped with the racial aspects of her explorations, she herself became a resource for her cousins in regard to these very concerns as a result of her school- and work-based explorations. In addition, her parents and their peers did prove to be an important resource for a family trip to Hong Kong that proved to be a "life-changing experience."

> I went with my mom and my dad, and [her husband] came too. And my aunt and her husband came. . . . I really wanted to see what it was like for my parents to grow up, because I was born there. I hadn't been back since I was, I mean, since I was two. And so it was really great, because we walked past the hospital where I was born, we walked, you know, through the market stands where my grandmother and my mom used to shop for groceries. And I still understood the language, even though they didn't understand my Chinese at all. I understood them. So it was good. But at the same time I felt very different because they could tell I wasn't from Hong Kong just by my body language. I didn't even have to say anything. They just knew! [*laughs*] I mean, it was definitely a life-changing experience. To go and see what it was like and what my life would have been like if we stayed there.

Even Sandra, however, has become less interested in further exploration through social exposure:

> I think at this point now I'm involved but [mostly] marginally. I mean, I'm really inspired by those people who are, like, a lot older than I am and who are still very much involved politically. But sometimes I don't feel like I have the energy anymore. I feel like I did that all when I was in my early twenties. And I just want to live my life and play with my dog and enjoy my husband and play with my kitties.

In sum, even after a substantial record of social exposure exploration, individuals like Sandra find themselves ready to "retire" to more personal or family-centered ethnic activities, not unlike their cultural heritage counterparts. Sandra's example captures how interest in pursuing ethnic exploration can wax and wane over different life stages. After an active period of exploration during early adulthood and continuing effort in later adulthood, Sandra now found herself pulling back.

CONCLUSIONS

In this chapter, we examined whether and how adoptees and non-adoptees explored their ethnicity in later adulthood. We found that exploration depended on whether they had explored at earlier life stages, whether opportunities were available, and whether the available activities fit the adoptees' interests. Of the two types of activities, exploring cultural heritage commanded wider interest but resulted in more superficial ethnic involvements. We also found that the extent and form of exploration in early adulthood channeled the extent and form of exploration in later adulthood; specific early experiences led in myriad ways to specific subtypes of later exploration. And finally, through our comparison of Korean adoptees and non-adopted Asian Americans, we found that Asian families played a critical role as a unique resource for increasing ethnic exploration, well into adulthood. As non-adoptees reached adulthood, their ties to their Asian parents and kin provided resources that enabled ethnic exploration. Korean adoptees, however, lacked these familial resources and therefore could find their equivalents only through participating in Asian social networks.

In short, the opportunities that adoptees pursued or did not pursue in early adulthood had significant bearing on whether they explored later in life. While there were certainly exceptions, including Margaret Houston, with whom we opened this chapter, most adoptees stayed within the track or trajectory they pursued in early adulthood. However, most who remained or became non-explorers in later adulthood also expressed interest in exploration and a level of frustration in their lack of opportunity to do so.

This suggests the importance of finding venues during the earlier life stage. Adoptees need opportunities to explore, and those opportunities need to be meaningfully compatible with their interests if exploration is to satisfy their apparently persistent interest in ethnicity. Those interests can wax and wane over the life course and take on different forms, but for those who manage to satisfy their interests, especially through early social exposure, ethnic exploration and ethnic involvement can become lifelong habits. Natalie Johnson comes to mind as someone who illustrates this profile: she started pursuing social exposure while in college, lived in Japan and traveled in Asia for several years as an adult, and now pursued personal exploration while living in a predominantly white community, raising her toddler, and being a "stay-at-home" mom.

In the next chapter, we move to the third central question guiding this study: how do Korean adoptees choose to identify, and what meanings do they attach to those identities?

CHAPTER 6

The Ethnic Identities of Adult Adoptees

When asked about his current identification, Brandon Luebke, a twenty-eight-year-old river-rafting guide, stated without any hesitation, "American." Despite engaging in cultural exploration in early adulthood through college coursework and study abroad, he did not consider himself knowledgeable enough to claim an ethnic label: "To consider myself Korean American . . . I would probably have to know a lot more about Korea itself. You know, I'd want to be able to say that I knew a little bit of the language and knew a little bit about the culture and the way that their society runs itself." In contrast, identifying as an American felt appropriate to him: "[Identifying as American] means to me that I grew up in America in a very white background and environment, and my values and the way that I present myself and the way that I think of myself are all based on the environment that I grew up in. So, [a] very, very white urban-rural environment."

In this chapter, we examine how Brandon and other adoptees in our study currently identify. In particular, we pay close attention to the meanings that adoptees attached to their identities, the contrasts they perceived between different labels, and the contexts that turned labels into salient identities for them. We also address the impact of earlier exploration, or lack thereof, on their adult identity choices. First, we describe how adoptees characterized their identity options. Second, we examine the cluster of meanings and situations that accompany each of the major ethnic labels—for example (for adoptees), American, Korean, Korean American, and Asian American. Third, we compare the identities of the adoptees with their non-adoptee counterparts. We conclude with a theoretical discussion of how the practice of ethnic identification occurs in certain social conditions that have less to do with questions of ethnic and national loyalty than with continuing social perceptions of Asian Americans, even adoptees, as foreigners.

ETHNIC LABELS AND THEIR CONNOTATIONS

According to Alejandro Portes and Rubén Rumbaut (2001), members of the second generation typically choose one of four common labels as their ethnic identity: (1) a foreign national-origin identity; (2) a hyphenated American identity; (3) an American national identity; or (4) a panethnic minority-group identity, such as Mexican, Mexican American, American, or Latino (or Hispanic). They argue that changes in label choice reveal trends in identity assimilation, defined as the balance of allegiance to the group versus to the nation. Their findings document the direction of these choices for different groups and reveal how behavior is correlated with labels; however, a shortcoming of their research is that it does not include questions about the reasoning behind the choices.

In our examination of adoptee identity development, we recharacterize Portes and Rumbaut's four types as: (1) a singular ethnic identity, for example, "Korean"; (2) a compound ethnic identity, for example, "Korean American"; (3) a singular national identity, for example, "American"; and (4) a compound panethnic identity, for example, "Asian American." Whereas Portes and Rumbaut infer the foreignness of a national-origin label like "Korean," our respondents emphasized its ethnic character—that is, its embeddedness *within* the American nation. Portes and Rumbaut infer the nationalism of the hyphenated and American labels, but our respondents also emphasized the inclusiveness of the former and registered the efforts it took to be recognized as the latter. And finally, Portes and Rumbaut infer the denationalized quality of the panethnic labels, but again, our respondents emphasized the ethnic embeddedness of such labels and distinguished the label "Asian American" from the singular "Asian," which was chosen by none of our respondents. We found two additional identity paths that were also compound identities in the sense of identifying equally with multiple labels or identifying with a unique label that signaled mixed-race ancestry. However, these paths drew on the same calculus of choice that motivated the more common pattern of primarily identifying with only one of the four main labels.

We also found considerable variation in the meaning and function of particular labels as identities. Probing the reasons for our respondents' choices, we distinguished (1) primary identities or the labels with which participants in our study chose to identify from, (2) secondary labels used in special situations but without identification, and (3) disidentifications or labels that our respondents hesitated to employ even under duress. Since these supplemental identifications used the same four labels, they add more dimension to our analysis of the primary identities. In brief, the majority of adoptees primarily identified with a singular label, either American or Korean, rather than a compound label such as a hyphenated panethnic or ethnic label, a combination of labels, or a label indicating mixture.

Finally, we found a distinct set of meanings for identity beyond allegiance in the ways that respondents voiced different meanings for the same labels and invested the different labels with the same meanings. Portes and Rumbaut argue that experiences with discrimination have moved second-generation identities in the direction of ethnic militance, with increases in both national-origin loyalty and denationalized panethnicity. Our analysis suggests that identity becomes salient for our respondents less as a matter of allegiance conditioned by overt prejudice and discrimination and more in the course of managing specific interpersonal interactions that are common to both adoptees and non-adoptees. These interactions challenge them to defend, accept, make sense of, anticipate, or strategically redefine their "place" in U.S. society. Ethnic identity is salient not so much because they are treated as inferior to whites as because they are regularly presumed to be less American than whites. Table 6.1 shows the distributions of primary identities and disidentifications among participants in our study.

THE MEANINGS BEHIND THE LABELS
Identifying as American

Theories of assimilation have long predicted that ethnic identities vary with length of residence in the host country, most notably with the shift from the first or immigrant generation to the children of immigrants or the second generation, to the grandchildren of immigrants or the third generation (Gordon 1964; Hansen 1938; Hughes et al. 1950; Lieberson and Waters 1988). The

Table 6.1   Distribution of Ethnic Identities in Adulthood

Ethnic Labels	Korean Adoptees		Non-Adoptees	
	Primary Identity	Disidentifications	Primary Identity	Disidentifications
American	28.1%	29.8%	21.4%	50.0%
Korean or equivalent	29.8	14.0	14.3	10.7
Korean American or equivalent	14.0	12.3	25.0	7.1
Asian American	17.5	1.8	17.9	10.7
Asian	0.0	10.5	0.0	14.3
Mixed	3.5	0.0	3.6	0.0
Multiple	7.0	0.0	17.9	0.0
Total	57	31	28	18

Source: Authors' calculations.
Note: The disidentifications sum to more than 100 percent because individuals could express multiple disidentifications.

process of assimilation, however, is not expected to be unidimensional (Portes and Zhou 1993). Each generation chooses a different identity label, but the choice reflects their aspirations rather than their actual level of acculturation. Across three generations, studies of pre-1965 immigration found that new Americans identified first by their singular ethnic label (for example, "Italian"), second by a singular national label ("American"), and third by their compound ethnic label ("Italian American"). In their actual cultural practices, however, new Americans began as ethnic in the first generation ("Italian") before becoming bicultural ("Italian American"), and finally assimilated, albeit adorned with symbolic ethnicity ("American").

Although popular advocates of assimilation regard identification as American to be the desired twilight of ethnicity (Alba 1990), sociologists have long regarded choosing the singular national label as an aspiration that masks a reality of bicultural socialization. Indeed, scholars of assimilation regard identifying as American as an indicator of the transition generation that will raise the fully assimilated—even if proudly ethnic—third generation.

Among the adoptees in our study, we found somewhat different patterns. Those who identified as Americans did not do so as an aspiration. For the vast majority (thirteen out of sixteen), identifying as American simply reflected their sense of cultural belonging. Some explained this sense of belonging by citing their personal distance from Korean culture, and others pointed to their upbringing or the sureness of their connection to American culture. Only a small group identified as American in an instrumental way—namely, to achieve social belonging with whites—and for these respondents, identifying as "plain American" without any hyphenation was one of many interactional tools for putting whites at ease with their visible racial differences.

Furthermore, adoptees who identified as American were more likely to have neither attended college nor explored their ethnicity in later adulthood. As we discussed in chapter 4, college has been a critical context for adoptees to experience opportunities for exploration and to think of themselves in ethnic terms. Adoptees who had never explored their ethnicity were thus more likely to embrace a singular national identity as American. Last but not least, American-identifiers were less likely to have experienced any discrimination as children and adolescents, suggesting that race was less salient to them from the start.

Still, almost all American-identifiers felt that they had to negotiate the recognition of that identity with strangers and acquaintances. They believed that these negotiations were necessary to counter the perceptions and expectations raised by individuals who were curious about their ethnic background, by civil servants administering government forms, and by their own self-consciousness about their racial appearance. For example, Bianca Spencer, a thirty-seven-year-old homemaker and manager of a group home, had dealt with her share of situations in which someone expressed disbelief about her identifying as American. She related an incident in which her personal identity was at odds with a civil servant's perception of her.

> BIANCA: When I was still living in Hawaii, I went down, my brother was stationed in Texas in the Air Force, and his buddies and stuff wanted to take me down to Mexico. So we went down, and when I came back, I had a hard time coming over the border. For some reason, the U.S. Customs guy couldn't figure out that Hawaii was the fiftieth state. I was delayed for, you know, quite a long time.
>
> INTERVIEWER: How did Hawaii come up?
>
> BIANCA: Because I was living in Hawaii at that time, so I had a Hawaii driver's license. And he said that I had to be a U.S. citizen, and I said,

"I am a U.S. citizen. Hawaii is the United States." And then he asked me who the president was, and I told him George Bush, and the vice president was Dan Quayle. And he asked me where Hawaii was, and I said, "Well, if you start from San Francisco or L.A. and fly in the, you know, in the southwest direction for about five hours." And he goes, "Don't get sassy with me, young lady!" And then my brother's friend, who's a captain in the Air Force like my brother, he says, "Let's go get your brother." I said, "Oh, yeah, that'll be really good." My brother is six feet tall, blond hair, blue eyes. This guy can't even figure out that the fiftieth state is Hawaii. He's not going to believe that this blond-haired blue-eyed guy is my older brother! [*laughs*] Things like that. Something that I thought was just so simple, just to come over the border, ended up being so complicated! [*laughs*]

Despite Bianca's efforts to minimize the incident as resulting from the Customs officer's ignorance about the state of Hawaii, we note that the officer never mentioned Hawaii as the reason for his unwillingness to approve her return to the United States. Instead, we suggest that her race and its stereotyped connotation of foreignness were the true precipitating factors that complicated her attempt to recross the border. Bianca minimized the incident as a "little thing," but had she not ultimately prevailed, the perceived conflict between her identity and her race might have had serious consequences.

In contrast to others who identified as American, John Davis, a forty-eight-year-old financial consultant and mixed-race adoptee, did not feel that he had to negotiate the acceptance of his identity. Instead, he simply underscored his sense of national belonging.

> **INTERVIEWER:** How do you identify yourself these days? Are you American? Are you Korean American? Are you Asian American? Are you . . . ?
>
> **JOHN:** I'm an American because I'm pretty much "red, white and blue." [*laughs*] I'm comfortable with that. I cannot really identify my Asianness. I'm just not, I'm not there.

Here John emphasized the sureness of his cultural belonging; however, his choice of words suggests that his belonging was somewhat residual. It seems that he was American not only because of his socialization but also because his sense of ethnicity was empty. Indeed, all of the adoptees in this group actively distanced themselves from the ethnic labels of "Korean," "Korean American," and "Asian American."

The most exceptional of the American-identifiers, however, were those who did not raise cultural or national belonging to explain identifying as simply American. Instead, they noted that their identification facilitated social acceptance from others, typically whites. Like other American-identifiers, Ok-kyun Hollander, a thirty-four-year-old executive assistant, introduced herself in person with her preferred label: "American. I don't even bat an eyelash." Ok-kyun recognized that her identity could cause cognitive dissonance for others. As we explored how she experienced identifying as American with new acquaintances, it became clear that she took significant pride in anticipating and successfully dissolving others' discomfort through humor.

> INTERVIEWER: So, because you make fun of yourself, people just accept that . . .
>
> OK-KYUN: Yeah. Well, like, for example, I have this one acquaintance, and she is like five-foot-nine, redhead, Irish, you know, and she is married to a Hawaiian. And her last name is Takahashi. We just laugh at that all the time. You know, like, Bill, her husband, he says, "Ornamentals," and I said, "God, I used to say that word too." I mean, we know we're a little bit different, you know, we're not really into our culture, you know? And it's not like we're making fun, it's just that we're not comfortable, we're not in that category. We're not, that's not us, you know?
>
> INTERVIEWER: So that's how you signal that you're not part of that category.
>
> OK-KYUN: Yeah. And also, I think some people feel uncomfortable, they don't know how to deal with you or what to say to you, or what's acceptable or not acceptable. You know what I mean? So if you kind of put them at ease, they're like, "Okay, this person's cool. They're okay with this. They're okay with who they are."

Ok-kyun likened her humor to that of a friend, who also referred to Asians by what could be considered a racial slur. Although she attributed their joking to their sense of distance from ethnic culture, the term "Ornamentals" also conjures the status of Asians as social "decor," a position that might describe

Ok-kyun and her friend in their predominantly white networks. She also emphasized the importance of humor for putting at ease people who are uncomfortable with the presence of someone "different." In such situations, Ok-kyun sought to communicate that she was "cool" and "okay with who she is" by making fun of her ethnicity. Ok-kyun's jokes are similar to the strategy of gaining acceptance with whites through self-mockery that we have previously documented among non-adopted Asian Americans (Tuan 1998). For adoptees like Ok-kyun, identifying as American and using self-deprecating humor were ways to achieve social belonging among whites.

Lastly, our analysis of those who distanced themselves from identifying as American reveals that this label marked the most significant divide among adoptee identity options. In contrast with the sixteen who identified primarily as American, seventeen adoptees disidentified from the same label—most commonly because they felt that it was *not socially acceptable* to claim the identity while looking Asian.[1] Revealingly, only two adoptees—both Korean-identifiers—ever used "American" as a secondary label, making it the least popular among the secondary identities.

Identifying As Korean

Most adoptees who identified as Korean were really American-identifiers at heart. That is, they saw themselves as American inside but identified as Korean in response to questions about their background. Some minimized their identity as simply a *ready answer* for a common inquiry, while others treated their experiences as a *source of perspective about society.* Adoptees in both of these groups did not invest the label with even a modest level of ethnic meaning. Instead, they were motivated by a social burden—the recurring need to respond to questions about their ethnicity.

Furthermore, adoptees who identified as Korean were more likely to be female, to not be racially mixed, and, significantly, to have not explored their ethnicity until later adulthood. Holly Littell, a twenty-six-year-old who sold television commercials, was representative of adoptees in this group. She described the matter-of-fact reasoning behind her identity choice.

> **INTERVIEWER:** Do you describe yourself as Korean, Korean American, just American, or anything else?
>
> **HOLLY:** Korean.

INTERVIEWER: And what does it mean to identify as Korean versus being just American?

HOLLY: Well, I don't necessarily, I mean, when people ask, it's mainly when people ask, you know, "Where are you from?" It's not like I, I don't know, that's when it comes up. And it doesn't ever come up any other way, usually.

For Holly, identifying as Korean gave her a ready answer to such inquiries and had no deeper meaning beyond that. Although she was aware that her identity might have different connotations for others, she regarded it primarily as a descriptive label.

Other adoptees experienced these inquiries with more emotion, ranging from negatively tinged amusement to significant annoyance. Samantha "Sam" Cawthorne, a forty-one-year-old air traffic controller, regarded such questions with outright frustration.

SAM: People say, "Well, where are you from?" And I say [*exhales*], oh, I get so mad at the question, because I hate that question. You know, like, "Where are you from?" and I say, "Well, I'm from my birth mother. Where are you from?" [*laughs*] I just get so . . .

INTERVIEWER: It's an intrusive question to you?

SAM: It's just a, just a, I hate that question. And so, I say, because I know what they mean, I say, "I'm from California. I was adopted." [And they say,] "Ohh, okay." It gets dropped.

Sam recognized that this question is not actually an open question about geography but instead a question about her ethnicity and probably also the apparent conflict between her racial appearance and how she perceived herself. Her reaction was similar to those of non-adoptees who were irritated by the same question and its assumptions (Tuan 1998), but Sam's standard answer presumed that the asker was familiar enough with Asian adoption to know that follow-up questions would be irrelevant. Nevertheless, she resented the question for putting her in the position of confirming the racially premised assumption that she was somehow less American than the asker.

Some Korean-identifiers viewed the question more philosophically, using the recurring experience as a source of perspective about society. To be clear, they did not take reactive perspectives that criticized the racial assumptions behind the question; instead, they voiced a curiosity and even amusement about societal perceptions and misperceptions. Jennifer Welch, a forty-one-year-old corporate manager, provided a good example.

> INTERVIEWER: Would you describe to me how being Korean is different from being American, if at all?
>
> JENNIFER: [*pause*] That's a really hard question. I guess the way I would answer it would be, for me it has to do with the visuals. Because I don't have a lot of the cultural overlap or interaction. And the American part is the part of who I am. Rather than the visible.
>
> INTERVIEWER: How comfortable would you feel calling yourself just a plain old American? How do the visuals play into that as an option?
>
> JENNIFER: That's a very good twist on that point. That doesn't feel right to me because it seems like so much of what has shaped me and what I know people see when they see me. This ongoing feedback is something other than "American." And I think "Korean" to me identifies the forces that have made my personality out to be what it is.

The "ongoing feedback" that Jennifer received confirmed that the American label was not fully appropriate for her. As a result, she "goes with the Korean part" to accommodate societal perceptions.

We found only a handful of Korean-identifiers ($n = 5$) who voiced any ethnic reasons for identifying as simply Korean. Some voiced a sense of ethnic pride, but it was not rooted in an appreciation of Korean history and culture or a sense of group exclusion. Instead, it was primarily a recent personal development that did not compete with a longer-standing identification as simply American. For example, Ross Green, a forty-two-year-old construction foreman, attributed identifying as Korean to his personal acceptance of not fitting the common image of an American—namely, someone white.

> ROSS: I, just now, I probably see myself more Korean. Or at least more aware of it, more accepting of it. That's a better term.
>
> INTERVIEWER: Would you ever consider calling yourself just an American?

Ross: No. You know, I do think of myself as American too. But, of all those choices, I'd just pick the Korean.

Interviewer: Has the way you identify yourself changed over time?

Ross: Mm hmm. Yeah, I've probably become less embarrassed or intimidated by it, and more accepting. I was probably like a closet Korean! [*laughs*]

Even though Ross saw himself as American, he declined to identify as such because he associated openly doing so with his years of feeling shame for being Asian after many childhood encounters with racism. In the present, he seemed to have come to terms with being Korean, although his qualification ("more accepting of it") still betrayed a measure of hesitation.

Our analysis of those who did not identify as Korean but used the singular ethnic label as a secondary identity shows that the label possesses a salience for adoptees that rivals that of the American label. In addition to the seventeen adoptees who identified primarily as Korean, another twelve adoptees, mostly American-identifiers, also used the singular ethnic label as a secondary label under questioning and under special circumstances. In other words, fully half of the adoptees identified with the singular ethnic label at some level, primarily because it was how strangers and new acquaintances sought to classify them. By contrast, only eight respondents distanced themselves from identifying as Korean—either because they did not feel *culturally competent* to claim to be Korean or because they perceived the label as *incomplete* in comparison to the compound ethnic label of "Korean American."

Identifying As Korean American

In popular discourse, hyphenated identities, or what we term compound ethnic labels, suggest either that the nation lacks and needs a more complete process of assimilation or that the nation needs to recognize that it is a culturally plural society rather than a true melting pot. For scholars, identifying as Korean American or as Italian American indicates both less "failure" and less "success," respectively, than is presumed by advocates of assimilation and cultural pluralism. Above all, they regard compound identities as "made in America" rather than as a more equal combination of ethnic and national loyalties and cultures (Portes and Rumbaut 2001). Identifying by the compound ethnic label can be a symbolic practice, even a desperate but hopeless effort to recover ethnicity by the third generation, especially those raised by American-identifying parents (Waters 1990). Alternatively, the compound ethnic identity might describe the second generation's bicultural lifestyle even as they aspire to be simply American (Hansen 1938). For yet others, typically those in the second and later generations, it may mark a lifestyle populated by coethnics but highly assimilated in content—as demonstrated, for instance, in the emergent ethnicity of ethnic sports leagues and ethnic "beauty pageants" (Tuan 1998; King-O'Riain 2006).

Adoptees in our study who identified as Korean American were more likely to come from a family that fostered a shared fate and pursued social exposure exploration in early adulthood. Almost all attended college and were not racially mixed. Furthermore, identifying as Korean American came out of a range of motivations, most of which rested on a desire for an inclusive category. Mona Brown, a twenty-eight-year-old county corrections security officer, illustrated how Korean American–identifiers anticipated the common question about their ethnicity by formulating a response that was inclusive of being both Korean and American.

> INTERVIEWER: And what does [identifying as Korean American] mean to you?
>
> MONA: It means I was born in Korea; I've got the Korean features. But I live here in America. And I'm a U.S. citizen.
>
> INTERVIEWER: And how is that different from just calling yourself American? Would you ever consider calling yourself just American?
>
> MONA: No. To me, it's, you know, it's the one thing I can claim. [*laughs*]

Mona's combination of being Korean and being American is a "Korean but" version of inclusive identity. In response to inquiries, she admitted her birthplace and her visible characteristics but emphasized her current community and nationality. At the same time, her ethnic admission was less reluctant than it was for the adoptees who identified by the singular national label. Indeed, she distanced herself from identifying simply as American because she felt that including Korean in her identity granted her a special distinction. In the context of her largely white networks, identifying as Korean American allowed her to be different but not too different.

Others premised their identities not on inclusiveness but instead on being constrained by not being white. Significantly, none identified as Korean

American to signal biculturalism even as aspiration; instead, their identity accepted their distinction from other Americans while still emphasizing their Americanness. Zachary White, a twenty-eight-year-old golf course grounds-keeper, serves as an example.

> ZACHARY: [I identify as] Korean American. Korean but, you know, raised in America.
>
> INTERVIEWER: Well, how is that different from just saying "American"?
>
> ZACHARY: When I, I would say it's just a matter of, you know, of being, you know, quote unquote, white. If I was to tell someone who I'd never met, say on the cell phone, that I was American, and I showed up, and I looked the way I did, you know, whether they'd say anything or not, they would think. . . . [If] I was to tell someone over the phone, if I said I was American, they would assume that I was Caucasian. Now, I don't know if that's weird or not, but when I think of American I think of someone who's white, unless they say, you know, "I'm Asian American or African American." That's just, you know, the society we live in, you kind of have to, you know, you have to tell people [and] not have them assume something that's not true.

Although Zachary began with the same "Korean but" frame for his identity, his explanation was less about a sense of cultural belonging to the United States and more about his responsibility to warn other Americans that his voice might mislead them into thinking he was white. In his mind, not informing others that he was Asian was tantamount to practicing a deception.

Whereas eight adoptees identified as Korean American, seven others disidentified from the label for reasons that depended on their primary identity. The American-identifiers and Asian American–identifiers disqualified themselves as not having the *cultural competence* to identify as Korean American, whereas the Korean-identifiers regarded "Korean American" as communicating a wide range of *inaccurate or unwanted associations* about having been born in the United States, having mixed ancestry, or promoting ethnic politics. Although these reasons reveal how some adoptees conceptualized what it means to be Korean or Korean American, it is also revealing that only one-quarter of adoptees either identified or disidentified with being Korean American. The greater salience of the American and Korean labels suggests that adoptees as a group experience a pressure to choose between national labels that crowds their free-dom to select other options.

Identifying As Asian American

In recent decades, the panethnic label has succeeded the hyphenated label as a symbol of either national fragmentation or diversity. Even more than the com-pound ethnic label, the panethnic label signals a balkanization of American cul-ture because panethnicity falls along the lines of race, which has long been regarded as less dissolvable than ethnicity. For scholars, identifying as Asian American or Hispanic American can indicate a reactive alienation from soci-ety. Indeed, Portes and Rumbaut (2001) imply that it marks a more intense alienation by characterizing panethnicity as denationalized rather than ethnic. Other scholars regard panethnicity in weaker terms—not as part of an extra-national or transnational movement, but rather as the symbolic ethnicity of those whose cultural assimilation is so complete that they have only the most diffuse attachment to their national-origin label (Waters 1990). Yet others characterize panethnicity as an emergent ethnicity born of the contradictions between the inevitability of acculturation and the continuing significance of race in American life (Espiritu 1992; Tuan 1998).

Among adoptees in our study, two non-exclusive motivations were offered for identifying as Asian American: *social constraints* against alternative identifi-cations and *affirmative reasons* for identifying panethnically. In brief, a mixture of social experiences and personal aspirations motivated adoptees to identify by the compound panethnic label. Unique to Asian American–identifiers was the absence of any effort like that among other adoptees to distinguish between external classification, personal classification, and a real self. Instead, they saw social perception as having shaped their real self, and they classified themselves accordingly. Even more so than identifying as Korean American, identifying as Asian American appeared to be a more fully "achieved identity" that confronted social expectations directly and resolved them in meaningful ways.

Furthermore, adoptees who identified as Asian American were more likely to come from families that had not fostered a shared fate, and they were also more likely to have pursued exploration in early adulthood. Almost all had experienced childhood discrimination and attended college. Natalie Johnson, the forty-one-year-old homemaker with an MBA, comes to mind as typical of adoptees in this group. Her adolescence was marked by embarrassment over being Asian and frequent teasing, which she overcame during her college days at Berkeley. In college she immersed herself in ethnic networks and actively explored what being Korean, Asian, and adopted meant to her. And what did identifying as Asian American mean to her now? She laughed and replied: "That I look different. And that I'm interested in Asia, not just Korea."

Lisa Packard, a twenty-six-year-old interior designer, also preferred to identify as Asian American. When asked to comment on what the identity meant to her, she replied, "I'm a person of Asian descent, and I'm a U.S. citizen." In response to the next question, she elaborated:

INTERVIEWER: Why Asian American as opposed to Korean American?

LISA: Good question. Probably because, again, I've never had [*pause*] . . . I don't know much about the Korean culture. I know more about [my husband's] Filipino culture [and] my girlfriends' Chinese culture. I do know a little bit of the Korean culture, what I learned in class. [*laughs*] But nothing like . . .

INTERVIEWER: Would you ever identify as plain old American? "I'm an American"?

LISA: It depends on who's asking and what context it's going to be used in.

INTERVIEWER: And what context would you . . . ?

LISA: If I was just talking to someone on the phone and they were talking about, like, the Mexicans trying to get into the California border or whatnot, then I would say "Hey, I'm an American just as much as a Mexican American."

Lisa distanced herself from identifying as Korean American on the basis of cultural competence or her lack thereof. In fact, identifying as Asian American made sense to her because, among her family and friends, she felt more culturally competent with the other Asian ethnic cultures. She fell back on the singular national label only when she sought to strategically promote an ethnically inclusive definition of the United States. We suggest that this strategy revealed her awareness of both the common association of American nationality and white race and its potential use in marginalizing nonwhites.

Adoptees who identified as Asian American also mentioned a range of affirmative reasons for their primary identities. Natalie Johnson illustrated this combination of reasons by weaving back and forth between the constraints and affirmations of this identification.

> **INTERVIEWER:** Would you feel comfortable identifying as a plain old American, without hyphenation?
>
> **NATALIE:** No. And people have tried to, like my family's tried to say, "We just see you as American." It's like, "No." Because I can't, I really can't say that, because it just seems so false. Because when people look at me, they see me as Asian. As a younger person, I wanted that [Asianness] not to be there. I wanted them to just see me as American, and my family [would say], "Well, when people ask you where you're from, why don't you just say, 'I'm from California'? When they ask you again, just say, 'California.'" And it's like . . . [*sound of frustration*] . . . I know what they're asking me. They want to know where, you know, what ethnicity I am. And that is part of who I am. And I did tell my parents that. I said, "You know, I can't ignore that I was born in Korea. And I look different." So, yeah, I sort of take pride in being different. And I don't see myself as just American.

Here Natalie revealed the complex thinking process she went through in negotiating the identity choices and constraints she encountered. Her earlier ethnic explorations during college had significant bearing on how she framed the identity landscape and where she situated herself. Natalie's understanding of the identity constraints confronting her revealed a level of sophistication typically associated with individuals who have taken ethnic studies or race relations courses. She recognized that a geographic answer would be tangential to the recurring question about her ethnicity—and worse, that it would confirm that being different was undesirable. Although a reactive sense of racial pride was not the sole reason for her primary identity, we suggest that it was the most important, and in fact the necessary, component.

Identities Beyond the Major Labels

Some adoptees chose to identify not with one of the four major labels, but instead with either multiple labels or unique labels that signaled their mixed ancestry. Two adoptees identified with *multiple labels* rather than with a primary label followed by secondary labels for superficial interactions or official classifications. Neither voiced any disidentifications. Margaret Houston, a forty-three-year-old ceramic tile business owner, was mostly a Korean-identifier for reasons of ethnic pride, but she was also occasionally an American-identifier for the purposes of making political statements about diversity in the United States—for example, identifying both Latinos and herself as Americans when complaints about illegal migrants arise. In brief, Margaret asserted different identities depending on the immediate situation, a practice that scholars have referred to as situational ethnicity or identity (Joshi 2006; Kaufert 1977; Okamura 1981).

Several adoptees identified with *unique labels* associated with their mixed ancestries. Without exception, these adoptees were racially mixed, had attended college, and had not pursued early exploration. Put another way, adoptees with mixed-race ancestry identified by the usual labels—American, Asian American, sometimes Korean—only if they had not attended college or if they had pursued any ethnic exploration in early adulthood. Sherwin Wright, a forty-four-year-old finance manager, identified as "half Korean" but did not immediately share this label with questioners. He preferred to play with them in a joking way to put them at ease. In other words, his identity was, like Korean-identifiers, sometimes a ready answer and sometimes a source of some perspective on the social compulsion to classify by race. Tracey Tulane, a forty-seven-year-old music teacher, identified as "Korean Irish," partly to assert a pride in the Korean contribution to her genes and "physical inheritance" but also to play with questioners because she privately identified as American out of cultural belonging. In short, the mixed and multiple identifications suggested two additional identity paths, though they invoked the same motivations and experiences as the major paths.

NON-ADOPTEE VARIATIONS

Whereas adoptees chose singular identities more often than compound identities, non-adoptees tended to prefer compound identities (see table 6.1). All twenty-eight non-adoptees voiced a primary identification, and among them, slightly fewer than half also voiced secondary identities.

Identifying As American

Similar to adoptees, the most common reason that non-adoptees offered for identifying as American was cultural belonging. In all cases, non-adoptees achieved recognition of their identities through some level of negotiation with strangers and new acquaintances. In contrast to adoptees, non-adoptees were not motivated to achieve social belonging with whites and instead had the distinct goal of making a political statement. Wayne Liu, a twenty-seven-year-old computer consultant, identified as American to embrace the freedom and choice available in the United States and contrasted that stance with their unavailability in his birthplace, China. In a different vein, Edward Chen, a thirty-seven-year-old engineering project manager, identified as American to express his distaste for the ethnic self-segregation in his profession and his preference for an occupational rather than ethnic-occupational identity. Edward admitted, however, that he was proud of the "accomplishments" that could be found in Chinese history, although his pride was tempered by good-humored awareness of "also some pretty crappy things."

Similar to adoptees, almost all non-adoptee American-identifiers employed secondary labels. For forms and official purposes, they fell back on the pan-ethnic label of "Asian American"; when personally questioned, they relied on singular ethnic labels such as "Chinese" or compound ethnic labels such as "Vietnamese American." Deborah Kuohung, a thirty-four-year-old investment banker, fell back on "Chinese American" only under intense questioning and expressed frustration about how often strangers would immediately ask for her ethnicity upon being introduced. Only Paul Vo, a thirty-seven-year-old architect, refused to employ a secondary identity. As a consequence, he often had to engage in substantial and not always successful negotiations to have his primary identity recognized, such as when a white friend responded to Paul's identifying as American with the retort that Paul "lived in America [only] because it's convenient." Paul was stunned by this comment:

> That's just not true. I didn't know how to respond to him right away. But later I go, "Hey, wait a minute, wait a minute. That's not true. I want to be American as much as . . . I think I am American as much as the white people are."

Among all American-identifiers, both adoptee and non-adoptee, Paul's identity came the closest to the theoretically expected aspirational character of identifying as American. It is revealing, however, that once again it was race that challenged the social acceptance of his identification.

Whereas six non-adoptees identified with the singular national label of American, *fourteen* respondents disidentified with the label. As among adoptees, the issue of *social acceptance* was a common reason; indeed, among non-adoptees it was the most frequently cited reason. These individuals largely associated the label "American" with being white, with a desire for social acceptance, and, uniquely, with *denying and being ashamed of their ethnicity*. With less heat, a couple of respondents simply saw identifying as American as socially unacceptable given their racial appearance, unless they were traveling abroad.[2]

Identifying by Korean-Equivalents

Although "Korean" was the most common label for adoptees, a singular ethnic label (such as "Vietnamese," "Chinese," or "Japanese") was the least common choice among the four main labels for non-adoptees. The reasons offered for this identity preference included: having ethnic pride, feeling social constraints against identifying as American, and appreciating that ethnicity grants some modicum of distinction from a more generic American identity. Most significant was the *complete absence* among non-adoptees of the most prevalent meaning of this identity for adoptees: a ready answer to questions about their ethnic heritage.

Similar to adoptees, non-adoptees defined their ethnic pride within the American context rather than against it. For Peggy Chang, a thirty-four-year-old senior accounting technician, identifying as Korean showed an appropriate level of pride, whereas she perceived identifying as Korean American as offensive because of its similarities to the label "African American," which she associated with ethnic politics and separatism. Most unique was Lindsay Yang, a thirty-year-old college bookstore supervisor, who distanced herself from identifying as American because of the international stereotypes of "ugly Americans" as self-centered and culturally ignorant tourists.

Several non-adoptees disidentified with singular ethnic labels because they felt that such a label was less personally resonant than alternative labels like "Chinese American" or "Asian American" or because it was less patriotic than a compound label that included "American." Significantly, these non-adoptees differed from their adoptee counterparts in *not invoking cultural incompetence* as a reason for dissociating from their singular ethnic labels.

Identifying by Korean American–Equivalents

Although "Korean American" was the least common label among adoptees, a compound ethnic label was the *most common* primary identity for non-adoptees. Like the majority of their adoptee counterparts, all of these non-adoptees identified as Chinese American, Japanese American, or Vietnamese

American to communicate an inclusive identity. Some refused to choose between Asian ethnic and national labels to signal not so much biculturalism as a sense of being culturally American combined with a pride in being "different." Feeling American was foundational in their daily lives, but their racial visibility set them apart. In fact, for two respondents, identifying as Chinese American served as a corrective to a preexisting shame in their earlier years about their racial visibility.

For other non-adoptees, an inclusive identity came with a *deeper biculturalism* than was apparent among their adoptee counterparts. Despite being a fourth-generation American, David Yamaguchi, a forty-one-year-old account manager, voiced the most substantial example of cultural fusion as he discussed what identifying as Japanese American meant to him.

> **DAVID:** If it was on a form, I'd check "Japanese American." But if they wanted my feeling, and they had a few minutes, you know, I would state that "I'm very much a mix." You know, I've grown up in a Japanese American home. As a fourth-generation Japanese American, I'm pretty much apple pie. And at the same time, I've had experiences in my life, for example, my time in Japan, which really helped me identify with some parts of me that are very Asian American, Japanese American, very Japanese. And so, it wouldn't be a real easy answer for me.

> **INTERVIEWER:** In your mind, what's the difference between Asian American and Japanese American?

> **DAVID:** I think there's not a whole lot of real differences between, when you get to where I'm at, as a yonsei [fourth-generation American], the difference[s] between Japanese American and Asian American are, just pretty blurred. There's just certain things with respect to being Japanese American that you can relate to that you can't as an Asian American. I can relate to the internment of Japanese Americans. I can relate to the feelings toward the Japanese with respect to World War II, a lot of animosity toward the Japanese. But in terms of being an Asian American versus being a Japanese American, there's very little difference.

David's answer ranged far and wide, from official classification to childhood socialization, to similarity with mainstream America, to experiences in Japan, to similarity with an emergent Asian American experience, to Japanese American history. Rather than only indicating his racial visibility, his sense of being Japanese was rooted in family culture, ethnic history, homeland travel, and a feeling of convergence with other Asian Americans. We suggest that a sense of ethnic group belonging is critical to the more bicultural version of inclusive identity.

Even though no one singled out the inability to be recognized as simply American as the sole or primary reason for choosing this label, we suggest that the desire to make peace with or resolve the issue of not being white was a factor in non-adoptees' identities. Most non-adoptees who chose compound ethnic identities distanced themselves from identifying as American because they regarded the identity as socially unacceptable for an Asian person in the United States; as referring only to whites; as associated with an earlier, immature desire for acceptance among whites; and, particularly, as a self-hating denial of their ethnicity.

In comparison with the seven non-adoptees who identified with compound ethnic labels, only two individuals distanced themselves from these labels. One who identified with a singular ethnic label echoed a reason cited earlier: a wish to avoid the recurring association between compound identities and a certain kind of ethnic consciousness exemplified by the label "African American." The other regarded the compound ethnic label as too narrow relative to her pan-Asian interests. In contrast to their adoptee counterparts, however, these non-adoptees did not explain their choice by saying either that they did not feel culturally competent to identify with an ethnic specific label or that they associated a compound ethnic label with being U.S.-born or having mixed ancestry.

Identifying As Asian American

Similar to adoptees, the five non-adoptees who identified as Asian American explained their identities in terms of social constraints and affirmative themes. Unlike adoptees, non-adoptees pursued pan-Asianism not because of their interest in Asian nations but because of their affinity for other Asian Americans. Milli Park, a forty-two-year-old engineering manager, attributed her panethnic identification to her experiences in school and at work.

> MILLI: You know, I feel like Asian American . . . if people insist on categorizing me! [*laughs*] Most people view me as a Korean American, but I feel pretty pan-Asian.

INTERVIEWER: Is it because you're married to somebody who's Japanese—

MILLI: And also because, I guess, because of [my college] experience. And at [my workplace] I have close friends who are other Asian Americans, Chinese American, Indian American, Japanese American. . . . [So] I feel very close to their culture. Very, very close.

INTERVIEWER: So, a sense of affinity even? Or is that too strong?

MILLI: Yeah, and you know, I'm always mistaken at work for being one or the other. I always have people think that I'm Miriam, who's a Chinese American, who's like ten years younger, and I'm delighted! [*laughs*] You know, just things like that.

Milli identified as Asian American because she felt very close to the pan-Asian American network of friends that she had had since college. It is perhaps not surprising that she was also in an interethnic marriage, much like adoptee Lisa Packard, who was also an Asian American–identifier. Milli's sense of closeness to other Asians had also been reinforced by ethnic lumping—specifically the frequent confusion of her for another Asian American who was not only of another ethnicity but also significantly younger. Whereas pan-Asianists like Milli did not actively distance themselves from other labels, those who defined the panethnic label as an inclusive identity dissociated themselves from both the singular national label and the alternative ethnic labels. They rejected identifying as American, either because doing so would be a denial of their ethnicity or because of its association with whites; whereas at the same time, they declined singular ethnic labels like "Chinese" for being too ethnic and the compound ethnic labels like "Vietnamese American" for still being too narrow. Like others who chose an identity out of a desire for inclusiveness, these individuals explained this desire as a new sense of pride in being Asian after earlier years of anxiety about limited racial acceptance among whites.

Identifying with Multiple and Mixed Identities

Although only two adoptees reported multiple primary identifications, five non-adoptees voiced multiple primary identifications, all including a compound ethnic label. Unlike adoptees, only one non-adoptee reported switching between labels depending on the content of an interpersonal situation.

Beth Lum, a twenty-seven-year-old infant development specialist, identified as Asian American when she felt that race mattered, but shifted to Chinese or Chinese American when she felt that race was not salient in the situation. For most non-adoptees, however, label switching depended not on the topic in a situation but on the composition of the audience. Several non-adoptees distinguished between a "private" ethnic label reserved for interacting with Asian Americans and a "public" panethnic label used with non-Asians and on official forms. As Sandra Chan, a thirty-one-year-old academic adviser, explained:

> It depends on what group I'm with. If I'm with other Asian Americans, I'll identify as Chinese American. If I'm with other people of color, it'll be Asian American—and I think overall I would identify as Asian American. Unless I need to be really specific. Then I would say [that] I'm a first-generation Chinese American woman.

Unlike adoptees who switched between ethnic-specific and national labels, Sandra switched between ethnic-specific and panethnic labels, in no small part because the interactions in which her identity became salient were primarily with colleagues who were Asian American and people of color, not those with white strangers and new acquaintances. Furthermore, non-adoptees like Sandra tended to distance themselves from the singular national label for reasons associated with social acceptance: identifying as American signaled a denial of ethnicity or an attempt to be white, or it simply was not acceptable for someone who looked Asian to claim to be simply American.

Only one non-adoptee voiced an identity communicating her mixed ancestry, but like her adoptee counterparts, she had familiar reasons. Courtney Perry, a thirty-one-year-old underwriter, identified as "biracial, half Japanese" to acknowledge her "100 percent Japanese American" father and her white American mother. Not surprisingly, she disidentified from the labels "American" and "Asian" as incomplete identities by comparison with her more inclusive identity. She recalled that her parents had originally encouraged her to identify as "mixed," but she discovered in school that the term "mixed" was less recognized than the term "biracial." None of her adoptee counterparts reported any institutional correction of this sort. We suggest that the reason for this difference lies in Courtney's relative youth in comparison with the adoptees, most of whom were in school in an earlier decade.

CONCLUSIONS

Previous research has found that Korean adoptees do not identify strongly in ethnic terms (Feigelman 2000; Feigelman and Silverman 1983; Friedlander 1999; Grotevant et al. 2000; Huh and Reid 2000; D. S. Kim 1977, 1978). Our research lends further support to this literature, although with some intriguing modifications. At first blush, the roughly equal numbers of adoptees in our study who identified as either American or Korean might suggest that their interest in their ethnicity was growing, relative to the very low bar set by previous research. On the contrary, most Korean-identifying adoptees did not invest the label with even a modest level of ethnic meaning or pride. Instead, their identity choice was a strategy they used as a simple description to address recurring questions about their background.

This finding points to an internal tension that adoptees had to negotiate as they made their identity choices. Like Asian ethnics, Korean adoptees were not entirely free to identify as they wished (Tuan 1998). When adoptees made ethnic identity choices, they had to navigate assumptions about race, ethnicity, and nation that cast them forever as foreigners. Most of those who identified simply as American still had to persuade strangers and new acquaintances to accept their identity. Those who identified with ethnic labels encountered the same assumptions but resolved the questions and expectations in a variety of ways. Many simply accepted these racial moments as inevitable parts of their life and prepared a ready, expected answer, though often with mixed feelings (most Korean-identifiers). Some anticipated these assumptions with an inclusive identification that deflected the implied choice between nation and ethnicity (most Korean American–identifiers and some Asian American–identifiers), while others stressed their nationality but resigned themselves to being seen as different (some Korean American–identifiers and some Asian American–identifiers). Still others tried to transcend this social reality by taking pride in their ethnicity (some Korean-identifiers) or their race, albeit on panethnic terms (most Asian American–identifiers). And as can be seen in this summary, the specific response or strategy chosen had less to do with a particular label and more to do with the rationale behind the choice.

Adoptees shared with other Asian Americans the regular experience of being reminded of their racial visibility and presumptive status as less American; however, these reminders appeared to be more salient for adoptees than for non-adoptees. Both experienced being questioned and having their citizenship questioned, but it was primarily adoptees who mentioned these experiences in explaining their identity choices. An important reason is that being raised in white families raised their expectations for social acceptance. Another reason, however, is that these moments simply cut deeper for adoptees.

Our research suggests that adult ethnic identity, whether for adoptees or non-adoptees, should be characterized less as a contest between national and group allegiances and more as a way to define a place for oneself within the nation in the face of group-based assumptions that diminish one's social citizenship. For Korean adoptees, this act is uniquely challenging because most were raised to think of themselves as white and to assume a sense of belonging to white society. When this family assumption collides with, or is violated by, comments grounded in group-based assumptions, a medley of reactions (outrage, resignation, confusion) may ensue. For adoptees, these group-based assumptions not only distance them from their nation but also sever them from their families. Given these more intimate, if not categorically greater, stakes, it is unfortunate that most adoptees in the study felt compelled to answer with a singular identity and did not feel free to choose a compound identity that could call those assumptions into question.

CHAPTER 7

Choosing Ethnicity, Negotiating Race

In this concluding chapter, we take a step back from examining the "ground-level" experiences of Korean adoptees to reflect upon the larger significance of our findings. An assumption we have made throughout this study is that identity exploration is important for Korean adoptees to pursue. Many scholars have documented the link between identity development, psychological well-being, and mental health (see especially Arroyo and Zigler 1995; Basow et al. 2008; Erikson 1963; Martinez and Dukes 1997; Thoits 1983; Vleioras and Bosma 2005; Wakefield and Hudley 2007). Jean Phinney (1989, 1992, 1996b), in particular, has emphasized the importance for racial minorities of engaging in identity exploration to counteract shame or the development of a negative self-image from being considered undesirable or inferior by white norms. Exploration is important for racial minorities because it enables them to make sense of who they are in a society where race matters and gives them a chance to develop a healthy self-image. A strong ethnic and racial identity can also offer protection from negative stereotypes by providing a positive counternarrative about one's group (Lee 2003b, 2005; Rivas-Drake 2008).

The unique life circumstances of Korean and other transracial adoptees make identity exploration especially important to pursue. But exploration is also a more complicated process given that adoptee families are white (Friedlander 1999; Hollingsworth 1997; Johnston et al. 2007; Lee 2003a; Song and Lee 2009;

Westhues and Cohen 1998; Yoon 2001, 2004). As Susan Basow and her colleagues (2008, 474) have argued, "In contrast to minority individuals whose parents are also members of racial minorities, transracial adoptees with Caucasian families must be deliberately exposed to ethnic and racial groups other than the dominant one within their homes if they are to experience cultural socialization."

We now return our attention to Caleb Littell, whom the reader may remember as the adoptee who became caught up in armed robbery, drugs, and general debauchery during his youth. We opened this book with a detailed discussion of his adolescence, and we return to him at the close because his narrative embodies many key elements of the Korean adoptee experience, albeit taken to extremes. Today Caleb is happily married and experiencing success as a producer of extreme sports videos. He is also taking small steps toward learning about Korean culture and interacting with other Asians, both of which he would have resisted until recently: "I'm finding myself, not drawn, but more interested in learning that stuff." Psychologists would view Caleb's current state as one where he is moving toward greater psychological health and an achieved identity. As sociologists, our attention is drawn to the broader social contexts and personal relations that compel adoptees like Caleb to give greater consideration to their identities.

In accounting for his gradual change in attitude, Caleb had a revealing conversation with the interviewer:

> **CALEB:** And I think the reason, the main reason why I do that for myself, is, so I don't have such a negative view on Asian people [*sigh*]. . . .
>
> **INTERVIEWER:** Okay. And why did you feel like you had to start working on that?
>
> **CALEB:** [*pause*] . . . My wife! [*laughs*] My wife told me I was racist! [*laughs*] I'd say things at dinner parties, or I'd say things around her that weren't, that to me were totally [*pause*] . . . whatever, normal. But I could see, either in other people's eyes or in her eyes, that that's not a normal way to talk. That's not a good way to be. . . . So I, [*pause*] . . . yeah. So when I say I had a complex with it, I mean I had a complex with it! [*laughs*] I was not a happy Asian person. And not happy with other Asian people.

Caleb's words speak volumes about the ambivalence that many Korean adoptees feel toward their ancestry and why exploration is so important to pursue. If Caleb had the option of ignoring his race, the stakes would be low. His feelings about being Asian would simply be a matter of individual preference. This is the case today for white ethnics, who can choose the racial and ethnic elements they wish to identify with or wish to discard (Alba 1990; Gans 1979; Waters 1990).

A different picture emerges for racial minorities and Asian Americans in particular (Macias 2006; Song 2003; Tuan 1998). As we have discussed elsewhere (Tuan 1998, 161):

> Today, Asian ethnics exercise a great deal of personal choice regarding the elements of traditional ethnic culture they wish to incorporate or do away with. . . . But in another very real way, being ethnic remains a societal expectation for them. They have yet to be embraced as bona fide longtime Americans and to be accepted as the highly acculturated Americans they are.

These words were written to describe the circumstances facing Asian ethnics who are highly acculturated and native-born Asian Americans, but they are equally applicable to Korean adoptees. Caleb remains bound to other Asians because of his race. The following example illustrates the point.

> **CALEB:** Um, recently, [I notice] when we go into small towns on the motorcycles. When everybody takes their helmet off, and I take mine off, and I'm the only Asian guy in, let's say, Kellogg, Idaho, or Ephrata or something like that. It's . . .
>
> **INTERVIEWER:** And they weren't expecting you when you took your helmet off.
>
> **CALEB:** Yeah. Or when I walk into a gas station in the middle of nowhere, and I speak impeccable English to the owner, and he looks at me like [*pause*] . . . "Holy shit, you speak English?"

Situations like these startle adoptees by taking them out of the moment and reminding them that others see and experience them differently from how they see themselves. One minute Caleb is a motorcycle enthusiast enjoying a ride with friends, and the next moment he is an Asian whose presence is unexpected and out of place. Attention is drawn to a dimension of his self that he does not necessarily identify with but that matters in terms of how he is treated.

Derald Wing Sue, Christina Capodilupo, and their colleagues (2007, 273) have popularized the concept of *racial microaggressions* to analyze situations in which minorities are pulled out of the moment because their race has become salient. They describe microaggressions as "brief and commonplace daily verbal, behavioral, and environmental indignities, whether intentional or unintentional, that communicate hostile, derogatory, or negative racial slights and insults to the target person or group." This concept is particularly useful for describing the everyday experiences of Korean adoptees and other Asian Americans (Sue, Bucceri, et al. 2007). As "model minorities," they encounter a more subtle and ambiguous form of racial subordination.[1] Although they may not be as likely to experience being followed around in a store and other overt forms of discrimination, Asians are more likely to endure "indignities"—comments calling into question their American heritage and loyalties, assumptions about their ties to Asian countries and culture, and encounters with the surprise or wariness of others at their very presence.[2]

Some might wonder why situations like these take on such symbolic importance to their recipients—though they present a nuisance or a mild annoyance, surely they are not harmful? We believe that these incidents cause harm precisely because they seem to be innocuous and are unpredictable. Such disruptions can happen anywhere at any moment, and over time such experiences can lead to a sense of vulnerability and confusion over who one is. Without engaging in some type of identity exploration to counteract the discomfort they may feel from these experiences, adoptees are susceptible to internalizing stereotypes, struggling with a negative self-image, and developing resentment toward other Asians. Caleb went as far as denigrating Asians to the point of making others around him uncomfortable, a response pattern known as internalized racism (Blauner 1972; Feagin and Cobas 2008; Pyke and Dang 2003; Scott 2003). Countless experiences had reinforced Caleb's aversion to Asians. However, rather than focus on the individuals making assumptions or comments, he had focused his resentment on Asians en masse for putting him in the position of being singled out.

In a society where race matters, it is important for Korean adoptees to understand the real and tangible ways in which race informs their lives and to foster a positive identity. We set out in this study to document how adoptees relate to the racial and ethnic groupings to which they are assigned, the ways in which they pursue ethnic exploration, and the factors that influence or diminish identity salience for them. We began by situating Korean adoption within the context of U.S. race relations and showing that the practice emerged during a turning point in this country's racial history. Despite adopting at a time when other racialized practices were being called into serious question, the soothing messages that Korean adoptive families received from the media and the general public encouraged them to believe that race did not have to matter in their child-rearing and family practices. These beliefs, in turn, led many parents to seriously underestimate the significance of race in their children's lives. Subsequent chapters showed how adoptees have negotiated the expectations they were raised with ("race does not matter") versus their actual experiences ("race does matter"), their forays into ethnic exploration, and, ultimately, their adult identity choices and what those choices mean to them.

We shift now to discussing the implications of our findings for understanding the current state of U.S. race relations and for understanding the Asian American experience. Before closing, we offer recommendations for both adoptive parents and agencies, and we also identify directions for future research.

WHAT CAN KOREAN ADOPTION TELL US ABOUT RACE IN THE UNITED STATES?

Race in the twenty-first century defies easy understanding. On the one hand, signs of barriers coming down can be readily found: the election of the first president of color, the first Latina appointed to the Supreme Court, impressive growth in rates of intermarriage, and, of course, the remarkable and increasing popularity of transracial adoption, just to name a few. On the other hand, stark inequalities persist in education, income, health, and other markers measuring quality of life. The picture, in short, is filled with promises and setbacks, reasons for optimism as well as for deep skepticism.

So what can Korean adoption tell us about race in America? Its first and most obvious lesson is simply that race continues to matter in the twenty-first century. Even for this highly acculturated group raised to think of themselves as more white than Asian or Korean, race remains a salient feature informing their lives. Korean adoptees still must navigate larger societal assumptions about race, ethnicity, and nation because they are not white. Their fate remains tied to a group they may not identify with but to which they are socially bound.

Second, the rising prevalence of Asian adoptions today signals a genuine form of interracial acceptance. Each year roughly ten thousand Asian children—today mostly from China—are issued visas to join their mostly white adoptive families in the United States (U.S. Department of State 2008). What this tells us is that more and more white Americans do not think twice about adopting an Asian child and see the practice as an uncontroversial way to create a family. Still, the practice also reveals the prevailing racial patterns and inconsistencies in American society. Asian adoptees, along with non-adopted Asian Americans, have come to occupy a unique position in contemporary U.S. race relations. Our findings lend support to the growing body of scholarship on racial triangulation and interminority hierarchy. Despite recent high-profile adoptions by pop culture luminaries such as Angelina Jolie and Brad Pitt and Madonna, adoptions from Africa are not viewed in the same light as adoptions from Asia. The juxtaposition of "desirable" Asian adoptees and "less desirable" African and African American adoptees raises provocative issues about racial hierarchy and the limits to racial acceptance.

Third, our research captures the gross misuse by some of the concept of color-blindness in the wake of the civil rights era. A white adoptive parent can claim to be color-blind because she adopted a child of color, but that same parent can admonish her child for dating anyone not white. Such inconsistency, unfortunately, is both cause and symptom of what Michael Omi and Howard Winant (1994) characterize as the messy state of racial affairs today. Abundant research is available documenting the gap between the liberal principles that white Americans express regarding racial integration and the daily decisions they make—where to live, who to befriend, what political legislation to support, how to raise their children—that actually perpetuate racial separation. The Korean adoption phenomenon offers more evidence of the discrepancy between principle and practice.

Fourth, our research reveals both the power and limitations of individualism as the solution for racial problems. Adoptees are accepted by whites on the basis of being exceptions to popular assumptions about Asians, Asian Americans, and other nonwhites. For most adoptees, racial acceptance is an individually achieved exemption from the exclusion of Asian Americans as a group from authentic Americanness (N. Kim 2007b). Contrary to predictions that Korean Americans and other Asian Americans will en masse become honorary whites (Bonilla-Silva 2003) and may even begin identifying as simply white (Yancey 2003), our findings suggest that honorary whiteness is an *individually negotiated status* that is based on social distance—if not active social distancing—from not only blacks but also other nonwhites, other Asian Americans, and even other Korean adoptees. The manner in which most adoptees have successfully cultivated a status as tokens in their white social networks suggests that these predictions of

Asian American racial assimilation confuse the acceptance of Asian American individuals for their acceptance as a group. Instead, the experience of Korean adoptees shows that racial assumptions and stereotypes remain salient hurdles for nonwhites despite, or indeed because of, their integration in predominantly white families, social networks, and neighborhoods.

HOW DOES THE KOREAN ADOPTEE EXPERIENCE COMPARE TO THE EXPERIENCE OF ASIAN AMERICANS?

According to Elizabeth Rienzi (n.d.), Korean adoptees are both "a part and yet apart" from other Asian Americans. We wholeheartedly agree with this assessment. Adoptees share with other Asian Americans the regular experience of being reminded of their racial status and presumed foreignness. Regardless of generation or degree of acculturation, anyone with Asian features is presumed to have a closer affinity and identity with Asia than the United States. However, this state of affairs is particularly hurtful to adoptees because they have higher expectations for social acceptance from whites. Adoptees were raised to think of themselves as white and are both outraged and confused when their expectations are not met. Non-adoptees also feel outrage and confusion but do not have the same level of expectation for acceptance.

A quotation we are particularly fond of is appropriate here. According to Ron Wakabayshi, former president of the Japanese American Citizens' League, "Asian Americans feel like we're a guest in someone else's house, that we can never really relax and put our feet up on the table" (Moore 1988). As perceived "guests" in the United States, Asian Americans walk a delicate line. On the one hand, they reap certain benefits as a result of being good guests ("model minorities"), including more social acceptance compared to other racial minorities and greater access to material resources (better neighborhoods and schools). On the other hand, the price they pay for conditional acceptance includes a nagging sense of needing to be on their best behavior—of not being free to relax and feel at home.

"Home" is a particularly sensitive topic for Korean adoptees given that they literally were raised in white homes. As adoptees venture farther away from their families and the communities where they are well known, they encounter a world where they are regularly perceived as more Asian than American. Ironically, while adoptees are foreigners by birth, they are more outraged than many native-born Asian Americans over being seen as such. We believe that adoptees feel the affront more deeply because being viewed as foreign cuts them off not simply from their nation but more immediately from their white families. And if they do not belong with their families, then with whom do they belong? This fundamental question rests just below the surface and underlies the heightened aggravation that adoptees experience when they are assumed to be foreign "guests."

Both Korean adoptees and non-adopted Asian Americans must negotiate the "ongoing feedback" of being Asian and its impact on their sense of self.[3] We found that while both groups make identity choices with race in mind, they often arrive at different places. Non-adoptees frequently choose identities that reflect their sense of being culturally and politically American combined with an acknowledgment or sense of pride in being "different." They are more likely to choose a compound identity that stresses their American and ethnic roots as a way to make a statement about who they are. Adoptees, on the other hand, often make identity choices that help them manage inquiries about their background or unique family circumstances. Thus, identifying with the singular label of "Korean" provides them with a ready answer to common questions, even if the label holds little personal meaning. Especially for those who do not pursue meaningful exploration, their identity choice ends up functioning as a coping strategy to address recurring questions about their background.

By comparison, identifying as Asian American allows adoptees and non-adoptees alike to say something positive about not being part of the white mainstream. This label comes closest to being an achieved identity—a deliberate choice and answer to the question, "Where do I belong?" Far from being a denationalized oppositional identity, a panethnic identity can serve to recognize the racial basis of the social reality of being Asian in the United States—as evidenced, for instance, in inquiries putatively about their ethnicity—and can permit adoptees and non-adoptees to redefine that basis rather than evade or deflect it. To be clear, however, a disproportionate number of adoptees who identified panethnically came from families that failed to cultivate a shared fate during childhood, whereas adoptees who experienced a sense of shared fate with their family were more likely to identify as Korean American. In other words, while panethnicity provides the most "socially healthy" identity strategy, it may be the compound ethnic identity that indicates the psychologically healthiest life.

A part and yet apart, Korean adoptees are bound to other Asian Americans because of their race and, as a result, have overlapping experiences. However, their unique life and family circumstances make them a different type of Asian American: they harbor greater expectations for social acceptance from white people and experience greater disappointment when that acceptance is not forthcoming.

WHAT SALIENT DIFFERENCES INFORM THE KOREAN ADOPTEE EXPERIENCE?

We set out to capture the broad contours of the Korean adoptee experience, but we also looked for salient within-group differences informing adoptee adolescence, adult ethnic exploration, and identity development. Differences based on generational cohort, mixed-race ancestry, and gender were particularly salient and are discussed here in greater detail.

Generational Cohorts

Cohort differences matter in studying adoptee experiences. Put simply, adopting from Korea in the 1950s meant something quite different from a Korean adoption today. Family motivations for adoption, how adoptees and their families relate to difference, the resources available to assist them, and societal attitudes toward race and ethnicity are all informed by history, time, and place. Earlier generations of adoptees were urged to assimilate and leave behind their birth country, while international adoptees coming of age today are more encouraged to pursue cultural exploration and embrace their multiple identities (Johnston et al. 2007; Scroggs and Heitfield 2001; Tessler, Gamache, and Liu 1999). And they are supported by a well-developed infrastructure that provides social and material resources as well as emotional and practical support. In short, each cohort faces new challenges and opportunities as they experience adolescence, decide whether to pursue ethnic exploration, and engage in identity development.

We found cohort differences in:

1. *Motivations for adopting from Korea:* Religious faith featured prominently as a motivator for earlier cohorts but not for later cohorts.
2. *Adoptive family outcomes:* The majority of adoptees from the 1950s cohort, regardless of family strategy, were left to cope alone with trying situations, while adoptees from the 1960s and 1970s cohorts were more likely to come from families with a sense of shared fate.
3. *Ethnic exploration:* Both the level, type, and tracks available for exploration varied based on cohort and historic period.

Mixed-Race Ancestry

Twelve adoptees in our study were of mixed-race ancestry, and three more were unsure about whether they were racially mixed. Of these twelve (or fifteen) adoptees, nine were born in the 1950s. Anecdotal reports suggest that the pioneer generation of Korean adoptees first brought to the United States were predominantly the mixed-race children of Korean women and U.S. or European military men. Mixed-race adoptees in our study largely fit this profile, with the largest share being members of the 1950s cohort.

This group stands apart from other adoptees in our study in several important ways. With only one exception, all were raised to cope alone with trying situations, which raises provocative questions about what their families thought about raising a mixed-race child, especially during the 1950s and 1960s. Also, some chose unique ethnic identities in adulthood to signal their mixed ancestry, but most identified with one of the major labels, with the sole exception of "Korean American." Finally, greater ambiguity in their physical appearance may have served to lessen the salience of race in their lives, especially if their Asian ancestry was less obvious.

Gender

Differences based on gender emerged early on in our analyses. Most intriguing to us was the finding that female adoptees were more likely to come from families that rejected differences, while male adoptees were more likely to come from acknowledger families. Furthermore, only females came from families that rejected differences but still fostered a shared fate. Perhaps families believed that it would be easier to raise daughters "as their own" and with no need to acknowledge differences compared to raising sons. On the other hand, many of these same parents were quite willing to acknowledge differences when it came to the subject of who their daughters should date. These findings raise intriguing questions about what daughters symbolize to adoptive parents compared to sons. More research is needed on this subject.

As for identity choices, we found that female adoptees were more comfortable identifying with the singular label "Korean," whereas male adoptees preferred to identify as "American." Because we did not notice this pattern until long after data collection, we did not pursue it during the interviews and can only speculate as to the reasons. Perhaps the gendered racialization of Asians and Asian Americans as feminine relative to the putatively masculine West makes the singular ethnic label more attractive to female adoptees. Or perhaps male adoptees view the recurring efforts to negotiate an American identity as a test of their masculinity.

Other dimensions of difference worthy of further research include: urban versus rural differences; family structure (single child, adopted children only, both adopted and biological children); and region of the country (Midwest, East, South). With the benefit of hindsight, these are variables we should have explored more thoroughly in our study.

RECOMMENDATIONS

Our findings have implications for how families and adoption agencies can more thoughtfully support adoptees in developing substantive and meaningful identities, and to that end we make the following recommendations:

Recommendation 1: Encourage the Creation of a Shared Family Fate

Our study confirms the importance of fostering a shared fate within all adoptive families, but especially ones involving transracial placements. Families with a shared fate acknowledge the differences stemming from race and culture, openly share and cope along with their children in the uncertainties that arise from adoption, and are resources for their children as they negotiate the impact of race and other forms of difference on their lives. Having a shared family fate is not a cure-all and does not enable adoptees to avoid painful experiences, but it does ensure that adoptees do not feel alone as they encounter these situations.

CREATE A FAMILY ENVIRONMENT IN WHICH RACIAL AND CULTURAL DIFFERENCES ARE DISCUSSED   We believe that families should make sure that adoptees feel comfortable in asking provocative questions, sharing troubling experiences, and learning about the circumstances that made them members of their family. The current movement to promote bicultural socialization—led largely by families and researchers of Chinese adoption (Tessler, Gamache, and Liu 1999; Thomas and Tessler 2007; Johnston et al. 2007)—has recommendations that white parents can choose to follow or not. However, whether families committed to bicultural socialization choose to acknowledge the significance of race in addition to culture remains to be seen.

Families need to strike a balance between celebrating ethnic exploration and dealing with the tougher issues associated with race.[4] Our analyses suggest that families that avoid discussing difficult topics such as race, prejudice, and inequality miss an important opportunity to strengthen the family's sense of shared fate. Adoptees in our study raised the issue of being questioned about their ethnicity and race far more than non-adoptees did, not because it happened more often but because it more deeply violated their sense of belonging to their white families and, by extension, the nation. Adoptees need support from their families as they process their feelings, and at different life stages.

White parents often overestimate how comfortable their Asian children feel in all-white situations. As members of the racial majority, these parents experience racial acceptance in most social situations and see little reason why their adopted children should not feel similarly. Many families in our study were not prepared to help when their children came home after painful racially based experiences because they lacked the knowledge, awareness, and skills to respond effectively. We urge parents to educate themselves so that they can provide their children with empowering strategies to handle racial incidents and ethnic inquiries. This means developing greater stamina themselves for engaging in uncomfortable conversations about race and inequality, experiencing situations where they themselves are racial minorities, learning U.S. race relations history, and engaging in deliberate racial identity development (Tatum 1997).

SUPPORT ADOPTIVE PARENTS IN DEVELOPING GREATER CULTURAL COMPETENCE IN HANDLING RACIALLY AND ETHNICALLY COMPLEX SITUATIONS   Ambivalence remains in the adoption agency world regarding the wisdom of acknowledging racial differences. Some agencies pay attention to race, while others avoid it. In short, families are offered inconsistent and even contradictory advice from agencies regarding the "stance" they should take toward racial differences within the family and beyond (Kallgren and Caudill 1993).

Parents who adopt internationally today are more likely to put effort into cultural socialization and are encouraged to do so by agencies, but this is a relatively recent phenomenon and a shift in policy (Lee 2003a; Quiroz 2007; Scroggs and Heitfield 2001; Song and Lee 2009). Although we applaud this change, a strong statement is also needed about the importance of dealing with racial differences in the family and beyond. Agencies can and should play a more pro-active role in establishing early on an adoption culture that normalizes talking about and acknowledging the significance of race.

Many white parents avoid difficult conversations about race because they do not know how to broach the subject or how to provide useful advice. This is an area where agencies can play a much bigger role in providing pre-adoption and post-adoption services. As adoptive parents mentally and emotionally prepare for the arrival of their children, they can also be encouraged to think deeply and thoughtfully about what race has meant in the United States and what it means for a white person to parent a child of color today. After the adoption, parents need opportunities to develop their knowledge, skill, and awareness in handling racially and ethnically complex situations. Agencies could provide ongoing classes, workshops, and support groups, in-person as well as online. Alternatively, while their children attend agency-sponsored heritage camps, parents could participate in sessions that build their skills in handling the situations their children are encountering, suggest role-play strategies to them, and help them explore different response options. These are just a few possibilities, but they all point to ways in which agencies can play a more active role in helping families create a sense of shared fate.

Recommendation 2: Help Adoptees of All Ages Transcend Seeing Race As a Deficit

Given the ambivalence of adoptive families and agencies toward acknowledging race, it is no surprise that adoptees also feel ambivalent about being Asian. We believe that adoptees should have support from their families and agencies to move beyond a view of race as a "stigma" they need to manage and to embrace it as a healthy facet of their identity.

FAMILIES HELPING ADOPTEES ESTABLISH A LIFELONG HABIT OF IDENTITY EXPLORATION   Our findings indicate that the opportunities to explore their ethnic identity that adoptees pursue or do not pursue in early adulthood have significant bearing on whether they make such explorations later in life. This suggests that it is important for adoptees to become invested in exploration at an early age—to develop a habit of exploration. We believe that families must take a more active role in fostering this habit rather than waiting for their children to show interest or following their lead. Our analyses revealed that the adoptees most willing to explore typically came from acknowledger families with a shared fate who welcomed their children's questions about being different and created opportunities to engage in exploration. In contrast, the adoptees who were least willing to explore came from both acknowledger and rejecter families but were united by their discomfort over feeling different from the people they cared most about. These findings show that exploration should not be an isolating experience—recall Natalie Johnson's description of her parents' efforts: "I think they felt that I should be interested in it because it was something that was part of me. But I didn't feel like they thought it was that interesting for themselves." Activities involving the entire family can reduce the likelihood of discomfort and instead create a shared experience.

Childhood explorers were also more likely to reside in racially diverse communities with abundant opportunities for exploration. The subject of where white parents choose to raise their nonwhite children needs to be openly discussed and deliberated. Clearly, many factors inform a family's decision about where to live, including work opportunities, the presence of extended kin, family history, and friendship networks, to name a few. We are not suggesting that families prioritize living in racially diverse communities over other priorities. We do suggest, however, that families seriously consider the racial geography of where they raise their children and the doors that are opened or closed as a result.

One way in which adoptive families in our study promoted ethnic exploration was by encouraging their children to socialize with other Asians, typically other adoptees and their families. We urge families to continue fostering relationships with other adoptees, but also to forge relationships with Asian Americans and Asian immigrants so that they and their children can experience the depth of diversity that exists under the umbrella term "Asian." Too often we found that adoptees held narrow and stereotypical views of Asians because they relied largely on media depictions rather than firsthand knowledge. Similarly, their beliefs about Asian cultures were often based on exotic and static depictions. Where possible, families should expose their children to a cross-section of Asians and Asian Americans, pursue relationships with diverse Asians, and increase their experiential knowledge base.

What adoptees might be interested in pursuing varies by life stage and, of course, individual temperament. Several years ago, one of the authors was dropping her daughter off at kindergarten when a little girl, adopted from China by white parents, ran up to her and proudly declared, "You're Chinese, and I'm Chinese too!" The little girl continued to gravitate to the author for the rest of the school year.[5] By the start of first grade, however, she had moved on to bigger and better personalities and was no longer interested in discussing things Chinese with her. A recent conversation with the girl's mother revealed that she is now interested in visiting China, something her parents would like to arrange. We share this story to illustrate the different forms that exploration can take, from casual conversations with a cultural consultant (Carstens and Julia 2000) to declaring a desire to visit the birth country. Families should look for and create ample opportunities to spark their children's curiosity. Sometimes those opportunities will emerge spontaneously, while at other times deliberate effort will need to be made.

AGENCIES SUPPORTING ADOPTEES IN DEVELOPING A LIFELONG HABIT OF ETHNIC EXPLORATION   Adoption agencies should put more effort into designing programs of interest to adoptees at various life stages. Although some agencies sponsor motherland tours and host adoptee forums and chat rooms on their websites that may interest adults, their greatest energy is devoted to developing programs and resources for adolescents. We believe that more should be done to meet the needs of adults. Our analyses show that non-adopted Asian Americans have familial resources for facilitating exploration well into adulthood that are unavailable to adoptees. Adoption agencies could play a more active role in facilitating social networking and exposure between adoptees and non-adopted Asian Americans by providing space, both physical and virtual, where adoptees could convene with Korean, Korean American, or Asian American groups. Agencies could invite organizations such as college student groups (Asian American Student Union, Korean Society), religious groups (Korean churches), or activist communities to socialize with adoptees. These events could be targeted for adoptees at different life stages. Similar online programs could be offered as a way to connect adoptees with welcoming Asian and Asian American networks.

DIRECTIONS FOR FUTURE RESEARCH

We set out in this study to satisfy our curiosity and answer questions that we, as Asian Americans and scholars of the Asian American experience, had about Korean adoptees. In the end, our efforts to find answers have led us to ask even more questions, ones that we hope other scholars will find relevant and worth pursuing.

To start, how do the experiences of Korean adoptees compare to those of other international and transracial adoptees? Chinese adoptees and their families immediately come to mind, given their current dominance in the international adoption scene. While Korea may be the pioneer of Asian adoption, China is clearly its present and future. The number of Chinese children being placed with Americans continues to jump each year. Meanwhile, Korea has moved in the inverse direction after decades of dominating the international adoption scene. Equally compelling are comparisons with adoptees from Russia,

Ethiopia, and Guatemala, whose experiences would illuminate how much white skin privilege mitigates white adoptees' interest in ethnic exploration, how much foreign birth moderates the ethnic identity development of black adoptees (as it does for the non-adopted children of black immigrants), and how the racial foreignization of Latinos shapes adoptions from Latin America and the experiences of Latino adoptees. Also, we would welcome efforts to update research comparing Asian and African American adoption experiences, such as that conducted years ago by William Feigelman and Arnold Silverman (1983).

More research is also needed on adoptive families that reject differences but still foster a shared fate. According to Kirk (1964/1984), only families that acknowledge differences are positioned to do so, but we encountered rejecter families that did indeed foster a shared fate. Is this a sophisticated version of color-blindness? Given that the only adoptees in our study to be in this category were women, is this an exception that rejecter families make to protect their daughters? If not, what are the unique circumstances that lead some rejecter families to successfully maintain close ties to their children?

We have additional questions concerning family structure. What is the impact of having multiple children adopted from the same country on identity development and attitudes toward exploration? What about the effects of having mixed-race parents, one white and the other a person of color? With only one adoptee in our study, Ella Scott, who fit this profile, we had too few cases to explore this question in any detail. Future research could shed light on this provocative subject. Similarly, what about the experiences of mixed-race adoptees? Unfortunately, we only began to scratch the surface of this topic—if given the chance to redo our study, we would pay significantly more attention to this important subgroup of adoptees.

We have further questions regarding identity development: Why are females more likely to identify as Korean? Why do mixed-race adoptees not identify as Korean American? What is it about coping alone that pushes adoptees to embrace an Asian American identity as opposed to a Korean American identity? What is it about coming from a family with a shared fate that pushes adoptees toward a Korean American rather than Asian American identity? We are also intrigued by the impact of the Internet on adoptee identity exploration. All adoptees in our study came of age before the advent of the World Wide Web. For adoptees coming of age today, what role does the Internet play in facilitating exploration? What about its role for adult adoptees? What kinds of exploration do they pursue on the Internet?

Last but not least, more research is needed on how Asian adoptees relate to each other, especially across different identity strategies and even entirely different identity paths. The representativeness of our sample of Korean adoptee experiences comes with a cost: very few of our respondents had had significant interactions with other Asian adoptees, much less Korean adoptees, even by their forties. It was primarily this small subgroup that had had the experience of sharing, comparing, and reevaluating their individual strategies for racial acceptance with other adoptees. Apart from the adoptees who identify as Asian American for affirmative reasons, the individuals with adoptee networks may be the ones who are most likely to advance a vision of social citizenship that does not require their racial isolation. In addition, it is these adoptees who might collectively define an emergent ethnic identity that provides an alternative to both mainstream perceptions of Asians and the ethnic social identity defined by non-adopted Korean Americans (Dhingra 2007).

CONCLUSION

Today rapid demographic changes are pushing the boundaries of what it means to be an American. As the nation moves further away from its European heritage, the meanings attached to race, nation, and belonging in American society will continue to be fought over (Alba and Nee 2003; Bodnar 1993; Kivisto 2005; Omi and Winant 1994; Singh 2004). Where do Korean adoptees fit in this larger struggle? We believe that while their very existence challenges hegemonic whiteness, their daily actions and efforts to gain white acceptance do not. Adoptees in our study did not, by and large, question hegemonic whiteness but rather wanted to be accepted as white Americans. Adoptees sought this acceptance because the alternative—identifying as Asian American or Korean American—struck them as undesirable based on their perceptions of the larger racial hierarchy. It is only later in life and under the right social conditions that some adoptees are able to gain perspective, question assumptions they have internalized, and gradually claim being Korean, Asian, and transracially adopted on their own terms.

Heralded as symbols of racial progress and tolerance, Korean adoptees are more accurately seen, we believe, as symbols of the current state of race relations in the United States, a society where acceptance and possibility exist alongside contradiction and inconsistency.

APPENDIX

Table A.1   Adoptee Characteristics

First Name	Last Name	Age in 2001	Occupation	Arrival Cohort
Gabrielle	Anderson	43	Notary public	1950s
Carrie	Bennett	31	Counselor/management	1970s
Mona	Brown	28	Security officer, county corrections	1970s
Samantha	Cawthorne	41	Air traffic controller	1960s
John	Davis	48	Financial consultant	1950s
Marc	Dwinelle	47	Longshoreman	1950s
Kyung-Soon	Edwards	33	Insurance claims adjuster	1960s
Rufus	Fitzgerald	34	Naval officer fire control	1960s
Melissa	Garvey	29	Office manager/chiropractic assistant	1970s
Diane	Genovese	31	Director, international visitor program	1970s
Karen	Granger	26	Bookkeeper, family accounting firm	1970s
Faith	Green	43	Bookkeeper	1950s
Ross	Green	42	Construction foreman	1950s
Sharon	Harding	25	Student/human resources	1970s
Ryan	Hilyard	29	Sales representative, Internet banking	1970s
Linus	Hobart	46	Computer engineer	1950s
Ok-kyun	Hollander	34	Executive assistant to president of real estate development	1960s
Amy	Hollis	42	Secretary/owner, trucking company	1950s
Margaret	Houston	43	Owner, ceramic tile business	1950s
Judy	Hudson	42	Surgical dental assistant	1950s
Christopher	Hurley	51	Train engineer	1950s

Family Strategy	Coping Strategy	Childhood Neighborhood	Highest Education	Primary Identity
Reject	Cope alone	White rural	Some college	Korean
Reject	Cope alone	White rural	Master's	Asian American
Acknowledge	Shared fate	Diverse metropolitan	Bachelor's	Korean American
Acknowledge	Cope alone	White rural	Some college	Korean
Acknowledge	Cope alone	White metropolitan	Bachelor's	American
Acknowledge	Cope alone	Diverse rural	High school	None
Reject	Cope alone	White metropolitan	Bachelor's	Asian American
Acknowledge	Cope alone	White rural	Some college	Korean American
Reject	Cope alone	White rural	High school	Korean
Acknowledge	Shared fate	White rural	Bachelor's	Korean American
Acknowledge	Cope alone	Diverse metropolitan	Some college	Korean American
Reject	Cope alone	White rural	Some college	Korean
Acknowledge	Cope alone	White rural	Some college	Korean
Reject	Cope alone	White metropolitan	Bachelor's	Korean
Acknowledge	Shared fate	White metropolitan	Some college	American
Reject	Cope alone	White metropolitan	Some college	Asian American
Reject	Shared fate	White rural	Some college	American
Reject	Cope alone	White rural	Some college	Mixed race
Reject	Cope alone	White rural	High school	Multiple
Acknowledge	Shared fate	White metropolitan	Some college	Multiple
Reject	Cope alone	White metropolitan	Bachelor's	Asian American

(Table continues on p. 158.)

Table A.1   Adoptee Characteristics (*Continued*)

First Name	Last Name	Age in 2001	Occupation	Arrival Cohort
Nancy	Jacobs	31	Human services/management	1970s
Natalie	Johnson	41	Homemaker currently/has MBA	1970s
Charlene	Jones	30	Chemist	1970s
Linda	King	26	Graduate student/MSW in counseling	1970s
Mary	Klein	46	Accountant	1950s
Carmen	Krum	48	Office specialist, insurance agency	1950s
Caleb	Littell	28	Producer of extreme sports videos	1970s
Holly	Littell	26	Sales TV commercials	1970s
Brandon	Luebke	28	River-rafting guide	1970s
Jim	Moreau	40	Automotive painter	1960s
Susette	Morgan	29	Homemaker/administrative assistant	1970s
Stephanie	Muller	27	Finance	1970s
Duncan	Myers	34	Federal corrections officer	1960s
Marsha	Nelson	45	Computer network sales/ now retired	1950s
Kerry	Nowitsky	25	Computer support technician/student	1970s
Gwen	Owens	41	Office manager, real estate development	1960s
Brian	Packard	27	Technical writer for engineering firm	1970s
Lisa	Packard	26	Interior design for housing development	1970s

Family Strategy	Coping Strategy	Childhood Neighborhood	Highest Education	Primary Identity
Reject	Shared fate	White metropolitan	Bachelor's	Korean
Reject	Cope alone	White metropolitan	Master's	Asian American
Reject	Shared fate	Diverse metropolitan	Doctoral	American
Reject	Cope alone	White metropolitan	Master's	Korean American
Reject	Cope alone	White metropolitan	Bachelor's	Mixed race
Reject	Cope alone	White metropolitan	Bachelor's	Korean
Acknowledge	Shared fate	Diverse metropolitan	Some college	American
Acknowledge	Shared fate	Diverse metropolitan	Some college	Korean
Acknowledge	Shared fate	White metropolitan	Bachelor's	American
Acknowledge	Shared fate	Diverse rural	High school	American
Acknowledge	Cope alone	White metropolitan	High school	American
Reject	Shared fate	White metropolitan	Bachelor's	American
Acknowledge	Shared fate	White metropolitan	Some college	American
Acknowledge	Cope alone	White rural	Bachelor's	American
Reject	Cope alone	White rural	Some college	Asian American
Acknowledge	Cope alone	White metropolitan	Some college	Korean
Acknowledge	Shared fate	Diverse metropolitan	Bachelor's	Korean
Acknowledge	Shared fate	Diverse metropolitan	Bachelor's	Asian American

(Table continues on p. 160.)

Table A.1   Adoptee Characteristics (*Continued*)

First Name	Last Name	Age in 2001	Occupation	Arrival Cohort
Jenine	Peterson	38	Elementary schoolteacher	1960s
Maisie	Potter	44	Federal management analyst	1950s
Stephen	Pratt	48	Police training supervisor	1950s
Amanda	Quick	28	Student/mother	1970s
Julia	Reiner	31	Legal assistant	1970s
Matt	Riley	33	Farmer	1960s
Thomas	Ryan	26	Probation officer	1970s
Ella	Scott	27	Customer service manager and marketing assistant	1970s
Leslie	Shuford	44	Project manager, Kaiser Hospital	1950s
Bianca	Spencer	37	Homemaker/manager of group home	1960s
Emily	Stewart	27	Mother/homemaker	1970s
William	Sullivan	41	Computer programmer/ consultant	1950s
Marianne	Townsend	45	Accountant	1950s
Tracey	Tulane	47	Music teacher	1950s
Taylor	Vogel	29	Graphics coordinator	1970s
Ruth	Weasley	40	Homemaker	1960s
Jennifer	Welch	41	Corporate manager	1950s
Zachary	White	28	Groundskeeper, golf course	1970s
Sherwin	Wright	44	Finance manager	1950s
Kirsten	Young	29	Homemaker/nonprofit staff	1970s

Source: Authors' compilation.

Family Strategy	Coping Strategy	Childhood Neighborhood	Highest Education	Primary Identity
Reject	Shared fate	White metropolitan	Bachelor's	Korean
Reject	Shared fate	White metropolitan	Some college	Korean
Reject	Cope alone	White rural	Some college	American
Reject	Cope alone	White rural	Some college	American
Reject	Shared fate	Diverse metropolitan	Some college	Asian American
Acknowledge	Shared fate	White rural		
Reject	Cope alone	White rural	Bachelor's	American
Acknowledge	Cope alone	White metropolitan	Some college	Korean
Reject	Cope alone	White rural	Bachelor's	Asian American
Acknowledge	Shared fate	White metropolitan	High school	American
Reject	Cope alone	White rural	Some college	Asian American
Acknowledge	Cope alone	White metropolitan	Some college	Korean
Reject	Cope alone	White rural	Bachelor's	Korean
Acknowledge	Cope alone	White rural	Some college	Mixed race
Acknowledge	Shared fate	White rural	Some college	Korean American
Acknowledge	Shared fate	White rural	Bachelor's	Korean American
Reject	Shared fate	White metropolitan	Bachelor's	Korean
Reject	Cope alone	White rural	High school	Korean American
Acknowledge	Cope alone	White rural	Bachelor's	Mixed race
Reject	Cope alone	White rural	Bachelor's	American

Table A.2   Non-Adoptee Characteristics

First Name	Last Name	Age in 2001	Occupation	Highest Education	Primary Identity
Sandra	Chan	31	University academic adviser	Master's	Multiple
Peggy	Chang	34	Senior accounting technician	Bachelor's	Korean equivalent
Daniel	Chang	36	Pastor	Master's	Asian American
Edward	Chen	37	Project manager, engineering	Bachelor's	American
Kelly	Choy	26	Information technology engineer	Bachelor's	Korean American equivalent
Jessica	Ho	34	Mother/homemaker	Bachelor's	Korean American equivalent
Nicole	Kim	41	Marketing manager	Bachelor's	Korean equivalent
Brenda	Kitano	43	Computer systems manager	Bachelor's	Multiple
Deborah	Kuohung	34	Investment banker	Master's	American
Mary	Lam	26	Marketing	Master's	Korean American equivalent
Denise	Lee	29	Graphic designer	Bachelor's	Asian American
Wayne	Liu	27	Computer consultant	Bachelor's	American
Beth	Lum	27	Infant development specialist	Bachelor's	Multiple
Kenneth	Maxime	44	Driver, parcel delivery	Bachelor's	American
Thui	Nguyen	27	Human resources	Bachelor's	Asian American

First name	Last name	Age	Occupation	Education	Ethnicity
Milli	Park	42	Engineering manager	Bachelor's	Asian American
Courtney	Perry	31	Underwriter	Master's	Mixed
Alice	Root	43	Mother, substitute teacher, former accountant	Bachelor's	Korean American equivalent
Michael	Shin	41	Air Force program manager (major)	Bachelor's	American
Patricia	Song	24	Public relations, technology	Bachelor's	Multiple
Meredith	SooHoo	29	Computer marketing	Bachelor's	Asian American
Viet	Thai	29	Software engineer	Some college	Multiple
Andrea	Theanh	29	Corporate human resources recruiter	Master's	Asian American
Cai	Tran	28	Events manager, corporate	High school	Korean equivalent
Paul	Vo	37	Architect	Bachelor's	American
Camille	Wong	26	Accountant	Bachelor's	Korean American equivalent
David	Yamaguchi	41	Account manager	Some college	Korean American equivalent
Lindsay	Yang	30	College bookstore supervisor	Some college	Korean equivalent
Bobby	Yep	44	Director, food services department, entertainment	Bachelor's	Korean American equivalent

Source: Authors' compilation.

Table A.3   Age at Time of Adoption

Age	Percentage	N
Under one year old	46%	27
One to five years old	46	27
Six years and older	8	5

Source: Authors' calculations.

INTERVIEW QUESTIONNAIRE

Name: Comparison Group:

1. Early Experiences: Extrafamilial

To start, please tell me about the place or places where you grew up.

- [for biologicals] Is this where were you born?
- Racial/ethnic demographics of neighborhood(s)?

How about the schools (K–12) you attended. Would you describe them for me?

- Racial/ethnic demographics of schoolmates?
- Asians/Asian Americans present/absent?
- Racial/ethnic character of peer cliques?
- Racial/ethnic character of tracking system?

Now I'd like to ask you about any experiences you might have had with racism or discrimination when you were growing up.

- What happened?
- How often?
- Where?
- Perpetrators?
- Who came to your aid? What did they do or say?
- Can you describe to me how these experiences made you feel?
- Did you share these experiences with anyone? How did they respond? If not your parents, why not? How about other family members?

How much contact did you have with other Asians or Asian Americans (adoptee and non-adoptee) while growing up?

• Where did this happen?
• [for adoptees] Was any of this contact facilitated by your parents or other family members?
• Did your parents ever place themselves and/or you in an Asian adoptee support group, either formal or informal?
• Did they ever place themselves and/or you in an Asian American social network?
• Did they ever send you to or bring you on special programs such as an adoptee heritage camp, ethnic schooling, ethnic summer camps, a tour of Korea, or a visit to an Asian American area?
• [for biological] Did your parents ever place themselves and/or you in an Asian American social network?
• Did they ever send you to or bring you on special programs such as ethnic schooling, ethnic summer camps, a tour of Korea/China/Japan, or a visit to an Asian American area?
• Ethnicity, gender, adoptive, and/or generational status of these Asians?
• Feelings toward them?

So tell me about your friends growing up.

• Race/ethnicity of closest friends?
• [if Asians were part of friendship circle] Did you seek them out? Why/why not?

When you were growing up, how conscious do you think you were of being Korean/Chinese/etc.?

• What prompted this consciousness?
• When did this consciousness begin?
• Feelings toward this consciousness?

How conscious do you think you were of being Asian, i.e., racially different?

• What prompted this consciousness?
• When did this consciousness begin?
• Feelings toward this consciousness?

[for adoptees] How much contact did you have with non-Asian adoptees?

• Where did this happen?
• Was any of this contact facilitated by your parents or other family members?
• Did your parents ever place themselves or you in a non-race-specific adoption support group, either formal or informal?
• Ethnicity, gender, and/or generational status of these adoptees?
• Feelings toward them?

[for adoptees] How conscious do you think you were of being an adoptee?

• What prompted this consciousness?
• When did this consciousness begin?
• Feelings toward this consciousness?

[for biologicals] How much contact did you have with Asian or non-Asian adoptees?

• Where did this happen?
• Was any of this contact facilitated by your parents or other family members?
• Ethnicity, gender, and/or generational status of these adoptees?
• Feelings toward them?

Did you ever feel "different" from others? What made you feel different?

• Who were you comparing yourself to? (Fantasies about being "normal"?)
• How might it have been different had you been male/female?

1. Early Experiences: Familial
Now I'd like to ask some questions about your family. How important do you think it was to your family that you be familiar with [Korean or Chinese/Japanese/etc.] culture/values?

• What aspects?
• Who felt it was important and how did they express this to you?

- Who took responsibility to teach you?
- Was Korean/Chinese/etc. ever spoken at home? By whom?
- How often would you say your family ate Korean/Chinese/etc. meals?
- Home-cooked or restaurant?
- Which Korean/Chinese/etc. holidays, if any, did your family celebrate?

[for adoptees] How important do you think it was to your family that you be familiar with *their* ethnic (e.g., Irish/Italian/Jewish) culture?

- What aspects?
- Who felt it was important and how did they express this to you?
- Who took responsibility to teach you?
- Was Italian/Polish/etc. ever spoken at home? By whom?
- How often would you say your family ate Irish/Italian/etc. meals?
- Home-cooked or restaurant?
- Which Irish/Italian/etc. holidays, if any, did your family celebrate?

Did your family ever speak with you about racism or discrimination that you might face?

- What did they say to you?
- [for adoptees] How did your family deal with the fact that you're racially and culturally different from them?
- [for biologicals] **[*revise also*]** Did your family ever deny that you were racially different from most Americans?
- Did they suggest any coping strategies for dealing with incidents?
- How comfortable did you feel in talking about racism with them?
- If any incidents happened to you, did you share them with your family? Why/why not?

1. Early Experiences: Adoption History
(For Adoptees)
Please describe the circumstances surrounding your adoption.

- What was the year of your adoption?
- Direct from your birth family?
- Direct from an orphanage?

- Direct from a foster family home?
- Other important circumstances surrounding your adoption?

Please describe your adoptive family.

- Adopted by: Couple? Single mother/father?
- Tell me about your mother.
  Also adopted?
  An immigrant?
  Her race/ethnicity?
  Her age when you were adopted?
  Occupation?
  Education?
- Tell me about your father.
  Also adopted?
  An immigrant?
  His race/ethnicity?
  His age when you were adopted?
  Occupation?
  Education?
- Tell us about your siblings.

Name	Age	Race and Ethnicity	Adopted?	Year of Adoption?	Source Country?

- What memories do you have, if any, of arriving in the United States?
- What memories do you have, if any, of Korea?
- What photographs do you have, if any, of Korea or of arriving in the United States?
- What did your parents communicate to you about your adoption?
- What were their motivations for adopting you? (Religious?)
- How did your family acknowledge your adoption while you were growing up?
- How did your parents explain your adoption to others?
- Was your adoption or arrival regularly celebrated in your family?

1. Early Experiences: Immigration History
(For Biologicals)

When did your family immigrate?

Please describe the circumstances of your family's immigration.

- What did your parents communicate to you about it?
- Reasons for leaving motherland?
- Reasons for choosing the United States?
- Where did you settle and live while you were growing up?

Please describe your family.

- Mother's characteristics
  Occupation?
  Education?
- Father's characteristics
  Occupation?
  Education?
- Tell us about your siblings.
- What memories do you have of arriving in the United States?
- What memories do you have, if any, of the country from which you immigrated?
- What photographs do you have, if any, of Korea/China/etc. . . . or of arriving in the United States?
- How important do you think it was to your parents that you feel that immigrating to the United States was a positive event for the family, or at least for you?
- Who felt it was important, and how did they express this to you?

- Who took responsibility to make sure you really believed it?
- Was your immigration regularly celebrated in your family?

2. Postsecondary Years

Tell me what you did after high school.

- How much contact did you have with other Asians/Asian Americans/adoptees?
- How would you characterize those interactions?

[if respondent attended college] Where is it that you went to college? *(Make sure to probe for the following)*

- Racial/ethnic demographics

Tell me about your closest friends in college.

- Where you met
- Race/ethnicity
- [if Asians are part of friendship circle] Did you seek them out? Why/why not?
- Do you think you had a preference?

Some people say that college is a time for exploring one's identity. How true was this for you?

- [if yes] What motivated your interest?
- *(Probe race, ethnicity, and adoptee dimensions)*
- Sudden interest or there all along?
- What did you do to explore your identity (i.e., take classes, join clubs)?

[if the respondent did not attend college] Tell me about your closest friends after high school.

- Where you met
- Race/ethnicity
- [if Asians are part of friendship circle] Did you seek them out? Why/why not?
- Do you think you had a preference?

During this time, what interest did you have in exploring your ethnic/racial identities?

- [if yes] What motivated your interest?
- Sudden interest or there all along?
- What did you do to explore your identity?

3. Current Lifestyle and Ethnic Practices

Since your college years (*or* initial years after high school), has there come a point in your life where you've started to explore (*or* continued or further explored) your ethnic heritage and/or adoptee identity? If so, how have you explored it?
  (Probes for this question begin)

- [for adoptees] Have you ever placed yourself in an adoptee support group or regular social group?
- Did the group have a racial/ethnic specific mission? (e.g., Korean/Asian adoptees)
- If it was not a Korean-specific group, what were the races/ethnicities of the other participants?
- Was race or ethnicity ever explicitly discussed?
- What was that experience like for you?

Since your high school years, have you ever placed yourself in an Asian American (non-adoptee) support group or regular social group?

- Did the group have an ethnic-specific (e.g., Korean, Chinese) character or mission?
- If it was not a Korean-specific group, what were the races/ethnicities of the other participants?
- Was race or ethnicity ever explicitly discussed?
- [for adoptees] Did your being transracially adopted ever come up?
- What was that experience like for you?

[for adoptees] Since your high school years, have you ever attended special programs, such as an adoptee heritage camp or a panel or conference on adoptee experiences?

- Did the event have an ethnic-specific (e.g., Korean, Chinese) character or mission?
- If the event was not Korean-specific, what were the races/ethnicities of the other participants?
- Was race or ethnicity ever explicitly discussed?
- *What was that experience like for you?*

Since your high school years, have you ever attended special programs, such as an ethnic- or minority-related retreat, panel, or conference?

- Did the event have an ethnic-specific (e.g., Korean, Chinese) character or mission?
- If the event was not Korean/Chinese/etc.-specific, what were the races/ethnicities of the other participants?
- Did the event include (Asian) adoptee experiences?
- Was race or ethnicity ever explicitly discussed?
- *What was that experience like for you?*

Have you ever been to Korea/China/etc.?

- When?
- What were your motivations for going?
- [if not] Any interest in going? Why/why not?

Have you ever been to an Asian American–themed place (e.g., Koreatown, Japanese American Historical Museum, Angel Island Immigration Station, former internment camp, special historical exhibits on Asian American history)?

- When?
- What were your motivations for going?
- [if not] Any interest in going? Why/why not?

(Probes for the above question end)
   What do you currently do for work?

- Racial/ethnic demographics
- Availability of Asians/Asian Americans

Tell me about your closest friends these days.

- Where you met
- Race/ethnicity
- [if Asians are part of friendship circle] Did you seek them out? Why/ why not?
- Do you think you have a preference?

What do you do, if anything, to explore your ethnicity/race these days?

- Motivations?

How much contact do you have with other Asians/Asian Americans?

- How would you characterize those interactions?

(Additional probes follow)
     What about ethnic foods? How often do they figure into your diet these days?

- Do you prepare them yourself or go to a restaurant?
- What does eating these foods mean to you?

What about celebrating ethnic holidays?

- How do you celebrate?
- With whom do you celebrate?
- What does celebrating these holidays mean to you?

Can you speak or read Korean/Chinese/etc.?

- Where and when did you learn?
- Who do you speak with?

How knowledgeable would you say you are about Korean/Chinese/etc. culture?

- [if knowledgeable] What does it mean to you to have this knowledge?
- [if not] Interested in pursuing this knowledge? Why/why not?

Do you belong to any ethnic clubs or organizations?

- What were your motivations for joining?
- [if not] Any interest in joining? Why/why not?

(Probes end)
   What (else) do you do, if anything, to explore your adoptee identity these days?

- Motivations?
- How much contact do you have with other (transracial/Asian/Korean) adoptees?
- How would you characterize those interactions?

In exploring your ethnic and/or adoptee identity, have you experienced moments where you realized differences between what you anticipated feeling and what you actually felt? Now I'd like to ask you some questions about your dating history.
   (Disclaimers and normalizations if gender of interviewer and interviewee differs)
   What has been the race/ethnic background of people you have dated in the past?

- Any racial/ethnic preferences? *(Probe if preference emerges)*
- What about currently? Who do you find yourself attracted to?

In thinking about the people you have been in relationships with, what has been their racial/ethnic background?

- Any racial/ethnic preferences? *(Probe if preference emerges)*
- Do you think it might have been different had you been male/female? Why?

Are you married now or currently in a relationship?

- What is the race/ethnicity of your partner?

[for those in an interethnic marriage or relationship, including minority-majority, minority-minority, and interethnic] How did you meet your partner?

- How often, if ever, does the difference in your races/ethnicities come up as an issue in your relationship? In what ways?
- How did your respective families respond to your relationship?
- Is anybody else in your families involved in an interracial/interethnic relationship?
- To what extent does race or ethnicity shape the life you have created with your partner?
- Do you have children or plan to have children?
- How important is it to you that your (future) children know about their ethnic roots?
- What will you do/have you done to accomplish this?
- Will you speak/have you spoken with your children about racism or discrimination that they might face?
- What might/did you say?
- What coping strategies might you suggest/have you suggested?

[for those in an intraethnic marriage or relationship] How did you meet your partner?

- To what extent does ethnicity shape the life you have created with your partner?
- Do you have children or have you discussed having children?
- How important is it to you that your (future) children know about their ethnic roots?
- What will you do/have you done to accomplish this?
- Will you speak/have you spoken with your children about racism or discrimination that they might face?
- What might you/did you say?
- What coping strategies might you suggest/have you suggested?

4. Societal Perceptions and Personal Identity

Now I'd like to ask you some questions about the ways in which you identify yourself and how others might identify you. Do you describe yourself as Korean, Korean American, Asian American, biracial, Hapa, Korean-White, Asian-White, American, or another identity? *(Fill in with appropriate ethnicity)*

- What does that mean to you, to consider yourself _____?
- Would you describe for me how being _____ is different from being American, if at all?

- [if respondent did not choose "American"] Would you ever consider calling yourself an "American" without hyphenation?
- How has the way you identify yourself changed over time, if at all?

How common is it for people to comment on your racial or ethnic background?

- How do you typically respond?
- How do you generally feel when people ask/comment?
- Have you ever been mistaken for Japanese/Korean/etc.?
- Do you think most Americans can tell the difference between different Asian groups overall?
- Which other Americans have been better or worse at telling differences?
- Have you ever found yourself trying to prepare better responses to such comments and questions?

Have you ever felt out of place or uncomfortable because of your ethnicity/race?

- Where?
- What was the situation?
- Have you ever been in situations where your ethnicity or race was the norm?

Has anybody ever made assumptions about you based on larger ethnic or racial stereotypes?

- Is ethnicity or race more often the basis for the stereotypes?
- What types of stereotypes?
- What are your feelings when this happens?

Do you ever feel pressured to identify ethnically/racially?

- When and by whom?

Do you believe there is racial discrimination in the United States today?
   Before the civil rights movement, Asian Americans were subjected to significant amounts of discrimination.

- In your opinion, how aware do you think most Americans are of Asian American history?

- When were you first exposed to or taught that history, if ever?
- In your opinion, do Asian Americans still experience discrimination today?
- [if yes] What feelings do you have about this?
- In your opinion, do they experience more than/less than/the same amount as blacks? Latinos? Native Americans? Whites?

As an adult, have you ever experienced what you believe to be racism or prejudice?

- What happened?
- How often does this occur?
- What are your feelings when this happens?
- With whom do you discuss these experiences, if anybody?

If the United States were to go to war right now with Korea or any other part of Asia, how would your life be affected, if at all?

- How about if the United States went to war with Italy, Germany, etc.? Would the lives of Italian Americans, etc., be affected?
- Do you believe that an event such as the Japanese internment could happen again?

[for adoptees] In terms of comfort, with which racial/ethnic/adoptee groups are you the most socially comfortable? How about the least comfortable?

- Korean adoptees?
- Other Asian adoptees?
- Other minority adoptees?
- White adoptees?
- Korean American biologicals?
- Other Asians?
- Asian Americans?
- Other biracial or multiracial Americans?
- Other minorities?
- Whites?
- What makes them more or less comfortable for you?

[for adoptees] Looking back over your life, what advice would you give young adoptees who came to you for support?

- What challenges would you warn them about—based on any negative experiences?
- What advantages would you tell them about—based on any positive experiences?

[for biologicals] In terms of comfort, with which racial/ethnic groups are you the most socially comfortable? How about the least comfortable?

- Korean/Chinese/etc. Americans?
- Other Asians?
- Other Asian Americans?
- Other biracial or multiracial Americans?
- Other minorities?
- Whites?
- What makes them more or less comfortable for you?

[for biologicals] Looking back over your life, what advice would you give young Asian Americans who came to you for support?

- What challenges would you warn them about—based on any negative experiences?
- What advantages would you tell them about—based on any positive experiences?

NOTES

CHAPTER 1

1. To protect the privacy of those who participated in this study, all of their names have been changed. For the same reason, we also replaced the names of smaller and rural communities with names that we hope reflect some of the character and uniqueness of the actual communities.

2. For a demographic profile of the adoptees who participated in this study, please see the appendix.

3. For a descriptive summary of the non-adoptees who participated, please see the appendix.

4. We reason that our sample is directly biased by (1) the underrepresentation of adoptive families who moved away from the homes in which they raised their children and did not maintain contact with the agency, and (2) the absence of (a) adoptive placements that failed during childhood, (b) adoptees who broke contact with their families in adulthood, and (c) adoptees whose parents declined for whatever reason to inform their adult children of the opportunity to participate. The first bias may have increased the representation of adoptive families who either were more geographically stable or remained interested in receiving the agency's newsletter. The second set of biases may have reduced the representation of cases where family relations were more strained. Among our respondents, we found that a high level of family strain was often associated with not pursuing ethnic exploration during early adulthood. If this association also holds true for the nonrespondents, then the proportion of non-explorers in our sample may be an underestimate. In brief, our non-response rate is likely to indicate a level of sample bias that limits the statistical generalizability of our analysis.

CHAPTER 2

1. For a fuller discussion of the history of Korean adoption from a Korean perspective, see D. S. Kim's (2007) excellent chapter, "A Country Divided: Contextualizing Adoption from a Korean Perspective."

2. For the most part, such studies found that transracial placements do not place children at greater mental health risk, and in fact they do not differ significantly from same-race adopted children or non-adopted children once other factors are taken into consideration. Particularly significant mitigating factors include age at adoption, gender, geographical region, adoptive family structure, and pre-adoption history (Hollingsworth 1997). Differences did emerge in several studies in the areas of racial identity development, racial talk within the family, and exposure to same-race peers. Transracially adopted black children were less likely to identify as black, less likely to discuss racial differences at home, and much more likely to attend predominantly white schools where they infrequently encountered other black people (Grow, Shapiro, and Child Welfare League of America Research Center 1974; McRoy and Zurcher 1983; Simon and Altstein 1987). Perhaps not surprisingly, both supporters and opponents of transracial adoption found something in these outcome studies to validate their positions.

3. Harry Holt's actions were not without controversy. His approach, which defined parental suitability in Christian terms as families who were *saved* and *born-again,* stood in contrast to the procedures employed by social service agencies and U.S. state welfare departments (Choy 2007, her emphasis).

4. Although we stand by this assessment, it is important to acknowledge the growing body of scholarship that has taken a more critical stance toward Korean adoption and international adoption more broadly. For the most part, such work has come out of postcolonial and cultural studies. See especially Anagnost (2000), Dorow (2006b), Hubinette (2004), Johnson (2003), Marre and Briggs (2009), Shiu (2001), Trenka, Oparah, and Shin (2006), Volkman (2003), and Yngvesson (2000). In several cases, criticism has been led by scholars who are also adoptees.

5. Accessed February 28, 2010.

6. Sara Dorow (2006b) reminds us that there can be no "model" minority without less-than-model ones for them to be compared against. She argues that the desirability of Asian adoptees must be understood in relation to the undervaluation of black adoptees. While Chinese adoptees are defined as "baggage-free," desirably different, and "savable," the narrative attached to black adoptees is laced with images of damage, irredeemability, and marginalization.

7. Intriguingly, Jacobson's (2008) respondents did not feel that Asian adoptees would face much prejudice, since their family and friends generally embraced them, and they cited the model minority stereotype as a factor influencing their views.

CHAPTER 3

1. The term "racial and ethnic explorations" refers to the personal examination of one's racial and ethnic ancestry and its relevance for one's life. Racial and ethnic exploration is important psychologically because it moves identity development beyond a diffuse identity and toward an achieved identity (Phinney 1989, 1991). In more sociological terms, exploration marks a shift in attitude about one's ancestry from thinking of it as merely a descriptive category toward deriving a more meaningful sense of membership in an ethnic or racial group.

2. In practice, the color-blind approach did not eliminate race so much as it facilitated most parents' desire to bestow their own racial and social status on their adopted children (Dalen 2005). Parents saw themselves as raising their children to be "normal," with little awareness that their definition of normal was white-centered (Lipsitz 1998). And by normalizing whiteness, parents essentially socialized adoptees to be white and to see the world from a white—rather than color-blind—perspective. Thus, far from being color-blind, many white parents, consciously or not, redefined their Asian children as white children.

3. We pass no judgment here on whether a self-conscious community of Korean adoptive families and their activities in that community actually constitute Korean cultural activities. Like scholars who study the construction and emergence of multiracial communities (Daniel 2001; King-O'Riain 2006; Reich 2002; Root 1992, 1996; Spencer 1999; Spickard 1989; Williams-León and Nakashima 2001; Winters and DeBose 2002), our interest lies in understanding the impetus behind this communal emergence, what it means for adoptive families who participate, and its long-range viability.

4. Ten adoptees spent all or a significant portion of their adolescence in racially diverse communities. Primarily located in California, these places included San Jose, Santa Clara, Irvine, and Stockton.

5. ESL (English as a Second Language) refers to specialized programs in K–12 schools geared toward English-language learners. In a sense, the new students in Stephanie's school were sufficiently branded by their separate educational track that she did not see them as possible peers.

CHAPTER 4

1. This stands in contrast to whites, who have considerably more latitude in their ethnic options (Alba 1985; Waters 1990, 1999). In fact, psychologists regard ethnic identity development as evidence of majority-group dominance because it is primarily nonwhites who explore their ethnicity, and it is solely among whites that self-esteem does not correlate with ethnic identity development (Phinney 1992).

2. Practically speaking, however, they conflate exploration with ethnic involvement, creating methodological problems that are the inverse of the first version. By measuring exploration primarily at an already substantial level, they potentially miss the distinct effects of personal and less immersive explorations by conflating them with non-exploration.

3. Proponents of diversity policies have advocated for both kinds of resources in their recommendations to educational institutions—implying that organizational characteristics may influence the occurrence and quality of ethnic explorations among students (Duster 1991; Valverde and Castenell 1998).

4. Anecdotal evidence suggests the growing importance of adoption agencies as providers of "motherland tours" for adoptees. However, only a fraction of the adoptee population has participated in these tours, as evidenced by the fact that only one of our adoptee respondents had taken a motherland tour.

5. The "culture war" of the 1980s and 1990s over American higher education also suggests historical variations in the context for ethnic identity development. The criticism that colleges and universities have become excessively multicultural assumes not only a less tolerant past but also a contemporary mixture of pro-diversity and diversity-queasy sentiments (Shiao 2005). Indeed, some argue that the recent historical shift in American attitudes regarding diversity amounts less to an embrace of multiculturalism than to a reduction of racial barriers to the still-preferred route of assimilation (Alba and Nee 2003).

6. In general, however, adoptees were substantially less likely than non-adoptees to have pursued any level of ethnic exploration.

7. We sorted respondents into three categories of early adulthood cohort by the decade in which they spent their first five years after high school: the 1970s, the 1980s, and the 1990s. As traditional college students, respondents between the ages of forty and fifty-one would have started college no earlier than 1968 and finished no later than 1983. Similarly, respondents aged thirty to thirty-nine would have matriculated starting in 1980 and graduated by 1993, and those aged twenty-five to twenty-

nine would have entered in 1990 and left by 1998. By these approximate criteria, twenty-six adoptees and eight non-adoptees spent their early adulthoods during the 1970s, eleven adoptees and eight non-adoptees during the 1980s, and twenty-one adoptees and twelve non-adoptees during the 1990s.

8. The adoptees who were young adults in the 1970s correspond to those noted in earlier chapters as born in the 1950s. Those who were young adults in the 1980s correspond to those born in the 1960s, and those who were young adults in the 1990s correspond to those born in the 1970s.

9. At the other end of the exploration continuum, the percentage of non-explorers among "college only" and "college and other" respondents was less than half the percentage among "college dabbler" and "no college" respondents.

10. Specifically, college participation increased the odds of exploration from three-to-seven to seven-to-three, or by a factor of 5.4.

11. To be clear, our non-adoptee sample is less representative than our adoptee sample, even if we were to define the population as non-adoptees raised in the communities characteristic of those in which adoptees were raised. Missing from our sample are the military non-adoptees and a larger fraction of the urban non-adoptees encountered by the adoptees in employment in Asian businesses—that is, the children of entrepreneurs (Park 2005). We cannot discern how much this finding resulted from the under-representation of primarily non-school early adulthoods from the non-adoptee sample, rather than a broader distribution of early adulthoods among adoptees than non-adoptees.

CHAPTER 5

1. The Gathering is an event that took place September 9–12, 1999, in Washington, D.C. Billed as the Gathering of the First Generation of Adult Korean Adoptees, the event brought together nearly four hundred adult Koreans who had been adopted between the years 1955 and 1985 to share, connect, and build community.

2. Stephen shared a remarkable story about his parents' first meeting with the Holts. His narrative captures the informality of the practice in its earliest days:

> And by this time [they had] figured out that they weren't able to have children, and so they were starting, I guess, to think about adoption. And Mr. Holt by this time had gone to Korea, come back with the first eight, and was making, well, the news was out. . . . But anyway, they didn't have any

idea what Korean babies looked like or anything else, so they went down [to the Holts' farm], and of course the Holts invited them in. They took a tour and, you know, did all that on the farm. And so then they left and went to my uncle and borrowed two hundred dollars, because that's all it took. And my brother arrived. My adopted brother arrived.

3. Marianne's concern over her mother's feelings mirrors the worry that Jennifer Welch expressed in chapter 2 as an adolescent interested in learning about Korea and her birth culture. While Jennifer stifled her childhood interest to assuage her mother's feelings, Marianne, as a mature adult, found a way to solicit her mother's support.

CHAPTER 6

1. Two other reasons were offered: identifying as American was unnecessary since their white friends already accepted them as simply American, and the label was incomplete without an ethnic qualifier or was less distinctive than an ethnic label.
2. A minority of these non-adoptees voiced other reasons for disidentifying with "American": the label had less symbolic distinction; it carried an inaccurate association with being U.S.-born; it was incomplete given their mixed heritage; and, uniquely, it was a culturally meaningless category.

CHAPTER 7

1. Our point here is not to deny that Asian Americans also experience violence and other overt forms of racism, but rather to highlight how they typically experience racial subordination.
2. For a powerful discussion of the type of racial subordination that Asian Americans experience compared to African Americans, see Bill Moyers's interview of September 11, 2009, with Dr. Jim Yong Kim, Dartmouth College's seventeenth president, available at: http://www.pbs.org/moyers/journal/09112009/watch2.html (accessed May 13, 2010).
3. We first heard this expression from adoptee Jennifer Welch (see chapter 6).
4. It goes without saying that the goal here is not to overstate how adoptees differ from their families but rather to give adoptees permission to raise issues that trouble them and to support their burgeoning identity. We are mindful that, for some the adoptees

in our study, their family put excessive emphasis on the ways in which they were different while still leaving them to cope alone with prejudice.

5. "Gravitation" took the form of singling out the author and holding her hand during a school field trip and school picnic, asking questions ("Do you speak Chinese? I know how to say hello in Chinese. Do you?"), and expressing curiosity during a play date at the author's home ("Do you use chopsticks?").

REFERENCES

Abdullah, Samella. 1996. "Transracial Adoption Is Not the Solution to America's Problems of Child Welfare." *Journal of Black Psychology* 22(2): 254–61.

Adams, Gregory, Richard Tessler, and Gail Gamache. 2005. "The Development of Ethnic Identity Among Chinese Adoptees: Paradoxical Effects of School Diversity." *Adoption Quarterly* 8(3): 25–46.

Alba, Richard D. 1985. *Italian Americans: Into the Twilight of Ethnicity.* Englewood Cliffs, N.J.: Prentice-Hall.

———. 1990. *Ethnic Identity: The Transformation of White America.* New Haven, Conn.: Yale University Press.

Alba, Richard D., and Victor Nee. 2003. *Remaking the American Mainstream: Assimilation and Contemporary Immigration.* Cambridge, Mass.: Harvard University Press.

Altstein, Howard, and Rita James Simon, eds. 1991. *Intercountry Adoption: A Multinational Perspective.* New York: Praeger.

Anagnost, Ann. 2000. "Scenes of Misrecognition: Maternal Citizenship in the Age of Transnational Adoption." *Positions* 8(2): 389–421.

Ancheta, Angelo. 1998. *Race, Rights, and the Asian American Experience.* New Brunswick, N.J.: Rutgers University Press.

Andresen, Inger-Lise Kvifte. 1992. "Behavioral and School Adjustment of Twelve- to Thirteen–Year-Old Internationally Adopted Children in Norway: A Research Note." *Journal of Child Psychology and Psychiatry* 33(2): 427–39.

Andujo, Estela. 1988. "Ethnic Identity of Transethnically Adopted Hispanic Adolescents." *Social Work* 33(6): 531–35.

Arroyo, Carmen, and Edward Zigler. 1995. "Racial Identity, Academic Achievement, and the Psychological Well-being of Economically Disadvantaged Adolescents." *Journal of Personality and Social Psychology* 69(5): 903–14.

Baden, Amanda. 2002. "The Psychological Adjustment of Transracial Adoptees: An Application of the Cultural-Racial Identity Model." *Journal of Social Distress and the Homeless* 11(2): 167–91.

Baden, Amanda, and Robbie Steward. 2000. "A Framework for Use with Racially and Culturally Integrated Families: The Cultural-Racial Identity Model as Applied to Transracial Adoption." *Journal of Social Distress and the Homeless* 9(4): 309–37.

Bai, Tai Soon. 2007. "Korea's Overseas Adoption and Its Positive Impact on Domestic Adoption and Child Welfare in Korea." In *International Korean Adoption: A Fifty-Year History of Policy and Practice,* edited by Kathleen Bergquist, M. Elizabeth Vonk, Dong Soo Kim, and Marvin Feit. New York: Haworth Press.

Bakalian, A. P. 1992. *Armenian-Americans: From Being to Feeling Armenian.* New Brunswick, N.J.: Transaction Publishers.

Bartholet, Elizabeth. 1995. "Race Separatism in the Family: More on the Transracial Adoption Debate." *Duke Journal of Gender Law and Policy* 2(2): 99–105.

Basow, Susan, Elizabeth Lilley, Jamila Bookwala, and Ann McGillicuddy-DeLisi. 2008. "Identity Development and Psychological Well-being in Korean-Born Adoptees in the U.S." *American Journal of Orthopsychiatry* 78(4): 473–80.

Benet, Mary Kathleen. 1976. *The Politics of Adoption.* New York: Free Press.

Benson, Peter L., Anu R. Sharma, Eugene C. Roehlkepartain, and Search Institute. 1994. *Growing Up Adopted: A Portrait of Adolescents and Their Families.* Minneapolis: Search Institute.

Bimmel, Nicole, Femmie Juffer, Marinus Van Ijzendoorn, and Marian Bakermans-Kranenburg. 2003. "Problem Behavior of Internationally Adopted Adolescents: A Review and Meta-Analysis." *Harvard Review of Psychology* 11(2): 64–77.

Blauner, Robert. 1972. *Racial Oppression in America.* New York: Harper & Row.

Bloom, Allan David. 1987. *The Closing of the American Mind.* New York: Simon & Schuster.

Bobo, Lawrence, James R. Kluegel, and Ryan Smith. 1997. "Laissez-Faire Racism: The Crystallization of a Kinder, Gentler, Antiblack Ideology." In *Racial Attitudes in the 1990s: Continuity and Change,* edited by Steven Tuch and Jack Martin. Westport, Conn.: Praeger.

Bobo, Lawrence, and Camille L. Zubrinsky. 1996. "Attitudes on Residential Integration: Perceived Status Differences, Mere In-Group Preference, or Racial Prejudice?" *Social Forces* 74(3): 883–909.

Bodnar, John. 1993. *Remaking America: Public Memory, Commemoration, and Patriotism in the Twentieth Century.* Princeton, N.J.: Princeton University Press.

Bonilla-Silva, Eduardo. 2003. *Racism Without Racists: Color-Blind Racism and the Persistence of Racial Inequality in the United States.* Lanham, Md.: Rowman & Littlefield.

Bonilla-Silva, Eduardo, and David Embrick. 2006. "Black, Honorary White, White: The Future of Race in the United States?" In *Mixed Messages: Multiracial Identities in the "Color-Blind" Era,* edited by David Brunsma. Boulder, Colo.: Lynne Rienner.

Bremner, Robert. 1974. *Children and Youth in America: A Documentary History,* vol. 3, pts. 1–4. Cambridge, Mass.: Harvard University Press.

Brodzinsky, David. 1987. "Adjustment to Adoption: A Psychosocial Perspective." *Clinical Psychology Review* 7(1): 25–47.

———. 1990. "A Stress and Coping Model of Adoption Adjustment." In *The Psychology of Adoption,* edited by David Brodzinsky and Marshall Schechter. New York: Oxford University Press.

Brodzinsky, David, and Marshall Schechter. 1990. *The Psychology of Adoption.* New York: Oxford University Press.

Brooks, Devon, and Richard Barth. 1999. "Adult Transracial and Inracial Adoptees: Effects of Race, Gender, Adoptive Family Structure, and Placement History on Adjustment Outcomes." *American Journal of Orthopsychiatry* 69(1): 87–99.

Carp, E. Wayne. 2000. *Family Matters: Secrecy and Disclosure in the History of Adoption.* Cambridge, Mass.: Harvard University Press.

———. 2002. *Adoption in America: Historical Perspective.* Ann Arbor: University of Michigan Press.

Carstens, Carol, and Maria Julia. 2000. "Ethnoracial Awareness in Intercountry Adoption: U.S. Experiences." *International Social Work* 43(1): 61–73.

Cederblad, Marianne. 1982. *Children Adopted from Abroad and Coming to Sweden After Age Three.* Stockholm: Swedish National Board for Intercountry Adoption.

Cederblad, Marianne, Borje Hook, Malin Irhammar, and Ann-Mari Mercke. 1999. "Mental Health in International Adoptees as Teenagers and Young Adults: An Epidemiological Study." *Journal of Child Psychology and Psychiatry and Allied Disciplines* 40(8): 1239–48.

Chestang, Leon. 1972. "The Dilemma of Biracial Adoption." *Social Work* 17(3): 100–105.

Child Welfare League of America (CWLA). 1960. *Adoption of Oriental Children by American White Families: An Interdisciplinary Symposium.* New York: CWLA.

Chimezie, Amuzie. 1975. "Transracial Adoption of Black Children." *Social Work* 20(4): 296–330.

Cho, Grace. 2008. *Haunting the Korean Diaspora: Shame, Secrecy, and the Forgotten War.* Minneapolis: University of Minnesota Press.

Choy, C. C. 2007. "Institutionalizing International Adoption: The Historical Origins of Korean Adoption in the United States." In *International Korean Adoption: A Fifty-Year History of Policy and Practice,* edited by Kathleen Bergquist, M. Elizabeth Vonk, Dong Soo Kim, and Marvin Feit. New York: Haworth Press.

Clark, E. Audrey, and Jeanette Hanisee. 1982. "Intellectual and Adaptive Performance of Asian Children in Adoptive American Settings." *Developmental Psychology* 18(4): 595–99.

Courtney, Mark. 1997. "The Politics and Realities of Transracial Adoption." *Child Welfare* 126(6): 749–79.

Cross, William E. 1978. "The Thomas and Cross Models of Psychological Nigrescence: A Review." *Journal of Black Psychology* 5(1): 13–31.

Dalen, Monica. 2005. "International Adoptions in Scandinavia: Research Focus and Main Results." In *Psychological Issues in Adoption,* edited by David Brodzinsky and Jesús Palacios. Westport, Conn.: Praeger.

Dalen, Monica, and Barbro Saetersdal. 1987. "Transracial Adoption in Norway." *Adoption and Fostering* 11(4): 41–46.

Dalton, Harlon L. 1995. *Racial Healing: Confronting the Fear Between Blacks and Whites.* New York: Doubleday.

Daniel, G. Reginald. 2001. *More Than Black?* Philadelphia: Temple University Press.

Day, Dawn. 1979. *The Adoption of Black Children: Counteracting Institutional Discrimination.* Lexington, Mass.: Lexington Books.

Dhingra, Pawan. 2007. *Managing Multicultural Lives: Asian American Professionals and the Challenge of Multiple Identities.* Stanford, Calif.: Stanford University Press.

DiVirgilio, Letitia. 1956. "Adjustment of Foreign Children in Their Adoptive Homes." *Child Welfare* 34(9): 15–21.

Dorow, Sara. 2002. " 'China R Us?': Care, Consumption, and Transnationally Adopted Children." In *Symbolic Childhood,* edited by Daniel Thomas Cook. New York: Peter Lang.

———. 2003. "Spirited Crossings: The Political and Cultural Economy of Transnational Adoption." Ph.D. diss., University of Minnesota.

———. 2006a. *Transnational Adoption: A Cultural Economy of Race, Gender, and Kinship.* New York: New York University Press.

———. 2006b. "Racialized Choices: Chinese Adoption and the 'White Noise' of Blackness." *Critical Sociology* 32(2–3): 357–79.

D'Souza, Dinesh. 1991. *Illiberal Education: The Politics of Race and Sex on Campus.* New York: Free Press.

Duster, Troy. 1991. "The Diversity Project: Final Report." Berkeley: University of California, Institute for the Study of Social Change.

Eckert, Penelope. 1989. *Jocks and Burnouts: Social Categories and Identity in High School.* New York: Teachers College, Columbia University.

Eng, David. 2003. "Transnational Adoption and Queer Diasporas." *Social Text* 21(3): 1–37.

Erikson, Erik. 1963. *Youth: Change and Challenge.* New York: Basic Books.

Espiritu, Yen Le. 1992. *Asian American Panethnicity: Bridging Institutions and Identities.* Philadelphia: Temple University Press.

Fanshel, David. 1972. *Far from the Reservation: The Transracial Adoption of American Indian Children.* Metuchen, N.J.: Scarecrow Press.

Feagin, Joe, and Jose Cobas. 2008. "Latinos/as and White Racial Frame: The Procrustean Bed of Assimilation." *Sociological Inquiry* 78(1): 39–53.

Feigelman, William. 2000. "Adjustments of Transracially and Inracially Adopted Young Adults." *Child and Adolescent Social Work Journal* 17(3): 165–83.

Feigelman, William, and Arnold R. Silverman. 1983. *Chosen Children: New Patterns of Adoptive Relationships.* New York: Praeger.

Fogg-Davis, Hawley. 2002. *The Ethics of Transracial Adoption.* Ithaca, N.Y.: Cornell University Press.

Frankenberg, Ruth. 1993. *White Women, Race Matters: The Social Construction of Whiteness.* Minneapolis: University of Minnesota Press.

Freidmutter, Cindy. 2002. "Testimony of Cindy Freidmutter, Executive Director, Evan B. Donaldson Institute before the House Committee on International Relations," 22 May 2002. Available at: http://www.adoptioninstitute.org/policy/ hagueregs.html (accessed January 9, 2008).

Freundlich, Madelyn, and Joy Kim Lieberthal. 2000. *The Gathering of the First Generation of Adult Korean Adoptees: Adoptees' Perceptions of International Adoption.* New York: Evan B. Donaldson Adoption Institute.

Friedlander, Myrna. 1999. "Ethnic Identity Development of Internationally Adopted Children and Adolescents: Implications for Family Therapists." *Journal of Marital and Family Therapy* 25(1): 43–60.

Friedlander, Myrna, Lucy Larney, Marianne Skau, Marcus Hotaling, Marshia Cutting, and Michelle Schwam. 2000. "Bicultural Identification: Experiences of Internationally Adopted Children and Their Parents." *Journal of Counseling Psychology* 47(2): 187–98.

Gans, Herbert J. 1979. "Symbolic Ethnicity: The Future of Ethnic Groups and Cultures in America." *Ethnic and Racial Studies* 2(1): 1–20.

Gelles, Richard, and Joel Kroll. 1993. *Barriers to Same Race Placement.* St. Paul, Minn.: North American Council on Adoptable Children.

Gill, Owen, and Barbara Jackson. 1983. *Adoption and Race.* New York: St. Martin's Press.

Ginsburg, Kenneth R. 2007. "The Importance of Play in Promoting Healthy Child Development and Maintaining Strong Parent-Child Bonds." *Pediatrics* 119(1): 182–91.

Glazer, Nathan. 1997. *We Are All Multiculturalists Now.* Cambridge, Mass.: Harvard University Press.

Glenn, Evelyn Nakano. 2002. *Unequal Freedom: How Race and Gender Shaped American Citizenship and Labor.* Cambridge, Mass.: Harvard University Press.

Goossens, Luc, and Jean S. Phinney. 1996. "Commentary: Identity, Context, and Development." *Journal of Adolescence* 19(5): 491–96.

Gordon, Milton Myron. 1964. *Assimilation in American Life: The Role of Race, Religion, and National Origins.* New York: Oxford University Press.

Grotevant, Harold, Nora Dunbar, Julie K. Kohler, and Amy Lash Esau. 2000. "Adoptive Identity: How Contexts Within and Beyond the Family Shape Developmental Pathways." *Family Relations* 49(4): 379–87.

Grow, Lucille J., Deborah Shapiro, and Child Welfare League of America Research Center. 1974. *Black Children, White Parents: A Study of Transracial Adoption.* New York: Child Welfare League of America Research Center.

Hansen, Marcus L. 1938. "The Problem of the Third Generation Immigrant." Rock Island, Ill.: Augustana Historical Society.

Herman, Ellen. 2007. "African American Adoptions." The Adoption History Project, 11 July 2007. Available at: http://www.uoregon.edu/~adoption/topics/African American.htm (accessed January 4, 2008).

Hoksbergen, Rene. 1991. "Intercountry Adoption Coming of Age in the Netherlands: Basic Issues, Trends, and Developments." In *Intercountry Adoption: A Multinational Perspective,* edited by Howard Altstein and Rita James Simon. New York: Praeger.

Hollingsworth, Leslie Doty. 1997. "Effect of Transracial/Transethnic Adoption on Children's Racial and Ethnic Identity and Self-Esteem: A Meta-Analytic Review." *Marriage and Family Review* 25(1–2): 99–130.

Holt, Bertha. 1995. *The Seed from the East.* Eugene, Oreg.: Holt International Children's Services.

Hoopes, Janet. 1990. "Adoption and Identity Formation." In *The Psychology of Adoption,* edited by David Brodzinsky and Marshall Schechter. New York: Oxford University Press.

Howe, David. 1992. "Assessing Adoptions in Difficulty." *British Journal of Social Work* 22(1): 1–15.

Howe, Ruth-Arlene. 1995. "Redefining the Transracial Adoption Controversy." *Duke Journal of Gender Law and Policy* 2(2): 131–64.

Hubinette, Tobias. 2004. "International Adoption is Harmful and Exploitative." In *Issues in Adoption: Current Controversies,* edited by William Dudley. San Diego: Greenhaven Press.

Hughes, Everett C., Charles S. Johnson, Jitsuichi Masuoka, Robert Redfield, and Louis Wirth. 1950. *The Collected Papers of Robert Park.* Glencoe, Ill.: Free Press.

Huh, Nam Soon. 2007. "Korean Adopted Children's Ethnic Identity Formation." In *International Korean Adoption: A Fifty-Year History of Policy and Practice,* edited by Kathleen Bergquist, M. Elizabeth Vonk, Dong Soo Kim, and Marvin Feit. New York: Haworth Press.

Huh, Nam Soon, and William Reid. 2000. "Intercountry, Transracial Adoption and Ethnic Identity: A Korean Example." *International Social Work* 43(1): 75–87.

Jacobson, Heather. 2008. *Culture Keeping: White Mothers, International Adoption, and the Negotiation of Family Difference.* Nashville, Tenn.: Vanderbilt University Press.

Jennings, Patricia. 2006. "The Trouble with the Multiethnic Placement Act: An Empirical Look at Transracial Adoption." *Sociological Perspectives* 49(4): 559–81.

Jeung, Russell. 2002. "Southeast Asian Youth and Multiple Layers of Identity." In *Contemporary Asian American Communities: Intersections and Divergences,* edited by Linda Vo and Rick Bonus. Philadelphia: Temple University Press.

———. 2004. *New Asian American Churches: The Religious Construction of Race.* New Brunswick, N.J.: Rutgers University Press.

Johnson, Kevin. 2003. *Mixed-Race America and the Law.* New York: New York University Press.

Johnston, Kristen, Janet Swim, Brian Saltsman, Kirby Deater-Deckard, and Stephen Petrill. 2007. "Mothers' Racial, Ethnic, and Cultural Socialization of Transracially Adopted Asian Children." *Family Relations* 56(4): 390–402.

Jones, B. J. N.d. "The Indian Child Welfare Act: The Need for a Separate Law." American Bar Association. Available at: http://www.abanet.org/genpractice/magazine/1995/fall/indianchildwelfareact.html (accessed January 9, 2008).

Joshi, Kyati. 2006. *New Roots in America's Sacred Ground: Religion, Race, and Ethnicity in Indian America.* New Brunswick, N.J.: Rutgers University Press.

Kallgren, Carl, and Pamela Caudill. 1993. "Current Transracial Adoption Practices: Racial Dissonance or Racial Awareness?" *Psychological Reports* 72(2): 551–58.

Kaufert, Joseph. 1977. "Situational Identity and Ethnicity Among Ghanaian University Students." *Journal of Modern African Studies* 15(1): 126–35.

Kaye, Kenneth. 1990. "Acknowledgment or Rejection of Differences?" In *The Psychology of Adoption,* edited by David Brodzinsky and Marshall Schechter. New York: Oxford University Press.

Kennedy, Randall. 2003. *Interracial Intimacies: Sex, Marriage, Identity, and Adoption.* New York: Pantheon Books.

Kibria, Nazli. 1999. "College and Notions of 'Asian American': Second-Generation Chinese and Korean Americans Negotiate Race and Identity." *Amerasia Journal* 49(1): 29–51.

———. 2000. "Race, Ethnic Options, and Ethnic Binds: Identity Negotiations of Second-Generation Chinese and Korean Americans." *Sociological Perspectives* 48(1): 77–95.

———. 2002a. *Becoming Asian American: Second-Generation Chinese and Korean American Identities.* Baltimore: Johns Hopkins University Press.

———. 2002b. "Of Blood, Belonging, and Homeland Trips: Transnationalism and Identity Among Second-Generation Chinese and Korean Americans." In *The Changing Face of Home: The Transnational Lives of the Second Generation,* edited by Peggy Levitt and Mary Waters. New York: Russell Sage Foundation.

Kim, Claire J. 1999. "The Racial Triangulation of Asian Americans." *Politics and Society* 27(1): 105–38.

Kim, Dong Soo. 1977. "How They Fared in American Homes: A Follow-Up Study of Adopted Korean Children in the United States." *Children Today* 6(1): 2–6.

———. 1978. "Issues in Transracial and Transcultural Adoption." *Social Case Work* 59(8): 477–86.

———. 2007. "A Country Divided: Contextualizing Adoption from a Korean Perspective." In *International Korean Adoption: A Fifty-Year History of Policy and Practice,* edited by Kathleen Bergquist, M. Elizabeth Vonk, Dong Soo Kim, and Marvin Feit. New York: Haworth Press.

Kim, Eleana. 2007. "Remembering Loss: The Koreanness of Overseas Adopted Koreans." In *International Korean Adoption: A Fifty-Year History of Policy and Practice,* edited by Kathleen Bergquist, M. Elizabeth Vonk, Dong Soo Kim, and Marvin Feit. New York: Haworth Press.

Kim, Nadia. 2007a. "Finding Our Way Home: Korean Americans, "Homelands" Trips, and Cultural Foreignness." Paper presented to the annual meeting of the American Sociological Association. New York (August 11–14).

———. 2007b. "Critical Thoughts on Asian American Assimilation in the Whitening Literature." *Social Forces* 86(2): 561–47.

———. 2008. *Imperial Citizens: Koreans and Race from Seoul to L.A.* Stanford, Calif.: Stanford University Press.

Kim, S. Peter, Sungdo Hong, and Bok Soon Kim. 1979. "Adoption of Korean Children by New York Area Couples." *Child Welfare* 58(7): 419–27.

Kim, Wun Jung. 1995. "International Adoption: A Case Review of Korean Children." *Child Psychiatry and Human Development* 43(3): 141–54.

Kimmel, Michael. 2002. "This Breeze at My Back." *Tikkun* (November–December). Available at: www.tikkun.org/article.php/nov2002_Kimmel (accessed October 7, 2010).

Kim Park, Irene. 2007. "Enculturation of Korean American Adolescents Within Familial and Cultural Contexts: The Mediating Role of Ethnic Identity." *Family Relations* 56(4): 403–12.

King, Rebecca Chiyoko, and Kimberly McClain DaCosta. 1996. "Changing Face, Changing Race: The Remaking of Race in the Japanese American and African American Communities." In *The Multiracial Experience: Racial Borders as the New Frontier,* edited by Maria Root. Thousand Oaks, Calif.: Sage Publications.

King-O'Riain, and Rebecca Chiyoko. 2006. *Pure Beauty: Judging Race in Japanese American Beauty Pageants.* Minneapolis: University of Minnesota Press.

Kirk, H. David. 1984. *Shared Fate: A Theory of Adoption and Mental Health.* London: Free Press of Glencoe. (Orig. pub. in 1964.)

———. 1988. "Integrating the Stranger: A Problem in Modern Adoption but Not in Ancient Greece and Rome." In *Exploring Adoptive Family Life: The Collected Adoption Papers of H. David Kirk,* edited by B. J. Tansey. Port Angeles, Wash.: Ben-Simon Publications.

Kivisto, Peter. 2005. *Incorporating Diversity: Rethinking Assimilation in a Multicultural Age.* Boulder, Colo.: Paradigm Publishers.

Klein, Christina. 2003. *Cold War Orientalism: Asia in the Middlebrow Imagination, 1945–1961.* Berkeley: University of California Press.

Koh, Frances. 1993. *Adopted from Asia: How It Feels to Grow Up in America.* Minneapolis: EastWest Press.

Krieder, Rose. 2003. "Adopted Children and Stepchildren: 2000." *Census 2000 Special Reports CENSR-6RV* (October). Available at: http://www.census.gov/prod/2003pubs/censr-6.pdf (accessed May 20, 2008).

Ladner, Joyce A. 1977. *Mixed Families: Adopting Across Racial Boundaries.* Garden City, N.Y.: Anchor Press/Doubleday.

Lee, Bong Joo. 2007. "Recent Trends in Child Welfare and Adoption in Korea: Challenges and Future Directions." In *International Korean Adoption: A Fifty-Year History of Policy and Practice,* edited by Kathleen Bergquist, M. Elizabeth Vonk, Dong Soo Kim, and Marvin Feit. New York: Haworth Press.

Lee, David, and Stephen Quintana. 2005. "Benefits of Cultural Exposure and Development of Korean Perspective-Taking Ability for Transracially Adopted Korean Children." *Cultural Diversity and Ethnic Minority Psychology* 11(2): 130–43.

Lee, Jung-Sook, and Natasha K. Bowen. 2006. "Parent Involvement, Cultural Capital, and the Achievement Gap Among Elementary School Children." *American Educational Research Journal* 43(2): 193–218.

Lee, Richard M. 2003a. "The Transracial Adoption Paradox: History, Research, and Counseling Implications of Cultural Socialization." *Counseling Psychologist* 31(6): 711–44.

———. 2003b. "Do Ethnic Identity and Other-Group Orientation Protect Against Discrimination for Asian Americans?" *Journal of Counseling Psychology* 50(2): 133–41.

———. 2005. "Resilience Against Discrimination: Ethnic Identity and Other-Group Orientation as Protective Factors for Korean Americans." *Journal of Counseling Psychology* 52(1): 36–44.

Lee, Richard, Harold Grotevant, Wendy Hellerstedt, Megan Gunner, and the Minnesota International Adoption Project Team. 2006. "Cultural Socialization in Families with Internationally Adopted Children." *Journal of Family Psychology* 20(4): 571–80.

Lee, Sharon M. 1989. "Asian Immigration and American Race Relations: From Exclusion to Acceptance?" *Ethnic and Racial Studies* 12(3): 368–90.

Lee, Stacey J. 1996. *Unraveling the "Model Minority" Stereotype: Listening to Asian American Youth.* New York: Teachers College Press.

———. 2005. *Up Against Whiteness: Race, School, and Immigrant Youth.* New York: Teachers College Press.

Lieberson, Stanley, and Mary C. Waters. 1988. *From Many Strands: Ethnic and Racial Groups in Contemporary America.* New York: Russell Sage Foundation.

Lipsitz, George. 1998. *The Possessive Investment in Whiteness: How White People Profit from Identity Politics.* Philadelphia: Temple University Press.

Louie, Andrea. 2002. "Creating Histories for the Present: Second-Generation (Re)Definitions of Chinese American Culture." In *The Changing Face of Home: The Transnational Lives of the Second Generation,* edited by Peggy Levitt and Mary Waters. New York: Russell Sage Foundation.

———. 2004. *Chineseness Across Borders: Renegotiating Chinese Identities in China and in the United States.* Durham, N.C.: Duke University Press.

———. 2009. " 'Pandas, Lions, and Dragons, Oh My!' How White Adoptive Parents Construct Chineseness." *Journal of Asian American Studies* 12(3): 285–320.

Lovelock, Kirsten. 2000. "Intercountry Adoption as a Migratory Practice: A Comparative Analysis of Intercountry Adoption and Immigration Policy and Practice in the United States, Canada, New Zealand in the Post W.W. II Period." *International Migration Review* 34(3): 907–49.

Lowe, Lisa. 1996. *Immigrant Acts: On Asian American Cultural Politics.* Durham, N.C.: Duke University Press.

Macias, Thomas. 2006. *Mestizo in America: Generations of Mexican Ethnicity in the Suburban Southwest.* Tucson: University of Arizona Press.

Maldonado, Solangel. 2006. "Discouraging Racial Preferences in Adoptions." *UC–Davis Law Review* 39(4): 1415–80.

Martinez, Rubén, and Richard Dukes. 1997. "The Effects of Ethnic Identity, Ethnicity, and Gender on Adolescent Well-being." *Journal of Youth and Adolescence* 26(5): 503–16.

McRoy, Ruth G., and Louis A. Zurcher. 1983. *Transracial and Inracial Adoptees: The Adolescent Years.* Springfield, Ill.: Thomas.

McRoy, Ruth, Louis Zurcher, Michael Lauderdale, and Rosalie Anderson. 1982. "Self-Esteem and Racial Identity in Transracial and Inracial Adoptees." *Social Work* 27(6): 522–26.

Meier, Dani I. 1999. "Cultural Identity and Place in Adult Korean-American Intercountry Adoptees." *Adoption Quarterly* 3(1): 15–48.

Melosh, Barbara. 2002. *Strangers and Kin: The American Way of Adoption.* Cambridge, Mass.: Harvard University Press.

Miller-Loncar, Cynthia L., Susan H. Landry, Karen E. Smith, and Paul R. Swank. 1997. "The Role of Child-Centered Perspectives in a Model of Parenting." *Journal of Experimental Child Psychology* 66(3): 341–61.

Moore, Michael. 1988. "Scapegoats Again." *Progressive* 52(2): 25–28.

Nagel, Joane. 1994. "Constructing Ethnicity: Creating and Recreating Ethnic Identity and Culture." *Social Problems* 41(1): 152–76.

———. 1996. *American Indian Ethnic Renewal: Red Power and the Resurgence of Identity and Culture.* New York: Oxford University Press.

Ngabonziza, Damien. 1988. "Intercountry Adoption: In Whose Best Interest?" *Adoption and Fostering* 12(1): 35–40.

Nutt, Thomas, and John Snyder. 1973. *Transracial Adoption.* Cambridge, Mass.: Massachusetts Institute of Technology.

O'Brien, Jodi. 2008. *The Racial Middle: Latinos and Asian Americans Living Beyond the Racial Divide.* New York: New York University Press.

Okamura, Keith. 1981. "Situational Ethnicity." *Ethnic and Racial Studies* 4(3): 452–65.

Omi, Michael, and Howard Winant. 1994. *Racial Formation in the United States: From the 1960s to the 1990s.* New York: Routledge.

Osajima, Keith. 1988. "Asian Americans as the Model Minority: An Analysis of the Popular Press Image in the 1960s and 1980s." In *Reflections on Shattered Windows: Promises and Prospects for Asian American Studies,* edited by Gary Okihiro, Shirley Hune, Arthur Hansen, and John Liu. Pullman: Washington State University Press.

Park, Lisa. 2005. *Consuming Citizenship: Children of Asian Immigrant Entrepreneurs.* Palo Alto, Calif.: Stanford University Press.

———. 2008. "The Model Minority Myth in the Second Generation." *Social Justice* 35(2): 134–44.

Perry, Twila. 1993. "The Transracial Adoption Controversy: An Analysis of Discourse and Subordination." *New York University Review of Law and Social Change* 21(1): 33–108.

Phinney, Jean S. 1989. "Stages of Ethnic Identity Development in Minority Group Adolescents." *Journal of Early Adolescence* 9(1–2): 34–49.

———. 1991. "Ethnic Identity and Self-Esteem: A Review and Integration." *Hispanic Journal of Behavioral Sciences* 13(2): 193–208.

———. 1992. "The Multigroup Ethnic Identity Measure: A New Scale for Use with Diverse Groups." *Journal of Adolescent Research* 7(2): 156–76.

———. 1996a. "When We Talk About American Ethnic Groups, What Do We Mean?" *American Psychologist* 51(9): 918–27.

———. 1996b. "Understanding Ethnic Diversity: The Role of Ethnic Identity." *American Behavioral Scientist* 40(2): 143–53.

———. 2001. *Legacies: The Story of the Immigrant Second Generation.* Berkeley: University of California Press.

Portes, Alejandro, and Min Zhou. 1993. "The New Second Generation: Segmented Assimilation and Its Variants." *Annals of the American Academy of Political and Social Science* 42(1): 74–96.

Prashad, Vijay. 2001. *Everybody Was Kung Fu Fighting: Afro-Asian Connections and the Myth of Cultural Purity.* Boston: Beacon Press.

Pyke, Karen, and Tran Dang. 2003. " 'FOB' and 'Whitewashed': Identity and Internalized Racism Among Second-Generation Asian Americans." *Qualitative Sociology* 26(2): 147–72.

Quiroz, Pamela. 2007. *Adoption in a Color-Blind Society.* New York: Rowman and Littlefield.

Rabow, Jerry. 2002. *Voices of Pain and Voices of Hope: Students Speak About Racism.* Dubuque, Iowa: Kendall/Hunt.

Reich, Jennifer. 2002. "Building a Home on a Border: How Single White Women Raising Multiracial Children Construct Racial Meaning." In *Working Through*

Whiteness: International Perspectives, edited by Cynthia Levine-Rasky. Albany: State University of New York Press.

Rienzi, Elizabeth. N.d. "A Part Yet Apart: Exploring Racial and Ethnic Identities for Adult Transracial Adoptees." Ph.D. thesis, University of Oregon.

Rivas-Drake, Deborah. 2008. "Perceptions of Opportunity, Ethnic Identity, and Motivation among Latino Students at a Selective University." *Journal of Latinos and Education* 7(2): 113–28.

Root, Maria P. P. 1992. *Racially Mixed People in America.* Newbury Park, Calif.: Sage Publications.

———. 1996. *The Multiracial Experience: Racial Borders as the New Frontier.* Thousand Oaks, Calif.: Sage Publications.

Rothman, Barbara Katz. 2005. *Weaving a Family: Untangling Race and Adoption.* Boston: Beacon Press.

Said, Edward W. 1979. *Orientalism.* New York: Vintage Books.

Schlesinger, Arthur Meier. 1992. *The Disuniting of America.* New York: Norton.

Schuman, Howard, Charlotte Steeh, Lawrence Bobo, and Maria Krysan. 1998. *Racial Attitudes in America: Trends and Interpretations.* Cambridge, Mass.: Harvard University Press.

Scott, Lionel. 2003. "The Relation of Racial Identity and Racial Socialization to Coping with Discrimination Among African American Adolescents." *Journal of Black Studies* 33(4): 520–38.

Scroggs, Patricia, and Heather Heitfield. 2001. "International Adopters and Their Children: Birth Culture Ties." *Gender Issues* 19(4): 3–30.

Sears, David, Jim Sidanius, and Lawrence Bobo. 2000. *Racialized Politics: The Debate About Racism in America.* Chicago: University of Chicago Press.

Shiao, Jiannbin Lee. 2005. *Identifying Talent, Institutionalizing Diversity: Race and Philanthropy in Post–Civil Rights America.* Durham, N.C.: Duke University Press.

Shiao, Jiannbin Lee, and Mia H. Tuan. 2008a. "Shared Fates in Asian Transracial Adoption: Korean Adoptee Experiences of Difference in Their Families." In *Twenty-First Century Color Lines: Multiracial Change in Contemporary America,* edited by A. Grand-Thomas and G. Orfield. Philadelphia: Temple University Press.

———. 2008b. "Korean Adoptees and the Social Context of Ethnic Exploration." *American Journal of Sociology* 113(4): 1023–66.

Shiao, Jiannbin Lee, Mia Tuan, and Elizabeth Rienzi. 2004. "Shifting the Spotlight: Exploring Race and Culture in Korean-White Adoptive Families." *Race and Society* 7(1): 1–16.

Shireman, Joan. 1988. *Growing Up Adopted: An Examination of Major Issues.* Chicago: Child Care Society.

Shiu, Anthony. 2001. "Flexible Production: International Adoption, Race, Whiteness." *Jouvert* 6(1). Available at: http://english.class.ncsu.educ/jouvert/v6:1-2/shiu.htm. (accessed October 8. 2010).

Silverman, Arnold R. 1980. "Transracial Adoption in the United States: A Study of Assimilation and Adjustment." Ph.D. diss., University of Michigan.

———. 1993. "Outcomes of Transracial Adoption." *The Future of Children: Adoption* 3(1): 104–18.

Simon, Rita J. 1984. "Adoption of Black Children by White Parents." In *Adoption: Essays in Social Policy, Law, and Sociology,* edited by Philip Bean, London: Tavistock Publications.

———. 1994. "Transracial Adoption: The American Experience." In *In the Best Interests of the Child: Culture, Identity, and Transracial Adoption,* edited by Ivor Gabor and Jane Aldridge. London: Free Association Books.

Simon, Rita James, and Howard Altstein. 1977. *Transracial Adoption.* New York: Wiley.

———. 1987. *Transracial Adoptees and Their Families: A Study of Identity and Commitment.* New York: Praeger.

———. 1992. *Adoption, Race, and Identity: From Infancy Through Adolescence.* New York: Praeger.

———. 2000. *Adoption Across Borders: Serving the Children in Transracial and Intercountry Adoptions.* Lanham, Md.: Rowman & Littlefield.

Singh, Nikhil Pal. 2004. *Black Is a Country: Race and the Unfinished Struggle for Democracy.* Cambridge, Mass.: Harvard University Press.

Smolin, David. 2004. "Intercountry Adoption as Child Trafficking." *Valparaiso Law Review* 39(2): 281–325.

Song, Miri. 2003. *Choosing Ethnic Identity.* Cambridge: Polity Press.

Song, Sueyoung, and Richard Lee. 2009. "The Past and Present Cultural Experiences of Adopted Korean American Adults." *Adoption Quarterly* 12(1): 19–36.

Spencer, Rainier. 1999. *Spurious Issues: Race and Multiracial Identity Politics in the United States.* Boulder, Colo.: Westview Press.

Spickard, Paul R. 1989. *Mixed Blood: Intermarriage and Ethnic Identity in Twentieth-Century America.* Madison: University of Wisconsin Press.

Spickard, Paul R., and W. Jeffrey Burroughs. 2000. *We Are a People: Narrative and Multiplicity in Constructing Ethnic Identity.* Philadelphia: Temple University Press.

Steinberg, Stephen. 2001. *The Ethnic Myth: Race, Ethnicity, and Class in America.* Boston: Beacon Press.

Sue, Derald Wing, Jennifer Bucceri, Annie Lin, Kevin Nadal, and Gina Torino. 2007. "Racial Microaggressions and the Asian American Experience." *Cultural Diversity and Ethnic Minority Psychology* 13(1): 72–81.

Sue, Derald Wing, Christina Capodilupo, Gina Torino, Jennifer Bucceri, Aisha Holder, Kevin Nadal, and Marta Esquilin. 2007. "Racial Microaggressions in Everyday Life: Implications for Clinical Practice." *American Psychologist* 62(4): 271–86.

Suzuki, Bob. 1989. "Asian-Americans as the 'Model Minority'." *Change* 21(6): 13–19.

Tatum, Beverly. 1992. "Talking About Race, Learning About Racism: The Application of Racial Identity Development Theory in the Classroom." *Harvard Educational Review* 62(1): 1–24.

———. 1997. *"Why Are All the Black Kids Sitting Together in the Cafeteria?" and Other Conversations About Race.* New York: Basic Books.

Tessler, Richard C., Gail Gamache, and Liming Liu. 1999. *West Meets East: Americans Adopt Chinese Children.* Westport, Conn.: Bergin & Garvey.

Thoits, Peggy. 1983. "Multiple Identities and Psychological Well-being: A Reformulation and Test of the Social Isolation Hypothesis." *American Sociological Review* 48(2): 174–87.

Thomas, Kristy, and Richard Tessler. 2007. "Bicultural Socialization Among Adoptive Families: Where There Is a Will, There Is a Way." *Journal of Family Issues* 28(9): 1189–1219.

Tizard, Barbara. 1991. "Intercountry Adoption: A Review of the Evidence." *Journal of Child Psychology and Psychiatry* 32(5): 743–56.

Townsend, Jacinda. 1995. "Reclaiming Self-Determination: A Call for Intraracial Adoption." *Duke Journal of Gender Law and Policy* 2(11): 173–87.

Trenka, Jane Jeong, Julia Chinyere Oparah, and Sun Yung Shin. 2006. *Outsiders Within: Writing on Transracial Adoption.* Cambridge, Mass.: South End Press.

Tuan, Mia. 1998. *Forever Foreigners or Honorary Whites? The Asian Ethnic Experience Today.* New Brunswick, N.J.: Rutgers University Press.

U.S. Department of State. 2008. "Immigrant Visas Issued to Orphans Coming to the U.S." Available at: http://travel.state.gov/family/adoption/stats/stats_451.html (accessed April 30, 2008).

———. 2010. "Total Intercountry Adoption to the United States." Available at: http://adoption.state.gov/news/total_chart.html (accessed March 9, 2010).

Unger, Sanford. 1977. *The Destruction of American Indian Families.* New York: Association on American Indian Affairs.

Valk, Margaret. 1957. *Korean-American Children in American Adoptive Homes.* New York: Child Welfare League of America.

Valverde, Leonard A., and Louis Anthony Castenell. 1998. *The Multicultural Campus: Strategies for Transforming Higher Education.* Walnut Creek, Calif.: AltaMira Press.

Verhulst, Frank, Monika Althaus, and Herma J. Versluis-den Bieman. 1990a. "Problem Behavior in International Adoptees: I. An Epidemiological Study." *Journal of American Academy of Child and Adolescent Psychiatry* 29(1): 94–103.

———. 1990b. "Problem Behavior in International Adoptees: II. Age at Placement." *Journal of American Academy of Child and Adolescent Psychiatry* 29(1): 104–111.

Vleioras, Georgios, and Harke Bosma. 2005. "Are Identity Styles Important for Psychological Well-being?" *Journal of Adolescence* 28(3): 397–409.

Vo, Linda Trinh. 1996. "Asian Immigrants, Asian Americans, and the Politics of Economic Mobilization in San Diego." *Amerasia Journal* 22: 89–108.

Volkman, Toby Alice. 2005. *Cultures of Transnational Adoption.* Durham, N.C.: Duke University Press.

Vonk, M. Elizabeth, Sung Hyun Yun, Wansoo Park, and Richard Massatti. 2007. "Transracial Adoptive Parents' Thoughts About the Importance of Race and Culture in Parenting." In *International Korean Adoption: A Fifty-Year History and Policy and Practice,* edited by Kathleen Bergquist, M. Elizabeth Vonk, Dong Soo Kim, and Marvin Feit. New York: Haworth Press.

Wakefield, David, and Cynthia Hudley. 2007. "Ethnic and Racial Identity and Adolescent Well-being." *Theory into Practice* 46(2): 147–54.

Waters, Mary C. 1990. *Ethnic Options: Choosing Identities in America.* Berkeley: University of California Press.

———. 1999. *Black Identities: West Indian Immigrant Dreams and American Realities.* New York and Cambridge, Mass.: Russell Sage Foundation and Harvard University Press.

Westhues, Anne, and Joyce C. Cohen. 1998. "Ethnic and Racial Identity of Internationally Adopted Adolescents and Young Adults: Some Issues in Relation to Children's Rights." *Adoption Quarterly* 1(4): 33–55.

Wijeyesinghe, Charmaine L., and Bailey Jackson III. 2001. *New Perspectives on Racial Identity Development.* New York: New York University Press.

Williams-León, Teresa, and Cynthia L. Nakashima. 2001. *The Sum of Our Parts: Mixed-Heritage Asian Americans.* Philadelphia: Temple University Press.

Willis, Madge G. 1996. "The Real Issues in Transracial Adoption: A Response." *Journal of Black Psychology* 22(2): 246–53.

Wilson, William Julius. 1978. *The Declining Significance of Race: Blacks and Changing American Institutions.* Chicago: University of Chicago Press.

Winick, Myron, Knarig Meyer, and Ruth Harris. 1975. "Malnutrition and Environmental Enrichment by Early Adoption." *Science* 190(4220): 1173–75.

Winters, Loretta, and Herman DeBose, eds. 2002. *New Faces in a Changing America: Multiracial Identity in the Twenty-first Century.* Thousand Oaks, Calif.: Sage Publications.

Yancey, George. 2003. *Who Is White? Latinos, Asians, and the New Black/Nonblack Divide.* Boulder, Colo.: L. Rienner.

Yngvesson, Barbara. 2000. " 'Un Niño de Cualquier Color': Race and Nation in Intercountry Adoption." In *Globalizing Institutions: Case Studies in Regulation and Innovation,* edited by Jane Jenson and Boaventura de Sousa Santos. Burlington, Vt.: Ashgate Publishing.

Yoon, Dong Pil. 2001. "Causal Modeling Predicting Psychological Adjustment of Korean-Born Adolescent Adoptees." *Journal of Human Behavior in the Social Environment* 3(3–4): 65–82.

———. 2004. "Intercountry Adoption: The Importance of Ethnic Socialization and Subjective Well-being for Korean-Born Adopted Children." *Journal of Ethnic and Cultural Diversity in Social Work* 13(2): 71–89.

———. 2007. "Utilization of Structural Equation Modeling to Predict Psychological Well-being Among Adopted Korean Children." In *International Korean Adoption: A Fifty-Year History of Policy and Practice,* edited by Kathleen Bergquist, M. Elizabeth Vonk, Dong Soo Kim, and Marvin Feit. New York: Haworth Press.

Zelizer, Viviana. 1994. *Pricing the Priceless Child: The Changing Social Value of Children.* Princeton, N.J.: Princeton University Press.

INDEX